EUROPEAN FOLK DANCE

HUNGARIAN COSTUME
The most elaborate costume in Europe

EUROPEAN FOLK DANCE

ITS NATIONAL AND MUSICAL CHARACTERISTICS

By

JOAN LAWSON

Published under the auspices of
The Imperial Society of Teachers of Dancing Incorporated

WITH ILLUSTRATIONS BY

IRIS BROOKE

LONDON
SIR ISAAC PITMAN & SONS, LTD.

First published 1953
Revised and reprinted 1955

SIR ISAAC PITMAN & SONS, Ltd.
PITMAN HOUSE, PARKER STREET, KINGSWAY, LONDON, W.C.2
THE PITMAN PRESS, BATH
PITMAN HOUSE, BOUVERIE STREET, CARLTON, MELBOURNE
27 BECKETTS BUILDINGS, PRESIDENT STREET, JOHANNESBURG

ASSOCIATED COMPANIES
PITMAN MEDICAL PUBLISHING COMPANY, Ltd.
45 NEW OXFORD STREET, LONDON, W.C.1

PITMAN PUBLISHING CORPORATION
2 WEST 45TH STREET, NEW YORK

SIR ISAAC PITMAN & SONS (CANADA), Ltd.
(INCORPORATING THE COMMERCIAL TEXT BOOK COMPANY)
PITMAN HOUSE, 381–383 CHURCH STREET, TORONTO

MADE IN GREAT BRITAIN AT THE PITMAN PRESS, BATH
E5—(G.411)

For
DAME NINETTE DE VALOIS
With Gratitude and Admiration
Hoping it will answer in some part her
request for a classification of the
historical and musical foundation of
National Dance

Preface

THE famous Russian writer Gogol has said: "People living proud and warlike lives express that same pride in their dances; people living a free life show that same unbounded will and poetic self-oblivion; people of a fiery climate express in their national dance that same passion, languor and jealousy."

There is no such thing as a national folk dance—that is, a dance performed solely within the political boundaries as they are known to-day. Folk dances, like all other folk arts, follow ethnological boundaries; perhaps it would be possible to define the limits of a nation from a study of the dances the people perform and the arts they practise.

The African native of the great Bantu tribe who asks the stranger "What do you dance?" does so because he knows, perhaps instinctively, that the stranger's dance will help him to understand something of that man's country, customs, and ways of life. What is more important, through the dance he may also discover some elements that will link him to the visitor, not only in the social activity of making movement together, but also by way of some ancient family traditions reflected in those movements.

This linking of people through movements occurs despite the mass migrations, wars, and other upheavals which are continually changing the balance of the varied ethnic groups. It is still possible to find certain steps and movements combined with specific musical characteristics in the dances of many widely dispersed areas. They are also found among the modern folk and country dances, which originated with the patriotic and nationalistic movements of the late eighteenth and early nineteenth centuries. These features belonged originally to the ancestors of the modern nations who swept through and round Europe, Asia, and Africa before they settled down and intermarried. Dances built from such movements therefore reflect something of the many influences that have helped to form a people's customs, habits and work.

Among the many elements which can be said to fill in the background of folk dances still performed to-day are these—

1. The situation of the country, its climate and physical features, which help to determine the type of work done, the quality and style of movement performed.

2. The racial origins of the inhabitants and the influence of subsequent immigrations and of wars.

3. The forms of religion and the churches' attitude towards the dance, the relationship between the people and their government.

4. The relationship between the sister arts of music, drama, literature, and painting.

This book is an attempt to cover some of the background of European dance, and to help others to understand how dances will interpret a people's origins, character, lives, customs, and traditions.

The book is divided into two parts. Part I deals with the development of European folk dance in general, and describes how the various peoples are linked together by way of rituals and movements. Part II deals with particular characteristics found in the folk dances of each European country, which are associated with those specific musical features that constitute its national form of music.

These later chapters are admittedly uneven—but the dances of some countries are so much more interesting than those of others. Moreover, I have preferred to spend more time on those countries whose dances I have taken part in as a performer. It is for this reason that the dances of Portugal and the Basques are dealt with in very general terms. I have only watched these as a spectator, and then not in the country of their origin, which is essential if one is to get a real insight into their significance, meaning, and close relationship to the music.

To illustrate this book fully would make its cost prohibitive. Maps would be required to show the movements of people and the changing political boundaries for at least every fifty-year period, and many illustrations would be needed to cover the variety of costumes to be found in each country. Hundreds of dances, with their music, would have to be annotated. The aids given, it is hoped, will help students to realize the enormous ground to be covered in a study of folk dance.

Map 1 shows some of the major movements of tribes during the first thousand years of this era only. The physical contours give some idea of the types of ground danced on.

Map 2 shows the present political boundaries (1952) and the countries divided according to the language groups. This is not absolutely accurate. To avoid complications of symbol, Greece, the Basque Countries and Albania are left blank as they are not directly linked with other European groups; so is the Alpine area, because so many different dialects are spoken. England is also left blank, for although she belongs to the Teutonic group her dances are Celtic. The Celtic-speaking areas have been shown to cover the whole of Scotland, Ireland, Wales, and Brittany, which is no longer the case—it is the dances that remain Celtic.

The costumes illustrate the general principles of the two chapters on the development and influence of costume, and the drawings illustrate typical movements in the dances of the countries to which they belong.

This book is published under the auspices of The Imperial Society of Teachers of Dancing, Incorporated, whose National Dance Branch Committee have authorized this work as the official text-book for the examination syllabus of their Branch.

J.L.

Acknowledgments

THIS book could not have been written without the valuable help given to me by the following people, to whom I offer my most grateful thanks—

P. J. S. Richardson, O.B.E., who first suggested this book, and who generously lent me valuable material and allowed me to quote from many important articles in *The Dancing Times*, which appeared as part of his campaign "to teach Mary through the Dance"; Frank Howes, for his advice on musical problems and material from his book, *Man, Mind and Music;* Miss Iris Brooke, for her vivid illustrations and help on the costume chapters; John Bancroft, A.R.I.B.A., for his work in connection with the pin-men; G. S. Holland, of the Royal Geographical Society, for making the maps; Carol Moverley, for her advice on Celtic dance and her continual help; Hamlyn Dennis, for valuable advice and, with Phillip Bate, the S.C.R., and Poul Elthorp of Copenhagen, for the loan of books; D. G. MacLennan, for permission to quote from *Highland and Traditional Scottish Dances;* The Clarendon Press, publishers of the *Oxford Junior Encyclopedia*, for permission to quote from my article on Folk Dancing; Lijerka Sondic-Boenish, the Grand Council, and Mrs. I. Grandison Clark of the Imperial Society of Teachers of Dancing, for their encouragement; Messrs. Novello and Co., for permission to quote from the works of Cecil J. Sharp; finally the late Seraphina Astafieva, Edwin Evans, and folk dancers everywhere, who taught me the secret of enjoying folk dance and music and making it come alive.

Contents

xi

Plates

Maps

PART I

THE DEVELOPMENT OF EUROPEAN FOLK DANCE

CHAPTER I

The Development of Dance

AT all stages in man's development, from being a primitive savage hunting and gathering food as he wandered through the vast forests to his present state of mechanically-aided existence under comparatively stable conditions, he has performed dance rituals. In earliest times before he learnt to control natural forces, the ritual was simple. But as he learnt to control these forces by performing different kinds of work, so he changed the conditions under which he lived, and his dance ritual became more complicated. It was no longer performed entirely as the result of strong emotions, but partly as an old custom which helped to recall those emotions, and partly because of a superstitious belief in the magic properties of the dance, which played such a large part in early communal life. Moreover with the growth of the various religions, the new priests, if they did not try to suppress the rituals, encouraged the newly converted to continue to perform them, but changed their function by bringing them into the ceremonies of worship. In doing this they usually attached to them some allegorical significance in keeping with the new precepts they were preaching. Yet, despite many changes, it is still possible to recognize some of the strange beliefs and significant movements of these ancient rituals in the folk dances performed to-day.

To trace the evolution of the dance ritual accurately is impossible. The peoples of the world have not all gone through the varying stages of development, which have been roughly classified as—

1. Lower Hunters. Food gatherers and hunters with spears.

2. High Hunters. These used the bow and arrow and made the first attempts to domesticate animals.

3. Pastoral. Two stages, in the second of which cattle-raising is supplemented by a little agriculture.

4. Agricultural. Three stages, in the last of which the hoe is superseded by the plough.

Such classifications are, however, quite arbitrary. At any one time, one particular group may be at several different stages, for although in early days the standard of life of any group of people was dictated by the geographical and climatic conditions under which they had decided to settle, as they progressed they changed those conditions by their own labour.

The hand is the symbol of labour, and the part it played, and still plays, in many vital folk dances cannot be too strongly emphasized. As man developed the use of his hands,

3

he began to master nature's forces by utilizing flints and stone, and then by making spears, axes, and knives. Until this happened he was unable to gather more food than was offered by nature, therefore he was constantly migrating and struggling to win new feeding grounds. But when his development progressed to the making of tools, he was able to add meat to his vegetable diet, and to domesticate the wild animals and make them his servants. He could make fire, and taught himself how to live in varying climates and localities. The transition from the hot climate of what is believed to have been man's first home to colder regions, where the year was distinctly divided into summer and winter, brought the need for shelter and clothing. From this grew new and diversified spheres of labour. Agriculture was added to hunting, then cattle or horse-raising, then spinning, weaving, metal-working, pottery, and navigation; with these came the development of trade and industry, and ultimately of art and science.

Dance and religion are both products of some particular stage in these processes, and both changed with the growing powers of man. The first great social division of labour gave rise to the first consciously organized rituals, when the pastoral tribes separated themselves from the other barbarians. Then not only were more things produced, but different necessities of life arose, such as milk, more meat, skins, wool and other fabrics, and with these the exchange of goods became possible. With a development in the exchange of goods came the division of society into masters and slaves, followed by wars waged for plunder; all of this had a tremendous effect on dance.

The second division of labour occurred when handicrafts became separated from agriculture. This eventually led to the industrial development which was ultimately to kill folk dance. The ensuing paragraphs are designed to show how dances change with the changing labours of man, and why so many people scattered all over the world show the same types of dance, incorporating the same kinds of movement.

GIPSY FOLK DANCE

The first men were entirely nomadic, making no attempt to establish even a temporary home. They wandered through the vast forests, seeking shelter in natural caves and gathering food as they went. No such people exist to-day, therefore it is impossible to speak with any certainty of the ritual they might have performed. But it is important to note that the one truly nomadic group still existing, the gipsy, has no folk dances of its own; the gipsy tribes assimilate and perform the dances of the country in which they travel and live.

There is, however, a distinct gipsy manner of performance, which is often mistakenly accepted as the true folk dance of some Central European countries. This mistake arises because the gipsy often happened to be the only musician available for the feasts, weddings, and other celebrations, and he imposed his rhythms on those of the native dancers. The most important gipsy characteristics are the irregular rhythms and broken cadences of the music, which completely disrupt the tempo giusto (regular) rhythm of the true folk music, such as the Hungarian.

When the gipsies themselves dance, the features that immediately stand out are: their proud bearing and beautifully easy carriage; the woman's fascinating reticence when she is showing off her beauty to the man and the discretion with which she manipulates her shawl, skirt, or handkerchief; and finally the curious shaking of the shoulders. This last characteristic and that of the broken irregular cadences and rhythms are the only features that the varying gipsy tribes have in common. The shaking movements are most noticeable among the gipsies of Russia and Hungary, for they are never seen when the local folk dances are performed by natives.

TREE-DWELLERS AND THEIR WORSHIP

The extraordinarily large number of European point and hilt, long and short Sword, and Maypole Dances, and other May-day and Lent festivities in which Jack-in-the-green figures, are relics of the ancient tree-worshipping rituals practised by the first settlers in the enormous forests that once covered Europe. The tree provided these primitive men with their sole means of existence. Its fruit and leaves served as food. Perched in its branches, they were provided with some sort of shelter from the elements and protected from the wild beasts who continually prowled below.

The first form of tree-worship can still be seen among the most primitive tribes of Australia and up the Amazon. A solemn circling of the tree is followed by an ecstatic raising of the head and hands to the branches, leaves, and fruit. Hands are then gradually run down the trunk and finally the men kneel or lie grovelling at the roots. They hope that by so doing the strength of the tree will enter into them.

Man's belief in the power of the tree did not lessen even when he taught himself to twist osiers, leaves, and branches into a more permanent home, to protect his private parts from insect pests by wearing leaves, and to fashion crude axes and spears for hunting animals, birds, and fish for food, as well as to protect himself from beasts of prey. He now began to practise magic by using bits of the tree to increase the area of protection it could give him, and thus new elements were added to the ritual.

Firstly, he broke branches from the tree and swept them over the ground in an ever-widening circle, believing he could sweep away any evil lying within his path. Secondly, he linked his branch with the next man in the circle, ensuring that the enclosed space would remain clear of evil until the ritual was over and he would retain that close neighbourly collaboration which he had now learnt was an essential part of communal life. It was within this newly cleared and enclosed circle that the most important part of the ritual could be enacted, some vital fertility rite, which would ensure man's existence.

As society developed this vital rite went through many phases. Its first form was probably the enactment of the sexual act itself. The fairly widespread appearance of Jack-in-the-green, Green-men, Nüssler and similar leaf-clad figures, who are still made the focal point of a group dance, or who wander through the streets sprinkling the bystanders with water, suggests that primitive man not only used pieces of the tree to protect himself but also attempted to imitate the tree itself in his efforts to sustain life. This would happen when leaders began to emerge to direct the energies of the group. Dressed in branches, leaves and fruit, they danced in the middle of the circle and, having worked themselves into an ecstasy by vigorous movement, showed the tribe what they must do if existence were to continue.

Later, and derived from this, came the initiation rites to be undergone by each member of the tribe on coming of age. At this stage, what had originally been a ritual practised by everyone together became a closed rite to be performed by selected members of the community, such as the young men or the maidens. Finally there developed the complicated death and resurrection rites. In these a man might be sacrificed after having reigned as king for a year. Or, as sometimes happened, he was killed in mock battle and had to be re-born in a vivid representation of the baby coming from his mother's womb.

Although the tree as a direct object of worship was superseded by other nature gods fairly early in history, its association with primitive ritual has been preserved in many European dances. The tree itself has been transformed into the maypole round which the dancers swirl. Its branches are sometimes symbolized by the fluttering ribbons held in the dancers' hands, which serve as their link to the protector. Elsewhere the maypole is the focal point of the ritual and is topped by a large nosegay and festooned with garlands, and although it does not play an active part in the dance, the dancers usually carry wooden staves and wear bunches of flowers to symbolize their reliance on the protector. They touch wood!

The dance-ritual of the Romanian Calusari is the most fully preserved of these ancient tree rituals. The dancers carry their tree with them. Their short maypole is topped by a bunch of garlic, in itself a powerful protection against evil, and gay with ribbons. They wear nosegays and begin their ritual by beating each other on the body and soles of the feet with wooden staves, which next sweep the evil from the circle and link the dancers together. Once the circle is closed two "animal" men enact a courtship and marriage with this house made of staves. It is invaded and after a fight, the man killed is brought to life again. The group then moves on, repeating their ritual as they go, bringing good luck, and dancing with and over sick children in order to cure them. The day ends with general rejoicing, during which the whole community, particularly the unmarried girls, try to rub against the "Fairies," in order to acquire some of the powerful magic engendered in the ritual. The Bulgarian and Yugoslav Rusalii perform a similar function. The latter's wonderfully exciting dance is performed with swords and therefore acquires a warlike air.

ANIMAL DANCES

The tree was not primitive man's only object of worship. Watching the speed, strength and cunning of the animals and birds surrounding him and their ability to fend for themselves, he began to imitate their movements and dress himself in their skins. This was the first phase in the development of the animal dance, traces of which are still found in Europe. The most interesting are those of the Cossack imitating the eagle, and of the Finn and Yakut copying bears, seals and reindeer.

Such dances often became an important fertility rite, as can be deduced from the present-day Schuhplattler and other dances, where the boy struts round the girl, preening himself, flapping his wings and squatting, as the mountain cock does at the mating season. Certain steps used in these animal dances became part of the technique of classical ballet, such as the *Temps de Poisson*, in which the dancer leaps upwards curving both legs and body backwards as a fish leaps into the air. Some of these steps are particularly associated with horse-riding peoples and entered the vocabulary of classical dance through the famous horse-ballets of the fourteenth and fifteenth centuries.

Cabriole is still used in circuses, and denotes that movement where the horse rears up on his hind legs and beats his forelegs, or reverses this process. The dancer leaps from the ground beating his legs together either to the front or to the back. The Slavs also leap up and beat their legs together sideways, as the horse does when he swerves (*Holubetz*, Ex. 25, page 101).

Pas de Cheval: the dancer stands on one leg and beats the ground with the other foot, as a horse paws the ground in impatience. This is very prominent in certain Cossack dances.

Chassé or *Cwal* (Ex. 26, page 101) where the sound of galloping hooves and the horse's rocking movements are indicated.

Pas-de-chat is probably a misnomer. In Georgia and France the peasants perform the goat's leap (Ex. 6B, page 65) and call it the Kermatt or Il Chieb', which resembles the *pas-de-chat*, the sole difference being that the peasant does not turn out his knees, but keeps them well underneath his body and kicks out backwards. This step is always associated with mountain goat dances performed by shepherds.

Rue-de-vache is a strange movement in which the dancer kicks out sideways like a cow; it is found in France as well as in Ukrainian Cowmen's Dances.

Développé en avant, or crane step, is so called from the deliberate arching of the leg forwards, like a crane proceeding on its dignified yet jerky way. It is particularly associated with Slav, Catalonian, Greek, and Basque Fertility Dances.

The purely imitative Animal Dance sometimes developed into a Hunting Dance, when man felt the necessity of augmenting his diet of roots and berries, and discovered that by copying the action of animals, birds, or fish he was better able to catch them. With only a primitive spear for weapon, such an undertaking was fraught with danger;

therefore, before starting out, the leader of the group would make some magic by working the tribe up into the right mood for the hunt. He still does this in Africa, where he first imitates the characteristic movements of the animal to be hunted, then the necessary stalking movements, moments of waiting, a swift attack, and the kill. The tribe follow his example and, at the height of their enthusiasm, set out. Few such dances exist in Europe, although several Courtship Dances in remote areas show how the man hunts his girl. There are also the Hungarian Shepherds' Dances, which vividly depict the hunting and killing of the boar.

The widespread appearance of the Hobby-horse indicates the third phase of the animal dance. These strange creatures are possibly the last remnants of the horse-worshipping rites belonging to the nomadic tribes of Europe and Asia who domesticated this animal. The horse is an extremely useful beast, providing a means of transport as well as food and drink, and because it was a vital element in the struggle for survival, rituals evolved which man hoped would ensure its continued fertility. The leader would dress up in the horse's skin, make a head-dress of his skull, imitate his movements and indulge in activities which have now degenerated into those antics of the Padstow Hobby-horse, where he whisks a girl under his skirt, or noses round the girls' legs. These rituals became increasingly important as some tribes came to areas where it was impossible to graze horses or to travel further. Other tribes settling in more fertile areas also continued to worship the horse as a god or fetish, because he had brought them to the richer soil and it was necessary to ensure his survival in case they were forced by other tribes to move onwards.

As evidence of this it is notable that the Hobby-horse mostly survives either in pastoral areas, such as Romania or Spain; or in areas bounded by an ocean, from which a tribe hard pressed from the rear would find it difficult to depart, such as Padstow in Cornwall or the Basque Countries, or where horses could only have penetrated after having swum across narrow waters or been ferried over in primitive boats, such as Greece. The association of the horse with some water-crossing expedition may account for the curious legends of sea-horses in some countries, and also for the strange sea-monster appearance of some hobby-horses.

Strangely enough, among people still leading a nomadic existence and rearing and relying on horses, in particular the Turki-Tartar tribes, there are few rituals actually associated with the horse as a god to be worshipped, although his movements may be copied in the dance.

GUERRILLA DANCE

Watching the strange Young Men's dance of Yugo-Slavia, the Rusalii, where the men sweep their swords round in great circles as they leap and twist in an open Kolo, it is easy to imagine how primitive man tried to clear both earth and air before starting on

PLATE I

BASIC PEASANT COSTUME OF MANY SLAV COUNTRIES

PLATE II

GEORGIAN COSSACK COSTUME

This shows the tight trousers, special boots, and waisted coat.
The woman is wearing bag-shaped trousers

his vital ritual. The eerie sound made by the flashing swords is called "whiffling," and resembles the whine of the bull-roarer, which primitive man still uses to warn the uninitiated from the sacred rite. Similar elements are found in many Guerrilla Dances of the Balkans and the Caucasus. They have derived from man's first attempts to clear away evil with the magic properties of the tree.

The first evil spirits man encountered were undoubtedly the forest beasts, which could come upon him silently. By breaking off branches and "whiffling" he hoped to protect himself by both action and sound. At first the "whiffler" did not move far from the forest clearing where his tribe had made a home, but when he learnt to domesticate animals it became necessary for the early herdsman or shepherd to protect his flocks as well as himself as he sought fresh pasture. He did this by making the axe, which was a weapon as well as a valuable tool. The movements he made are still used by Romanian and Hungarian shepherds and Slav woodsmen, who sometimes depict tree-chopping and add strange cutting actions as if slashing at wild beasts.

As flocks and tribes multiplied, they had to travel further afield and in so doing encountered others; this added new elements to the dance, because man found it valuable to reconnoitre before he moved, or in time of famine suddenly to raid the flocks of another tribe, richer than his own. In time man had to fight for new land, and it was then that dance was used to inspire the battle. As the leader had conjured up the fighting mood for the hunt, so the leading warrior worked up the young men into a battle mood by showing them how to bring all their muscles into play before practising the vital thrusting and spearing movements. This was followed by stalking round in a circle and possibly a mock fight and its triumphant conclusion, thus ensuring, it was hoped, the desired result to the expedition.

This latter form of dance is still common in those mountain areas whose political boundaries have been in continual dispute, or where people have been driven into hiding by large conquering armies. They are quite distinct from those of a more settled community. Once the warlike spirit has been evoked in a common circle, every man acts independently as he moves further from the centre to combat the unexpected elements he may encounter. Nevertheless, the dancers all work to a common rhythmic base usually dictated by their leader to a drummer. Also, despite their individualistic movements, these are all directed towards a single point, the imaginary enemy, and each man is ready at any moment to go to the aid of another or step into the leader's place, should he fall in battle.

WORK DANCES

At first man imitated nature in his efforts to sustain life, but as he taught himself to control nature, so he began to think he could persuade nature to do what he wanted by enacting in his rituals the events he wanted to come about. This is noticeable in the traces of sun-rituals existing in European areas, where climatic conditions are unstable and the summer is short.

The sun became a vital object of worship as soon as man realized that, without its heat, existence was well nigh impossible. One form of sun-worship was associated with the rites of the Celtic Druids and, if we are to believe the Roman author Tacitus, some type of dance used to take place in which the relative position of the celebrants to that of the sun was carefully observed. It was performed within a circle of stones, at that moment when the rays of the rising midsummer sun struck the central altar. It seems more than likely that some ancient Celtic dances as At the Beginning of the World (Sellenger's Round, Ex. 56, page 170) with their constant weaving round a central point, are reflections of these rites.

The most common type of European sun-worship is that of dancing round the bonfires. It occurs at various periods of the year: in springtime (Sweden and Greenland) when the sun has to be encouraged to increase its heat to warm the earth after a long and weary winter; in many areas at midsummer, when it must ripen the crops; in the autumn when it must be begged to stay a little longer for the harvest; and round about the shortest day when man's energy is at its lowest ebb. Such a ritual probably developed with the discovery of fire, which was the first thing to make man realize he was not entirely at the mercy of the elements. This form of worship was intimately connected with the tree, and it can be imagined how the felling of the chosen trees for the bonfire, the triumphant procession to the sacred site and the ceremonial dance as the bonfire was lighted, came to be associated with man's plea to the sun to follow the fire's example and burn brightly.

In Teutonic countries another dance ritual is sometimes associated with the bonfires. This is a closed circle in which each alternate man thrusts his heels forwards into the centre, bracing them against those of another, whilst the entire group revolves rapidly like a mill-wheel. It probably developed with man's invention of the wheel, which was of great value in grinding corn, making pottery and generating heat—by imitating the wheel, man hoped his dance would prove a further encouragement to the sun.

Such dances as these are the exclusive prerogative of the man. Dances in honour of the moon are almost always performed by the woman. With the more permanent settlement of tribes, the types of work to be done increased, and were divided between men and women. Because the women's physical capacities naturally attached her to the home to rear children, sow seed, and fetch water, and because primitive man had a habit of linking like to like when making magic, women's rituals were particularly associated with those things he believed would ensure the continued fertility of his tribe and land. She was linked with the moon because her menstrual periods appeared to coincide with the phases of the moon and, as this was intimately connected with her fertility, he believed that the seeds planted by woman must be planted with the new moon, so that they would burst when it was full. Several Slav women's dances (Ex. 16

page 91) copy the waxing and waning of the moon in their floor pattern, as well as the types of work to be done during its various phases.

Because water-fetching was part of woman's work, rain-making magic was also woven into her dance. The Armenian Willow Dance, in which her fingers simulate the action of raindrops falling from the leaves as the arms toss and sway, is a living example. Other interesting movements are found in the Ukraine and elsewhere, such as a strange *pivot step* (Ex. 4, page 62), in which the heel of the following foot is thrust vigorously in front of and then behind the working leg as the hair is tossed backwards and forwards. This used to be danced in the fields of hemp and maize to encourage it to be as fruitful as the woman.

The richer the soil, the more the work to be done, and, with the invention of the plough and use of draught animals, the man also took part in the sowing and harvesting rituals. Some of the most interesting of these demonstrate the actual work process and are found at their best in the rich earth belt of the U.S.S.R. As the dancers circle they sow, mow, tie, stack, and thresh the corn, as children do in the Provençal Danse Ronde de la Civaia; or they vividly depict the gathering of grapes and making of wine, as in a few Portuguese, Greek, and Italian Vintage Dances. The Woodcutters' Dances of Karelia, Czechoslovakia, and Hungary have the same movements of chopping, sawing, and turning of logs as in the neat Soyotte (Ex. 52, page 158) from Champagne.

But, where men and women join together, other more erotic elements often enter the dance. Such are the vigorous throwing of the girl in the fertility leap, for they say that as high as her skirts fly, so high will the corn grow; and, if the man has already crouched down making the shape of the seed with his bent legs and then leapt up flinging his legs open as wide as possible in imitation of the seed bursting, then surely the leaves sent out will be many and strong.

In less fertile areas the work dances may not be so vigorously exciting, but the type of country may give rise to certain types of industry, such as the breeding of sheep, which leads to the weaving of cloth and carpets, and thus to the lovely Carpet Weaving Dance of Armenia, the Hebridean Weaving Lilt, and Swedish Renningen.

In the same way Fishermen's Dances have developed in coastal areas. Some of these, like the Hunters' Dances of Russia, contain elements of the purely imitative Animal Dance, for if the men wish their fishing expedition to be successful they feel it necessary to enact their wish before setting off, as in one strange fish-spearing dance of the Barents Sea area. For the most part, however, Fishermen's Dances depict the various tasks to be done and they are seen at their best in Portugal.

Some of the most important Work Dances are performed at weddings in Slav and Finno-Ugrian countries, where the bride is shown what her future work will be. The rocking of the cradle, baking of bread, feeding of guests, weaving of linen, sowing, harvesting, all have a place. Sometimes she sits whilst the mothers show her what to do; at others, the bridesmaids perform; or she herself must perform, encouraged by her maids and instructed by mother-in-law and aunts. The bridegroom often plays some part, if only to tie his wife's handkerchief over her head when the bridal wreath has been removed.

The list of Work Dances is endless and, oddly enough, the reason why so many have survived is surely that the magic they work is often successful. The practice of the varied movements in dance form not only stimulates man's interest, but actually helps him to perfect his work. The gesture, by being performed in rhythmic unison with others, who are equally concerned in the ritual, becomes heightened in activity and therefore more significant.

WAR DANCES

It is a mistake to suppose that the many European Sword Dances were originally associated with war. To decipher their development is always a problem. Only the Guerrilla type of dance is capable of a comparatively easy explanation, largely because in Slav and Turki countries and in Hungary it is possible to see it in its various stages of development— firstly the sweeping of evil by the branches of the magic tree; secondly the linked branches keeping evil away from the vital ritual; and thirdly the clearing of the air and development of tool or weapon for protection against seen and unseen enemies.

It is possible that the linked Sword Dance was part of a sun ritual amongst the Celtic tribes, who carried it through Europe. The custom of weaving the swords into patterns developed as the initiates stalked along, linked together in a chain, to the secret meeting-place. They then gradually wove their branches into a close formation until the leader could hold the Lock or Rose aloft as a symbol of the sun. This type of dance demanded the closest collaboration between the participants and was the exclusive property of certain members of a tribe, particularly with the growth of work processes with which such dances ultimately became associated.

It is important therefore to note that during the Middle Ages certain Trade Guilds are known to have practised such dances and were entrusted with the production of the Morality Plays. The popularity of these plays grew to such an extent that it became necessary to stage them in the town squares. Such dances were of considerable value in driving home moral points to the uneducated, because the Saintly Hero of the play could be raised aloft on the Lock, as he is in Provence, or laid on a bier, before being resurrected as he is in Basque and Slovak dances; or the devil or some evil character could be decapitated or hung. In addition to their play-making activities, the Guilds were often entrusted with the defence of particular bastions in a town in times of war, and as weapons were scarce, such implements as furriers' knives or skutching knives (to-day sometimes known as "rappers"), coopers' staves, axes and so on, had to serve instead. In this way Guild Dances became associated with warlike activities, and possibly when swords were more easily obtainable, they were substituted for the tool.

The geographical distribution of such dances in England suggests that they were taken over by the Northern nomadic tribes and probably practised by the soldiers coming to England, using either the short swords of the Danes or the long swords of the Vikings.

There is another type of Sword Dance in which the men actually practise fighting. Unlike the Guerrilla Dances, this is "set," and probably developed with the growth of the Greek City States, when, under more settled conditions, one particular group in the community had to concentrate on soldiering. Known as the Pyrrhic, it taught the boys the art of attack and defence, a method of instruction that was taken over by the Romans, elaborated and spread over the Empire, where it still exists in the cut-and-thrust dances of Montpellier and Pont-Aven in France and elsewhere, and the hitting of sticks in certain English Longways Morris Dances, such as Lads a Buncham or Bean-setting. In the latter the gestures made are mostly those of sticking poles into the ground. The hitting of the sticks together is only an added incentive to the rhythm that all must keep if the work is to succeed, but its likeness to that of soldiers parrying swords is inescapable.

The role of the soldier in disseminating and changing the meaning of dance cannot be too strongly emphasized. The development of the military band at the time of the Crusades, for example, played a tremendous part in changing the rhythm and context of earlier folk tunes, and helped to dispense with mouth music and pipes and tabor for dancing. An even better example of military influence is the linking of so many Sword and Morris Dances to the events of the Crusades. In every area through which the Crusading armies passed are found dances depicting Christians fighting Moors (such as the Morescas of Korčuk, Yugoslavia), or rescuing maidens from the Turks (Dalmatia), and similar subjects. These are often accompanied by folk plays of unknown origin, like the "Seven Champions of Christendom," and still surviving in France, Italy, Spain, Bohemia, and the Balkans; it has been suitably altered to fit the subject because its context implies an earlier association with vital fertility rites of death and resurrection.

The so-called Morris Dance which sometimes accompanies the play has a much deeper meaning still to be elucidated. It is a young men's dance in which they constantly jig up and down, generating tremendous energy and thus vital magic which thereby quickens all living things, and ensures the continued existence of man. Such a dance is not the exclusive property of any one nation, and therefore when Crusading armies met it among their allies, and their enemies, they might attach the name of "Morris" or "Morisco" to it. Probably, too, when attempting to dramatize current events, they would black their faces and pretend to be Moors. This may explain the curious Morris Dances of Bacup in Lancashire and Provence, where the dancers wear half coconuts on their knees, waists, and hands, and clap out intricate rhythms as they dance energetically, in much the same way that young men in certain Turki tribal rituals slap themselves with their bare hands. The use of the coconut reinforces the suggestion that this dance was a copy of Moorish antics, for the coconut is of African origin, just as the floating ostrich plumes of the Basque Morris dancers also originated in Africa.

Occasionally the fighting Sword Dance takes on yet another aspect, deriving perhaps from that triumphant moment when the victor seizes the sword of the vanquished in a hand-to-hand fight and dances exuberantly with or over it. In times of peace this may change into a dance of pure skill, in which weapons are laid on the ground and the dancer lightly weaves his way in, out, and over the swords, as he does in the most famous of Scottish dances, Gillie Callum, or over ice-axes as in the Carpathian and Tatra Mountains, or over crossed ribbons as in the Pyrenees.

The influence of military activities is also seen in the Celtic Three-handed Reels and other social dances in which two women are accompanied by only one man, who is supposed to make a choice. The Hungarian Verbunkós, with its peculiar characteristic of each man dancing opposite the one with whom he is most in harmony, led to the development of Recruiting Dances in many Slav countries, which first practised certain drill and then changed into a dance in which the boy said good-bye to his girl (Ex. 31, page 110). Possibly after the soldiers' return, or during wars when a shortage of young men made itself felt, the dance changed again into one in which the boy took on two girls. Many of these, like the Polish Troyak and North Yugoslav Kolos, are simple peasant dances, but others such as the Swedish Vingaker Dance show the influence of military activities and foreign dancing masters.

COURTSHIP DANCES

Although elements of courtship were already inherent in numerous fertility rites, as seen in those dances in which man or woman displays his or her physical ability or charm before the opposite sex, the pure Couple Dance did not begin to develop until the founding of the Provençal courts at the time of the Crusades. At this time a definite form of courtly dance different from that performed by the peasants is known to have been practised. It coincided with the establishment of a code of social behaviour when, with the development of language, the significant gesture of the peasant would be substituted by a politer one. For example, the man's forward thrust of the body and his embracing and carrying off the woman became the dignified kneeling before the lady of his choice, and the delicate giving of hands as he led her down the room; or the girl's violent gesture of repulse and attempt to escape became the admonishing shake of a finger and a shy turn of the head; and the triumphant flinging of the girl in the fertility leap became the dainty twist under the man's arm. The development of fashions helped to change the vigorous peasant steps into something gentler. It must also be remembered that it was not always the man who knelt before the woman. At times she was expected to submit to him, as she still does in Eastern dances, and thus the low curtsey was brought into the court dance, and is found in the Swedish Daldans (Ex. 42, page 138) when the woman kneels as the man throws his leg over her head.

Ultimately dances containing these politer elements were transmitted to the peasants whenever they lived in close proximity to their kings or overlords. Evidence of this is provided by the numerous Cushion, Shoemaker, and Finger Dances of Western Europe, in which man or girl chooses a partner. It is difficult to believe that they are not all derived from the same source. For example; Sweet Kate (Ex. 54, page 167) of Playford's *Dancing Master* (1670 Edition) is known in no less than nine countries—Finger Polka (Denmark), Mary Went to the Garden (Poland and Czechoslovakia), La Vinca (N. Italy), Driekusman (Holland), La Badoise (Savoy), Clap Dance (Sweden and Germany) and Come to Me (Westphalia). Whether it is English in origin would be difficult to prove. Most of the tunes resemble the Playford model and the gestures differ only in so far as the various nationalities have imposed their own character on to it. For example, the North German version is heavy and hearty, whilst that of Savoy is neat and gracious. It may have been taken abroad by seventeenth-century soldiers. On the other hand, its presence in Savoy suggests it may have originated there.

In other court dances the couple may flirt as they twist and turn under handkerchieves with Valse or Polka steps, as they do in Czechoslovakia and the Alpine Areas. They may exchange hats, as in the Lithuanian Kepurine, or perhaps the boy may steal a girl, as he does in many Austrian and Scandinavian dances.

The most fruitful source for the exchange of social customs influencing the Couple Dance were the complicated arrangements for alliance or conquest by marriage between the ruling royal and ducal houses of Europe, when bride or bridegroom would travel abroad, taking large bodies of retainers. As each court took a turn in outshining the others, so its particular fashions dominated the world. That of the North Italian courts followed closely on the inauguration of the Provençal modes, to be followed by that of France, when Catherine de Medici, with the help of Italian and French dancing masters, musicians, and philosophers, staged her great court ballets into which many peasant dances were incorporated. Spain made her influence felt in those areas where the alliance and treaties between France and herself were continually altering the political boundaries. England too played some part in influencing this type of dance, but her influence weakened when, having emerged as a first-class power, she began to practise the Victorian code of respectability.

The fascinating Valses and Polkas of the Austro-Hungarian Empire took the continent by storm after the Congress of Vienna. From then onwards, the majority of the Western European countries seem to have lost their hearts to the gay whirl of these dances played by military bands returning from the various wars. They often became part of older rituals and at times these newer dances completely superseded them. To-day they still hold pride of place, because they are often the only dances to be remembered by the older people.

RECREATIONAL DANCE

These later Couple Dances, like the seventeenth and eighteenth century Country
Dances and their offspring, are purely recreational, often specially arranged for social
occasions. Other true folk dances have become recreational, for although they have been
continually performed for hundreds of years they have gradually lost their significance
and are now danced as a mere pastime, as are those which have been revived during the
past fifty years. No folk dances have retained their original form and meaning. The
preceding chapters have tried to show how they keep spilling from one category into
another. As man learnt to control and improve the conditions under which he lived,
his ideas and beliefs changed, and as a result the dance altered. The development of
religion plays the strongest part in these changes. Study shows that each branch of the
Christian church has its own particular effect on the dance.

In countries where the Greek Orthodox Church predominates, folk dance remains
in an early stage of development. Many rituals retain the primitive unset Kolo and
Chain forms which arise spontaneously whenever the people are inspired by exciting
events, as well as on all vital occasions such as weddings, births, and even deaths. There
exists a deep sense of the community, and with this the priest is intimately connected—
indeed he often takes an equal part in the ritual with the other members of the group.
Some rituals are retained in an almost pre-Christian state, possibly because the tenets
of this church spread very slowly over the large areas where it is now paramount, and
it gradually took into its orbit many national and local heroes, both real and mythological,
before turning them into saints. In this way the peasants were kept in touch with their
pagan past. In addition most of the Greek Orthodox countries have had little contact
with the West. In the past the feudal lords of these areas lived in close contact with their
serfs and shared their entertainments, sometimes building theatres in which folk plays,
dances, and even ballets were performed by serf actors. Few of these actors had any
training in the court dance or theatrical technique until the late eighteenth century,
when they were occasionally sent to St. Petersburg to study. By this time theatrical
dance was purely professional and was technically different from that of the peasants,
but as folk dance was also studied a clear demarcation was always maintained. Moreover
it was considered an essential part of the serf dancer's skill to be able to return to his master's
theatre and not only entertain him, his guests, and serfs with the new-fangled ideas, but
also lead the true peasant dances.

As the Catholic church developed in power and became the official religion of
barbarian kings, the pagan elements were rigorously suppressed and the rituals brought
within the jurisdiction of the church. Except in France and Ireland, the Couple Dance
takes pride of place in Catholic countries. This has happened because the church and
state were in close alliance and completely dominated the peasant mind, this process
being furthered by the staging by spiritual and secular lords of magnificently spectacular

PLATE III

BRETON COSTUME (LE PAYS DE QUIMPER)—THE GAVOTTE
This shows the influence of court costume

PLATE IV

COSTUME FROM INNSBRUCK (ALPINE AREA)

An example of a specially designed peasant costume

processions and entertainments, which brought entire towns and villages into immediate contact with court fashions.

At first this led to a mutual exchange of ideas, court dancing masters borrowing folk dances and refining them, and peasants borrowing ideas of court behaviour and clothes, as the Trade Guilds borrowed church vestments to wear in the Morality Plays. But as the papal and ducal palaces grew in splendour and the ecclesiastical authorities organized the entire labour force of serfs and peasants on the lands they were rapidly annexing, so increasing economic pressure was applied to the peasants. They could not dance so freely and the court dancing masters ceased to bother with the folk dances and sought only to perfect the technique of the courtiers, or to entertain them with new dances. As the courtiers were by now interested almost solely in the Couple Dances, so these became more popular among the vast number of serfs in court service anxious to imitate their lords and masters.

In France, however, the Couple Dance had not the same hold. Until the establishment of official formulas for art by the philosophers and cardinals, and the building of Versailles, the French court dance exercised as much influence on the folk dance as that of the earlier Provençal and Italian courts. With the withdrawal of the court from Paris, and the absence of many princes and dukes from their own palaces to dance attendance on King Louis XIV and his heirs, it ceased to influence the people, and became the exclusive property of the aristocracy. Strangely enough it was when the French court isolated itself that the English and Scottish Country Dances began to find their way on to the Continent.

During the Tudor period, England played some part in influencing Western European art, if only by astounding foreign ambassadors with the liveliness of its music, plays, masques, and court dances, and the amazing prowess of Queen Elizabeth, whose performance of La Volta shocked many a diplomat. During the Cromwellian Revolution the English Country Dance was introduced by the English court in exile and gradually became popular because of its comparatively easy style, which was in opposition to the complicated technique demanded by the dancing masters. As England's ideas on the Reform of Government and more naturalistic style in art came to be studied by prominent philosophers such as Voltaire and Rousseau, these dances became even more popular. Rousseau's "Back to Nature" movement made it fashionable for the isolated French court to seek the so-called "rusticity" and to indulge in simple pastoral pastimes, and the Country Dance answered this demand. The abortive attempt of Bonnie Prince Charlie to capture the English throne sent many Scots abroad, which again helped to increase the popularity of these Country Dances. This was followed by the outbreak of the 1789 Revolution and the coming of English and Scottish Regiments during the Napoleonic Wars, which spread these dances to the peasants.

Similarly the lack of Couple Dances in Ireland can be explained because there never were any courts from which dancing masters could dictate a style that would penetrate to the peasants.

The greatest enemy of the folk dance was the Protestant church (see England and Germany, Chapters XIII and XIV). But although the wealthy Protestants did successfully stifle folk dance (since they were the leaders of industrialization and nothing kills folk dance so quickly as the building of factories and mechanization), they did encourage their own form of dance. The new dance spread wherever the example of the Protestants was followed. It is not surprising therefore that England's Country Dances were copied by other Protestant countries as they gradually emerged victorious from the battles against the Catholic kings and church. England had led North-western Europe in rejecting papal power. She was also the first to grow wealthy through industrialization.

It is perhaps significant that it is only in Protestant countries that folk dance has had to be revived. England, having been the first to kill its dance, was also the first to revive it, and Cecil Sharp was fortunate enough to find people alive who still were able to recall some of the old rituals. His example was followed by other researchers in the Teutonic countries, particularly among the physical training experts of Sweden, who began to find the practise of simple folk dance a valuable part of physical education.

England's revival was not, however, a consciously political event as the revival of folk dance was in Germany for the Hitler Youth, in Italy during Mussolini's dream of empire, and in Austria after the 1914–18 war. The movement to revive folk dancing in these countries was a deliberate attempt to arouse the strongest possible feelings of nationalism. In the same way, during the long periods when Poland, Hungary, Czecho-slovakia, Yugoslavia, and Scotland were suppressed by foreign rulers, there was a deliberate fostering of the dances by the native aristocracy and the military in an attempt to express their national patriotism. It was perhaps this desire to express themselves as actively as possible that led so many people in the various Resistance groups to revive and practise their old rituals and folk dances during the German occupation of the last war.

Throughout the centuries it has proved impossible to stop people dancing for one reason or another, and even if to-day a dance is purely recreational it is still a means of expression that all can enjoy. It can also tell an onlooker something about the people who dance it.

CHAPTER II

The Development of Dance Patterns

THE patterns made by the dancers' feet help to describe something of the development of the society in which a dance is performed. Although some patterns are common to many European countries, it appears that those who have been affected by a complex series of historical events possess dances with most complicated patterns, whilst those in a comparatively early stage of development retain the simple forms.

THE CIRCLE

The earliest and simplest form of dance, the closed circle, is found everywhere. It exists in its primitive state in the innumerable Yugoslav, Romanian, Bulgarian, and Middle-Eastern Kolos and Horas, Russian and Czech Khorovods and Kalamajkas, Breton Bondes, and the like. In these dances everyone is equal and sex is immaterial because all must enter into the ritual of circling round the object of worship, if the magic engendered within the ring is to be successful. Often there is no progression, while at the most there is a very gradual movement to left or right. The dancers hold each other's hands, wrists, shoulders, elbows or waist-belts, and face the centre.

As society develops and the ritual becomes more involved, so the circling becomes more complex. This is found in the Celtic Sellenger's Round (Ex. 56, page 170), and Circassian Circle, and in certain Russian and Yugoslav dances, such as Moonshine (Ex. 16, page 91) and Neda Grivny (Ex. 11c, page 83). The dancers now begin to move in and out of the circle as well as moving round. Although maintaining contact with each other during most passages of the dance, they also open out to perform individual movements. Men and women begin to stand alternately, or the dance may become the exclusive property of one sex. This signifies that at one stage people began to differentiate between the work to be done, because such dances deal with work processes to be performed exclusively by one sex. Amongst these are the Provençal Danse Ronde de la Civaia, depicting the sowing and reaping of oats, once danced by the shepherds but now a children's game, and the Russian Moonshine, a harvesting dance for girls.

Occasionally such dances develop complicated patterns, as the Armenian Carpet-weaving Dance, and the Hebridean Weaving Lilt, because the work process depicted demands an intricate shape. The most complicated of these are the English point and hilt Sword Dances, which contain no actual work movements, but can be interpreted as belonging

19

to that category. The implication of such dances as the Flamborough Sword Dance is obvious, for the men's flat wooden swords derive from a tool used in making mats and baskets. The movements are called "threedling," and the patterns made can be related to either trade. Similarly the Northumberland and Durham short swords or "rappers" are derived from the scutching knife used in dealing with flax, and the foot movements represent the work process of retting the flax before spinning it into linen, a process which is also shown in the patterning. Other dances where such elements appear can be related to the threshing of corn, the treading of grapes, and the weaving of cloth. Such dances were the particular property of one section of the community; firstly the males who had to conjure up the vital essence of the fertility rite before passing it on; and later the Trade Guilds, who had to teach their apprentices the secrets of their craft, so that their work could be carried on. All these processes demanded a constant rehearsal of the complicated figures to make them perfect. There are many ways of twisting in and out, and over and under the linked swords, and each particular group has its own methods.

Comparatively simple circular patterns are also found in many Morris Dances, in which the dancers twirl "slings" or handkerchieves. These dances have derived from the earlier simple Kolos, in which a bull-roarer or similar instrument was used to keep the uninitiated away from the place where the vital rite was being enacted. The patterns vary with the district in which they are performed and require special study, as do those of the point and hilt Sword Dances.

Another important form of Kolo is that derived directly from certain fertility rites. An outer circle or chain of women move round an inner circle of men, or vice versa. After they have increased the speed of their dance, the men seize the women and swing them round in the fertility leap, as in the Dalmatian Eagle Kolo. At other times, the sexes move from a common circle to face each other, as in La Tournidjaire (a bourrée from Auvergne) before dancing together. In other double-circle dances the couples enact some work process, as in Carillon (Île-de-France), now a children's game, where the couples are supposed to be swinging bells, and their stamps and claps represent the peal of sound.

THE CHAIN

The Chain Dance in its simplest form derived from the closed circle at a very early stage in the development of the ritual. It happened, so some authorities believe, when a gap was left in the circle either for evil to escape or for good to enter. In the double circle dances, however, particularly those in which a women's chain encircles the men's closed ring, it seems likely that the magic engendered within the closed circle was passed on to the women as the men swung them round in the fertility leap. The powerful magic made at that moment then passed through the open gap to the surrounding countryside.

PLATE V

COSTUME FROM GRAZ (ALPINE AREA)

This costume shows Italian influence on head-dress

PLATE VI
THE SCOTTISH KILT AND PLAID

The necessity for such an act arose from the fact that it was not always possible to find all the essential life-giving elements within the narrow confines of the early settlements where the ritual took place. This is certainly true of the pastoral areas of Greece, Yugoslavia and elsewhere, where the Chain Dance is widely found. After circling round a central point in the village, the leader guides the group over the rough ground and round the widely scattered houses and patches of cultivated land, to bring good luck to the entire community.

An interesting part of many of these dances, such as the Greek Kalamatianos (Ex. 8, page 70) is that the same man does not remain as leader. To ensure that the life-giving force originally conjured up at the starting-point is carried everywhere, the leader performs exciting leaps, turns, and other spectacular steps as the group travels. When he tires he hands a handkerchief to the next man, who energetically continues to weave the spell, again passing the handkerchief on as he tires. This continues until the group returns to their meeting-place. It is from these rites that the handing-on of a torch or other symbol in such events as a Marathon race has been derived. It is also a prominent feature of Guerrilla Dances, in which the next man immediately seizes the sword of his newly-dead leader to carry on the struggle.

These Chain Dances are often performed by everyone, as in the oldest Greek, Yugoslav, Faröe Islands, and Norwegian Chains. Sometimes they are danced exclusively by one sex, the leader carrying some symbol and making his or her path extremely tortuous. This happens because in earlier times the particular group were on their way to some vital initiation rite, which was kept secret from the rest of the community.

Occasionally, such dances are performed by men and women standing alternately, as in the many Coraules, Cramignons, and Chains, which are now walked or run to religious or semi-religious songs. In older dances of this kind, such as the Provençal Farandole (Ex. 51, page 156) and in the French, Italian, and Spanish versions of this dance, an extremely complicated serpentine pattern is made. This particular dance is supposed to represent the story of Theseus and the Labyrinth, a myth which has been interpreted as evolving from a complicated fertility rite. The dancers are linked together by handkerchieves, which represent the silken thread leading Theseus from the Labyrinth. The pattern of their steps represents the tortuous winding path through the maze, and the tight ring in which his fight with the Minotaur took place. His final triumphant exit is shown as the dancers gaily untwist through the arch made by the hands of the leading couple. The arch, which appears in many other ancient rituals, also has its significance. It is believed to symbolize the gateway through which the initiated enter their new life.

THE PROCESSIONAL

The Processional march or Promenade which opens so many Scandinavian and Teutonic dances was once a dance in its own right, and had its origin in two important tribal customs: the need of cleansing the community after the rigours of winter and the need of ensuring its continued fertility. England has preserved two of the more ancient Processionals in the Helston Furry Dance and the Abbots Bromley Horned Dance. There are other European examples. In the English Processionals, the whole community used to take part, dancing in and out of the houses and through the town, sweeping everything they met with branches of may or green broom. In some places these processions were led by a Hobby-horse or other animal, which not only nosed the onlookers, particularly the girls, to bring them good luck, but sometimes died and had to be resurrected by the man who led him.

The Abbots Bromley Horned Dance is unique, having only one counterpart in a ritual performed by the Yakuts of North Russia. It seems to epitomize primitive man's belief in ritual as a means to ensure fertility, a successful hunt, and to win the struggle for life. Six men carrying a set of reindeer antlers, three painted black and three white, followed by a Fool, Maid Marian, a Hobby-horse, and a boy with a cross-bow and arrow, dance through the village and fields. The leader of the black antlers often makes serpentine figures round those who hold the white, or, draws the dancers into a double file. The two sets challenge each other, swinging their great antlers downwards and upwards again as they advance to meet and back, cross and return to places. In the Yakut dance the implications are more obvious, as the leader wears the most powerful antlers, and after a fight takes first choice of the women onlookers.

Sometimes the processional dancers go in single file but more often they are in couples and from this second form one or two interesting dances have developed. One of these is the Breton Piler-Lan (Gorse-beating, Ex. 46, page 152), in which a file of men and one of women pause on their way at every ninth beat to strike the gorse, supposedly lying between them. Sometimes, however, the procession halts and the couples join hands to dance together before continuing on their way. It was from this later form of ritual that there developed first the early Processional Court Dance, then the English Longways Sets and their Continental versions, and finally the Couple Dances, which became most popular of all, and have remained the principal feature of so many later Scandinavian, Teutonic and Alpine dance forms. It was the close-turning form of these dances that so angered the church, no doubt because the tremendous energy expended was too apt to make the dancers lose their heads and indulge in fertility rites like their primitive ancestors. This fact was noted by stern Mamas when the Viennese Valse came to English ballrooms.

COMPLICATED PATTERNS

Circle and Longways Dances with most complicated patterns have developed from the early court and social dances. The Closed Circle still formed a part of seventeenth, eighteenth and nineteenth century Scottish Reels, Polish Mazurkas and Krakoviaks (Ex. 27, page 102) and of the English Country Dances, with their many Scandinavian and French descendants. It often serves as an opening or closing phrase, but the dancers soon break it up to exchange courtesies with each other and to introduce complicated figures. The simplest of these are found in the old Celtic Reels, but the more complicated were derived from the dances introduced into sixteenth and seventeenth century English Masques and French Ballets. These entertainments were devised by philosophers and literary men, whose aim was to display learning in presentations cloaked in mythological and allegorical allusions. Even the patterns made by the dancers' feet had to be symbolical by spelling out a magic hieroglyphic, or the name of some lord to be honoured.

The actual steps of these figured dances are usually very simple, but different ways of holding one's partner or other members of the group and interesting ways of changing places are often introduced. These are some of the holds found in these pattern dances.

Inside Hands Joined when facing the same way, or the same hands when facing opposite ways. The hands may be raised from these positions to form an Arch through which others dance.

Cross Hands Hold. Man holds woman's R. hand in his R. and her L. in his L. (R. hands on top.)

Two Hands Hold. Man takes the woman's R. hand in his L. and her L. in his R.

Ballroom Hold. Man holds woman's R. hand in his L., both arms are raised sideways. His R. hand is below her L. shoulder-blade and her L. hand is on or near his R. shoulder.

Arming. Partners turn with linked L. or R. elbows.

Ring Grasp. As many dancers as will, join hands and hold them high in a circle.

Thumb Grasp. Usually performed by two men standing with either R. or L. shoulders towards each other, each grasping the other's thumb firmly round its base.

Double Ring Grasp. Men and women standing alternately, each man places his R. hand in front of the waist of the woman on his right and grasps the next man's L. hand; and places his L. hand in front of the woman on his left, and grasps the next man's R. hand. Women do likewise, but join hands above the men's.

Reel Grasp. When dancing clockwise, partners face each other holding L. hands across, whilst placing R. hands on each other's shoulders. Counter-clockwise the hands are reversed.

Basket Grasp. For four dancers. Two men stand opposite each other holding their own L. wrists with their R. hands. With their L. hands they grasp the R. wrists of the opposite men. The two women thread their arms under and over those of the men.

Back Hold. Partners stand side by side facing in opposite directions and place their L. hands behind their own backs to take their partners' R. hands, which are opened to the side.

One-handed Mill. Four or more dancers grasp R. hand or wrist of the one in front, with arms outstretched and thumbs upwards to dance clockwise, using L. hands when dancing counter-clockwise.

Two-handed Mill. For two couples. The first couple take hands facing each other and the other couple join hands, but place R. arm over and L. arm under the ring formed by the first couple.

Swing. Partners skip round using Two-hands Hold (English Country Dance), or pivot turn with partner either linking elbows or with R. hands on partner's L. hip and L. arms raised, or using ballroom hold.

Some of the ways of changing places are—

The Grand Chain or *Hey.* An equal number of dancers stand facing their partners in a circle, ellipse or chain. They move round or up and down the set, passing those they meet first by the R. and then by the L. shoulders, until all have returned to their original places.

There are also *Heys for Three,* where a figure of eight is described, which is danced in two ways: in the English Morris the two outside men turn away from each other, the centre dancer following the leader and the third man first meeting the leader; in the Scottish version the two outside men face each other and the leader first meets the centre man. There are also *Heys for Four* and *Double Heys.*

The Half Poussette. Two couples with hands joined stand opposite to each other, and dance simultaneously outwards and inwards in a semi-circular or shuttle-like figure to change places.

The Full Poussette or Swing. This is the same as above but the couples complete a circle and return to their own places. Both these figures are performed by moving either in and out of a circle, in the centre of a circle, or in a column. Sometimes the couples themselves turn as they move (see *Swing* above).

Casting-off. One couple usually turns outwards and divides, to dance outside the general set. They are often followed by other members of the group.

Setting. The dancer faces his partner or another member of the group and takes a movement to the right and back to the left. This is often accompanied by a slight bow as the dancer moves sideways.

Siding. Two dancers, either partners or members of the group, change places by passing left shoulders, turn, and then return to their places along the same track.

There are many other figures to be found in the later Circle and Longways Dances, but these are mainly in the Lancers or similar dancing master's dances, such as the Quadrilles and Cotillions.

THE DIRECTION OF THE CIRCLE

The significance of the clockwise or counter-clockwise movement of a dance is difficult to determine. Among the Celts, who have sun-worshipping ancestors, it is usual for the dancers to move clockwise on all happy occasions, and counter-clockwise or "widdershins" in mourning dances. The Slavs, however, also possess sun-worshipping ancestors, and the vast majority of their dances move counter-clockwise, and clockwise in some mourning dances. It is possible to offer two solutions to this problem.

Firstly, the Celts, who were among the earliest known inhabitants of Europe, travelled from the east and moved south through the Mediterranean areas before turning north-westwards to fan out through France and into the British Isles. They followed, as it were, the path of the sun from its rising to its setting, and continued to do so in their dances. On the other hand the Turki and Finno-Ugrian ancestors of the Slav tribes commenced their travels in the east or north-east of Asia and journeyed north-westwards, before moving south and turning east again to fan out into the European Plains and Russian Steppes. Their travels thus influenced their dances to move counter-clockwise.

Alternatively, it is possible that some dances moving counter-clockwise may have originated south of the Equator, where the sun appears to travel east, north and west. Early tribes coming from South Africa or Southern India may have brought and retained certain sun-rituals as they journeyed to the Middle East.

CHAPTER III

The Development of Step

THE steps of all the dances mentioned range from the simple step-to-the-side and close of the Slavs to the complicated leaps, twists, and beats of the Georgians, Hungarians, and Scots. The principal variation in steps results from the climatic, geographical and economic conditions. Exceptions occur in countries where the original folk dances have been suppressed and then revived; where more modern musical instruments have been introduced and supplanted the original accompaniment of mouth music; or where civil or military dancing-masters have played some part in forming the dance. It is not true to suggest that intricate steps, like patterns, are an indication of complex historical influences.

Steps in the oldest known Circle Dances are extremely simple. Many are based solely on a step-to-the-side and close, and it is from this simple beginning that the most complicated enchaînements have been developed. The Yugoslavs have fifteen ways of performing this movement in the Kolos, without changing alignment. Some of these steps exist in several different countries.

(It is understood that the R. foot always moves first.)

1. Close L. ft. tightly to R. with relaxed knees.
2. Bring L. ft. up to inside of R. ankle (Ex. 11c, page 83).
3. Swing L. ft. inwards and slightly upwards with toe pointed in front or at the back.

(These three movements are almost universal.)

4. Bring L. leg up with knee bent and leg turned inwards.
5. Bring L. leg up with knee bent and leg turned outwards.
6. Bring L. leg up with knee bent and pointed forwards, foot resting behind R. calf.

(These three examples are common to Greece, Romania, the Caucasus, and parts of Russia.)

7. Roll L. ft. round in a semi-circle to outer side of R. ft. and transfer weight of body immediately the foot is placed on the floor (Ex. 10, page 80).
8. Cross L. ft. behind or in front of R., transferring the weight. This can develop into the *pivot step* found everywhere (Exs. 4, 8, 10, 47, 51 etc.).
9. Bring L. ft. up smartly to the R. and clip both heels together (Poland, Czechoslovakia, Hungary, and Russia; Ex. 20, page 99).
10. Bring L. ft. to centre of R. ft., both slightly turned outwards as in third

position of classical ballet technique (Scotland, Spain, and Portugal).

11. Slide R. ft. sideways and bring L. to it, rising on the toes. (This develops into the *gallop* known everywhere.)

12. Jump feet apart and close L. ft. to R., either with or without a jump or hop (France, Poland, Hungary, and Alpine areas; Ex. 51, page 156).

13. Bring L. toe slightly behind R. ft. at the same time bending R. knee, as in French curtsey or English honour. (Known also in Teutonic, Scandinavian, and Italian countries.)

14. Bring L. ft. up behind R. ankle and immediately bend R. knee as far as possible.

15. Bring L. ft. up bent and immediately sink on R. leg to kneel on L. knee. (Greece, Romania, and Georgia).

Altering the direction of the leading foot to move in and out of the circle introduces the first series of variations, moving forwards and backwards instead of sideways, thus forming more complicated patterns (Ex. 11c, page 83).

When the dancers turn their bodies to face the way they are going, there develops a second series of variations, which give rise to the group moving in chains or serpentine figures. These can be extremely interesting, as the dancers twist and turn towards and away from the line of dance. (See Exs. 8, 11, 47, 51.)

The quality of the movements can be varied a great deal. For example, the basic step may be hard, slow, or abrupt, and followed by a soft, quick, or lethargic one. The initial step can be jumped followed by a smooth closing, or glided and the feet closed with a jump. The ways of performance alter the rhythm of the original basic step, and it is the rhythm which finally gives a dance its unique quality and style.

When another step is added to this basic movement, and attention paid to the different ways of placing the feet, transferring the weight of the body and the creation of new rhythms, such well-known steps as the Czech polka without a hop (Exs. 30, 53), *pas-de-basques* (Exs. 5, 22, 37, 63), *pas-de-bourrées* (Exs. 13, 49, 50, 57), and valses are developed. For example: give a slight jump on to the R. ft., raising the body with a tiny circular movement, transfer the weight momentarily to the L. toe, and then fall back on the R. This is the English "setting." Exaggerate the first jump and turn out the legs before transferring the weight on to the L. toe, and then rock back on to the R. ft. and the Scottish *pas-de-basque* is seen. The possibilities offered are endless and are exploited by folk dancers everywhere.

Besides the simple basic step, there are many different ways of walking, running, skipping, and hopping, all of which can develop exciting and important rhythms, like the simple running walk of the Hebridean Weaving Lilt, with its accented step on the first beat of each bar, which makes the rhythm of the dancers so true to the work they depict.

In the earliest stage of man's development the nature of the step performed and its purpose determined the sequence of notes to be sung. It has been noted that in the most primitive parts of the world, where dances and steps have a small variety of movement, the tunes have a small compass of sound, but as soon as the dancers grow more excited or perform some significant gesture the tunes are punctuated with wider intervals. This is also true to some extent of the relationship between tunes and steps in Europe, most particularly in those areas where mouth music or primitive instruments still accompany the dance.

The mood of the dancers originally determined the steps and the tune, which were intimately related. At first the steps were simple, and so were the melodies. As soon as the steps became broader and more varied, larger intervals began to appear and with the increasing range, variety, and mixture of step, the melody increased in scope and variety.

Curiously enough certain musical intervals seem to be associated with certain countries and even with certain steps or ways of performing them. The following table will serve as a guide to these national characteristics which later chapters attempt to describe in fuller detail.

The Augmented Second is particularly noticeable in Yugoslavia and is associated with all the fifteen ways of performing the Slav Basic step.

Chains of Thirds are found in all Teutonic countries, but these are not associated with particular steps or methods of performances, as most of the dances originated in the seventeenth, eighteenth, or nineteenth centuries and are not danced to mouth music or early instruments, although the preponderance of steps and dances in triple time suggests that the Chains of Thirds lend themselves to this type of measure.

The Falling Fourth of Slav countries, particularly in Russia, is associated with methods of performing certain steps.

The Rising Fifth among the Chains of Thirds in Scandinavia and in some Celtic areas, as well as the Rising Sixth, another Celtic characteristic, is sometimes associated with leaps and jumps.

The Octave is often associated in Alpine areas with the Fertility Leap and methods of performance.

(See Ex. 1, page 52, for Musical Intervals.)

CHAPTER IV

Climatic Conditions

THE climatic conditions prevailing in any one area dictate the quality of the movement to be performed and, to some extent, the accompanying rhythm. In the hottest countries, such as India and others lying within the Torrid Zone, movements are fluid, flowing easily from one part of the body to the other. Little or no muscular strain is ever visible, and an accented step has not the same abrupt quality as the same type of step performed in a cold country, such as Poland. The foot, which is usually very broad and flexible, meets the ground in a relaxed state, but the moment the weight of the body has been transferred to the stepping foot the muscles tighten and contract, relaxing again almost immediately. This means that poses are seldom held more than momentarily in their most perfect state, in direct contrast to the firmly held pose of the colder areas. Instead, a continual rocking from foot to foot, or from hip to hip, often accompanies a held position of the upper half of the body. Or alternatively the upper half of the body, particularly the arms, may flow in undulating movements whilst the lower half is held immobile. Rhythms, once "set," vary very little and usually seem intricate to Westerners, but once they are understood one realizes that their patterns are evenly constructed.

Where there is a swift change of temperature between day and night, as in Spain and along the Mediterranean coast, it is usual to find a clear distinction made between hard and soft movements, which usually coincides with the rapid changes in the dancers' moods. Flowing languorous steps are abruptly alternated with clear and vigorous stamping or foot-work. The softly held pose may terminate in a sudden turn or in rushing feet; or the brilliant succession of swift, accentuated steps may end in a soft turn and pose. Rhythms change equally rapidly and their patterns, following the dance, are usually irregular.

In those countries, such as the Ukraine and the central parts of the U.S.S.R., where there is a strong contrast between the heat of summer and the bitter cold of winter, the dancers mark this distinct change by long phrases of contrasted step and rhythm. One of the most important elements in such countries is the strongly stressed contrary body movement. This is apparent in the slower and more flowing sections of a dance where broad sweeping movements predominate. The body sways easily from side to side at the waist-line. Feet and head mark the direction of the dance, and the arms swing easily in opposition to the feet, or else head and arms act as a counter-balance in more difficult steps. These features are evident in the vigorously marked quicker sections, but are more precise and clearly articulated. A vigorous pulling up and opening of the leg is accompanied by an equally vigorous bending and opening, or swinging across of the arm. The head marks precisely the swiftly changing direction of the feet or downwards and upwards movement of the dancer. This is stressed strongly in all turning movements, where the eyes always keep turning to one focal point.

In those countries, such as Germany, France, and England, where there is a more gradual change between day and night, and between the seasons, movements are equalized, as are their rhythms. It is possible to see something of the muscular strain required to make the contrast between an upward and downward, or a forward and backward movement. This is not usually very broad or flowing, the dancer tending to keep well within his own axis and rejecting anything which might result in a straining for effect.

This equalization of movement is most noticeable in England, where the constantly moist atmosphere has undoubtedly helped to prune any spectacular effects from the folk dances. In such an atmosphere, it is impossible to keep up any prolonged, vigorous physical effort, unless strength is carefully preserved in order to endure the strain. It is impossible to indulge in an excess of exuberance. Among the best folk dancers is found an evenness of movement and absence of muscular strain, and this enables them to skim lightly and easily over the dancing floor. But this very evenness, the well-balanced body and equally ordered rhythmic base, lends an air of similarity to all the dances and tends to make them boring to an onlooker, unless attention is drawn to the fascinating floor patterns.

It is important to note that a lack of specific arm movement in most dances of these temperate countries is not due to climatic conditions. The arm movements would seem to have been lost through other causes, such as the suppression of ancient ritual dance by the church, the early industrialization and mechanization of processes hitherto under-taken by hand, and the development of language as a means of communication.

The colder the country, the more vigorous are the movements made. The distinction between the various muscular strains, beginnings and ends of steps, and the various types of steps, are most noticeable. The steps are usually strongly accented and accom-panied by similarly stressed rhythms which are regular in form, although the accent does not always fall on the same beat of a bar.

Although climatic conditions influence the quality of movements made they do not dictate the tempo of the dance, which varies at all times and in all places. The speed at which a folk dance should be performed is originally dictated by the purpose lying behind it. For example: an occupational dance is never taken at a speed greater than the tempo of the work process it represents. If man is to continue working until a task is completed, it is essential to keep to an absolutely regular rhythm, as can be seen by studying a man scything. On the other hand, as the dancers' ecstasy grows in their concentration on the ritual, so the speed increases until they reach that pitch of excitement when they feel, as Sir Gilbert Murray has said about the Greeks, that the spirit or "Mana" of their god has entered into them and they can perform feats which at other times would be impossible.

CHAPTER V

Geographical Situations

THE climatic changes that the world has undergone have created its geological structure of deserts, rolling steppes, fertile plains, river valleys and mountains, in all of which man finds a home. The style of movement he performs is greatly determined by the kind of ground on which he dances, and it must be remembered that among some people the dances still retain an occasional characteristic movement of the land from which they originated, generations earlier. It is this mixture of movement that makes the dances of some people, such as the Russians, Hungarians, Czechs, and Spaniards, seem so varied.

In rich agricultural plains or river valleys, as the Danubian Plains and parts of France, Denmark, and Yugoslavia, movements are accented downwards as if the whole body were being drawn towards the soil and the rich earth were preventing the feet from rising. Steps may be large or small, but the feet are not very accurately placed owing to the uneven state of the ground. Large numbers of dancers perform at the same time, keeping close together, using the identical step, and the dance is usually "set." Among the more primitive Europeans, as in parts of Yugoslavia and the Balkans, or where the rich-soiled area does not extend very far, the closed circle form of dance, the Kolo, is most in evidence. The dancers are tightly linked together by little fingers, hands, elbows, or shoulders. Sometimes the dancers continue to do the same series of simple steps for hours at a time, working themselves into a frenzy. Their entire bodies shake from head to toe as the movement ripples through their arms to their partners. Elsewhere the circle may not be so tightly closed, or the dancers may sometimes place themselves some distance apart, and the patterning of their dance within the circle becomes involved, as it does in the English Sellenger's Round (Ex. 56, page 170). In areas with rich soil the dancers seldom travel very far with any one step and, if it is a figure dance, usually return to their original place in the circle or set.

In pastoral areas and rolling countryside, such as the lower slopes of the mountains in Greece, Romania, the Alps and the Pyrenees, the dancers travel much more, directing their movements along the surface of the ground. Their bodies move both upwards and downwards, but never in excess, and the whole dance appears buoyant and easy. As in the richer areas, comparatively large groups perform together but are not so tightly linked, and it is more usual to find the circle opening out into a chain. The dance is usually "set." That is, the chain performs a simple series of steps which are continually repeated. There are very few pattern dances. But in order to vary the series of steps the leader will often direct the chain into serpentine figures, breaking away at times to perform individual steps. This happens in the Greek Kalamatianos (Ex. 8, page 70), the Provençal Farandole (Ex. 51, page 156), and the Yugoslav Devojacko Kolo (Ex. 11B, page 82). Another strongly marked characteristic of these pastoral people is that although the dancers move forwards, they do so almost reluctantly, turning from side to side, stepping diagonally across or even backwards to or from the line of dance.

These pastoral movements are in great contrast to the travelling movements of the nomadic people of the enormous grasslands and steppes, stretching from the Ukraine to Mongolia. These latter dancers appear to skim over the surface of the ground, and travel with the widest possible variety of movement, in which easy leaps and swift, neatly executed running steps predominate. These are directed almost entirely forwards, and the dances are seldom "set." Although quite large groups may dance together, and each dance may have a generally accepted form of basic step, this step is elaborated at will by each individual. It often happens particularly in the men's dances, that each member of the group in turn will break into a spectacular solo, whilst the others continue to circle round him or mark his rhythms by stamping and clapping. The Ukrainian Gopak and the Georgian Cherouli are excellent examples of this type of dance.

Steppe-dwellers are usually great breeders and riders of horses, and this activity is reflected everywhere in their movement. The most noticeable points are their erect head and back, easy carriage and shoulder movement, and the arms held as if riding—they are seldom raised directly over the head. A number of their steps are directly derived from the horses' galloping, jumping, trotting, rearing, and "reined in" movements.

Movements of all mountain people are easily recognized. Being confined to smaller areas and hard ground, the dancers utilize every bit of space by performing exciting high leaps which are accurately placed and accompanied by neat stepping. The accent of such steps is nearly always upwards. These intricate dances are usually "set," but only very small groups dance together at a time. There is a great deal of individual display, and the easily carried body is usually balanced by upheld arms and a head that is continually keeping eyes alert to the difficulties of moving in such areas. The entire dance gives the effect of being as light and invigorating as the mountain air. Good examples of this are the Scottish Seann Triubhas and the mountaineer dances from the Tatra and Carpathian mountains.

In countries where the peasants may be said to scratch a bare existence from very poor soil, the movements are similarly poor in step and pattern. The dance is usually "set," and comprises a few simple steps. Nevertheless the difficulties a stranger can encounter when trying to join in are great. In parts of Yugoslavia and elsewhere in the Balkans, these simple movements are made interesting because of the performers' complete relaxation in the dance. As it gets quicker so their bodies appear to bounce softly on the ground and shake throughout, so that the whole group seems to tremble like leaves in the wind, and the rhythm becomes most intricate and syncopated, as in the Yugoslav Zhikino's Kolo (Ex. 10, page 80).

The movements of desert-dwellers, whether in the heat of Asia or Africa or in the cold areas such as the vast tundras of northern Russia, are what might be termed spasmodic. The dancers make sudden convulsive movements with their bodies as they constantly change their weight from foot to foot, as if the ground were either too hot or too cold to allow a pause. In cold countries the movement is more jerky and there is a great deal of arm movement from side to side and up and down. The hands are often allowed to touch the body as they move to and fro, as in the Eskimo dances. In hot areas the hands and arms have not the same vigour and are kept away from the body, except at those moments where slaps or claps are introduced to accent the rhythm. They are also often used to shade the head and eyes, as in Bedouin dances. Dances on both these types of ground are seldom "set." The group usually have a basic step and occasionally some member may feel inspired to break out into a solo. There is, however, nothing like the same individuality or spectacular variety of movement found in the dances of the steppe nomads.

Most European countries, as defined by the present-day political boundaries, show some variety of physical feature, therefore one usually finds in their dances a variety of movement. In Yugoslavia, Bulgaria, and Romania there are three quite distinct types, corresponding to the three types of physical features: the shaking and closed Kolos in the Northern Plains and other river valleys where the soil is rich, the hopping chains and open Kolos on the mountain slopes, and the trembling dances in the poorer areas, such as the Black Mountains of Serbia.

But physical features seldom help to mark the national boundaries, and this is one of the reasons why so many countries of Europe share certain dance features. As the rich-soiled Danubian Plains rise to the Alpine slopes in the South and the Carpathians to the North, so the predominating closed circle dance, with its downwards accent, is gradually replaced by the more open chains and buoyant ease of the rolling pasture and shepherd peoples, changing again into the neat upwards leaping dances in the high mountain villages. Then as the dancer crosses the vast Alpine mountain system and descends into France or Italy, so these leaps lose vigour and height, until they are lost in the low-stepping circles, chains, and processionals of south and central France and Italy, or are carried through the various passes and across river valleys to appear again in some of the fascinating Basque dances of the Pyrenees.

Map 1 (facing page 32) shows how migrating people and warlike excursions by conquering armies always took advantage of the natural features as they passed on their way, and this helps to account for some of the movements still found in Europe to-day. Dances in which elements of the horse-riding, steppe-dwelling people can be seen are found throughout such widely separated areas as Mongolia to the north-east, Turkistan, Georgia and the Crimea to the south, Hungary to the west and Poland to the north-west.

This is proof of the enormous influence exerted first by the Huns and other near Eastern tribes during the first to the fifth centuries A.D., and then by the Mongols under Genghis Khan in the thirteenth century A.D. Sweeping across the vast Russian steppes, the hordes at varying times found means of fording the Volga, Don, Dnieper, and Dniester rivers, as well as following up these river banks to spread out into Central Russia and as far as Poland. They also swept round the shores of the Black Sea, followed up the banks of the Danube and spread throughout the Danubian Plains, and finally penetrated into what is now known as Germany. As they travelled so their vigorous horse-riding dances gradually weakened in movement and rhythm as they met and intermarried with people of more sedentary cultures. It is sometimes difficult to recognize such movements in the simple stepping dances of the Pripet Marshes of Poland, or in the complicated leaps and turns of the Far Eastern mountain peoples. But in Hungary and the Ukraine and Armenia, such elements are still easily recognized among the more solid agricultural dance movements.

Other migrating and raiding people, like the Greeks and Vikings, travelled by sea routes, establishing themselves in coastal areas and only penetrating into other countries as far as they could by river. They too spread their own peculiar dance characteristics among those of the more stable peoples.

Sometimes the physical features of a land help the people to preserve ancient traditions, as well as to disseminate their culture. The very difficulty of getting into the mountainous or desert areas of some countries has prevented a conquering people from occupying all but the sea-ports and easily accessible areas in river valleys, or lower mountain slopes. The Basques, Greeks, and Georgians all possess what are possibly the oldest rituals and ceremonials in the whole of Europe. A glance at the map showing the physical features of those countries will help to explain why this has happened. The extremely high mountains, dangerously narrow mountain passes, and almost impassable river gorges prevent all but the most courageous of travellers and warriors from penetrating within, and such solitary travellers would have little influence on the prevailing customs and habits of the inhabitants.

CHAPTER VI

The Development of Costume

NATIONAL costume can be defined as being the dress common to the inhabitants of certain political and ethnological groups who also have common dances, music, art, customs, and habits. A study of the basic principles of such costumes reveals, however, that the distinctive dress of any one group has similar characteristics to those of any other group living similar lives, performing similar work, and having the same ancestors. This likeness occurs even though tiny regions within any one country may have their own distinctive ornamental elements. In order to understand how these regional differences have developed, it is first essential to define the common characteristics.

National costume serves three purposes: first, it is purely utilitarian, serving to protect the body from the elements and suitable for the life and work of each group; secondly, for adornment, serving to display either the charms of the human body or the wearer's status and wealth; thirdly and most important, to protect the body from evil influences.

The first factors to determine the form a costume will take are the geographical and climatic conditions. Wherever man lives he has evolved methods of making the raw materials he finds into garments suitable for his environment. By roughly sketching out man's evolution from his most primitive and nomadic state to the present-day groups of nomads, hunters, fishermen, pastoralists, agriculturists, mountain and town-dwellers and others, it is possible to discover why certain characteristics are held in common, with differences only in detail.

It is curious that in trying to make a study of the one true nomadic race still existing, the gipsy, one finds that there is no such thing as a common gipsy costume. As with their dances, each group utilizes what it finds in the country in which it travels and lives. In Spain, gipsies wear Spanish costume, in Hungary, Hungarian and so on. These may be ragged, but one particular country's features are evident. There are nevertheless in all countries some specific gipsy characteristics common to both men and women. These are their love of bright touches of colour, particularly red, orange, and cerise, their glittering coin ornaments, and the beautiful way in which they drape their shawls and kerchiefs.

THE APRON OR OVERSKIRT

Man first attempted to establish himself more permanently in forest clearings near water. Here he learned to plait osiers, creepers, and grasses and, with the help of enormous leaves, to build himself a primitive hut. At the same time he began to use large leaves and grasses to protect those parts of his body most sensitive to insect pests. This gave him one of the earliest known garments, which developed into the apron, or short over-skirt. Today this apron is common everywhere in Europe, where it is more than just a means of protecting the dress. One look at the exquisitely embroidered aprons of the Balkans, France, Scandinavia, Hungary, or Slovakia, where they are worn by both men and women, or those of the Ukraine, which play an important part in the wedding ceremonies, gives a clue to their older use. Their purpose is ostensibly to display the girl's capabilities as a needlewoman and, in some eastern countries, her dowry of gold coins and ornaments, with which it is lavishly decorated (Plate VII, page 36). It is also an added protection, covering the placket in the smock, skirt, or trousers, which is often left open.

THE OVERCOAT AND JACKET

When man began to settle he started to practise hunting and fishing in his search for food. This gave him pelts and fish-skins, which he used as an added protection from the elements, to which he became more sensitive as he learned the value of comfort. But garments of leaves, pelts, and fish-skins served other purposes. As man believed that the strength of the tree would enter in to him if he worshipped it in his rituals, so he hoped that if he wore its leaves he would be better able to withstand the elements. Similarly, he noted the speed, strength, and cunning of the animals and fish he hunted and hoped that by dressing up in their skins and imitating their movements he would not only acquire the qualities he most admired, but would also be better able to catch them.

It is because of this belief in the gaining of understanding of and command over animals by dressing up in their skins that one finds shepherds, guardians of flocks, and hunters everywhere who wear an outer coat or cloak made of the pelts or woven hair from the pelts of their flocks, or of the animals they hunt. The enormous sheepskin cloaks or "suba" of the Hungarian shepherds, which are like the "pelerine" of the French shepherds, their overcoat of felt cloth called a "szur," which is like the Ukrainian "schuba," the sheepskin waistcoats worn by shepherds everywhere, the all-enveloping reindeer coats of certain Finno-Ugrian tribes, the seal-skin jackets of Russian fur-trappers, the fox-cloaks of the Yakut hunters, the curious "burka" of the Georgian Cossacks made of alpaca wool, thickly felted until it stands up by itself, the fish-skin robes of the Karelian and Barents Sea fishermen, are just a few examples of the sympathetic magic practised by man in his dress. It must also be noted that some such garments not only act as a cloak but can serve as a temporary shelter if the wearer cannot get back to his home at night. This accounts for the curious tent-like shape of the Georgian "burka."

At a much later stage of development, after man had learnt to breed animals and spin wool, outer garments of hide or woven wool became necessary articles of attire.

PLATE VII

DALMATIAN COSTUME

The woman is wearing her dowry

PLATE VIII
THE GREEK AND MACEDONIAN SOLDIER AND GUERRILLA COSTUME
The origin of this costume is difficult to trace

This was particularly so in the colder countries, such as Scandinavia, and in all mountain districts, where large knitted shawls or thickly felted or knitted jackets became part of the national costume. In Slav countries, however, this outer garment is still made of animal skins. It is often sleeveless, and the fur is worn on the inside.

Other interesting articles of attire arising from man's desire to emulate, capture, or control some animal are the shoes made of the animal he hunted, as the deer or elk-skin shoes of the Scots. To this category also belong the eagle-feather head-dresses of the Red Indians, and the mountain cock's feathers stuck in the Tyrolean hats as the dancers fly round in the old mating dance.

The geographical situation played a large part in determining the form costume should take when man began to breed domestic animals and cultivate crops. The larger the area occupied and the richer the soil, the more varied is man's work and the more varied the materials for clothing. In swampy ground and in hot countries, such as Egypt, the main garments will be of cotton. In Europe, flax grows particularly well, therefore the principal garment of most European countries is made of linen, which can be from the coarsest to the finest of qualities. Where the soil is not so rich, hemp is made into coarse cloth. This is used a great deal in fertile areas like the Ukraine, where the work processes are so many that the strain on clothes is particularly heavy. Wool is widely used among pastoral peoples and in colder areas everywhere. Finally there is the natural silk, found wherever silk-worms are cultivated. In Asia this art was understood many years ago, but in Europe it is a modern development, except in those countries where the Mongol invaders settled and brought both mulberry-tree and silk-worm. That is why one finds in some Eastern European countries, particularly Romania, exquisitely fine silk veils, scarves, aprons, and embroidery, which are a genuine part of the folk costume, and not a later addition, as are the silk aprons of Western European countries.

THE BASIC SMOCK OR SHIRT

At first the woven material was very short and narrow. The most ancient Egyptian reliefs and pictures show that strips of it were wound round those parts of the body most in need of protection. Peasants still use these strips of cloth to protect themselves from strain, cold, and insect bites. When man evolved a method of weaving broader and longer strips he created the basic garment—the smock—made of a single piece of material. This is still the basic garment of male and female attire in all parts of Europe where they still use their own elementary looms. In its simplest form, the smock is made of a long strip of material folded in half; a slit is made horizontally in the fold and vertically down the front, and two extra strips are attached vertically to the folded end to serve as sleeves. It is still found in this form in Yugoslavia, Russia, Bulgaria, Poland, and Czechoslovakia, and among the poorest women it is often their only garment. Sometimes it is worn with an apron, a strip of cloth for head-dress, and a sleeveless jacket for winter (Plate I, page 8).

The division of mankind into classes led to the desire of the upper strata of society to distinguish themselves from the workers they employed. This led to an elaboration of the ornamental side of the basic garment, and the utilization of rare materials exclusively by the overlords. In time, it became possible however to weave longer and wider strips of materials and the basic form of the smock began to alter. In some places, notably the hot countries, it became fashionable to drape this extra material round oneself, altering the thickness of the draping with the varying temperature. The method of draping and the colour began to denote the particular category of society to which one belonged, as it did in the "chitons" and "togas" of ancient Greece. Elsewhere, extra sections of cloth were added to the existing smock. The two most interesting examples of this are the Scottish "plaid" and the Arab "burnous."

THE PLAID

The original Scottish costume was a smock of coarse linen dyed with saffron, with strips of the same material or untanned leather wound round the legs and a plaid wrapped round the shoulders. Later a length of plaid was laid on the floor and carefully pleated lengthways. The man lay on it so that its bottom edge came just below his knees, wrapped the two unpleated edges over the front of his body, and then strapped a belt round his waist to keep it on. The long upper end was slung over one shoulder and held with his clan pin, or else draped round the entire body to protect him from cold and wet. It is from this simple beginning that the present-day kilt and separate plaid have evolved (Plate VI, page 21).

THE TROUSERS

Not all men settled in rich soil. Some were content with a semi-permanent site, and as the group grew larger and the soil became impoverished they moved on to fresh pasture. There are races still living this nomadic herdsmen's type of life, and it was such people who created the last basic garment—the trousers. Most nomadic peoples are great lovers and breeders of horses, and it can easily be understood that neither the apron nor the overskirt, the overcoat nor the cloak, the smock nor the draperies were comfortable attire for horse-riding. The first men to evolve a more suitable garment were possibly the nomadic horse-breeders in the Asiatic steppes. They created a tight form of short trousers made of hide, to which they later added a primitive type of gaiter or boot. These trousers were brought to Eastern and Northern Europe by the barbarian tribes as they conquered the Roman Empire, and the leather breeches soon became a common article of attire for all horsemen and fighters (Plate II, page 9).

Fashion has changed the leather breeches considerably, particularly at the time when the overlords, no longer needing to lead their own troops into battle, found means of making them of material. This new idea was gradually copied by the peasants, and one can still see how the petticoat breeches of the court of Louis XIV were adapted and became the knickerbockers of France, as they did in other areas where a court lived in close proximity to its people (Plate III, page 16). The leather breeches retained their original form only in those areas where Western European fashions did not penetrate, and wherever horse-breeding and riding are still a major occupation. They are seen either in the short form, or in the long tight form of a later period amongst the Hungarians, Czechs, and Georgians (see frontispiece). The long tight form also exists in the mountainous districts, where riding, though necessary, is difficult and use is made of sturdy mountain ponies, as in the Carpathians and Tatra mountains. Although rarely seen in Scotland to-day, the Tartan "trews" were a favourite article of attire among the wealthy clansmen. Many of these long tight trousers were or are now made of cloth. In addition there are the short, somewhat wider, leather trousers of the hunters, which form a picturesque part of the recently evolved costume of Austria (Plates IV and V, pages 17 and 20).

The Arab and Turk also made their contribution to this article of attire. Unlike the steppe nomads, they preferred to drape large folds of material into long baggy trousers, which not only helped to protect them from the blistering sun of the desert highways, but also served as a padding against the rough hide of the horse or camel mount. Both men and women affected this type of garment, as entire families were continually on the move. Wherever Arab or Turk penetrated or conquered a country, the baggy trousers have become a part of national costume. This happened because the conquered races, in order to protect themselves and particularly their women, used the costume as a form of disguise. These trousers are little more than a long strip of cloth folded in half with two slits, either cut horizontally at each end of the fold, or with the side seams left open near the fold for the legs to slip through (Plate II, page 9).

At a still later stage in man's development, a new type of trouser began to be worn among all seafaring folk, and among the peasants of certain fertile areas. These were of three-quarter length and very wide. Occasionally they were worn, as they still are in parts of Denmark, as an extra protection over the long, tight trousers. Among seafaring races they gradually became full-length trousers, which could be easily rolled up and kept dry when working in the water and then let down to protect the legs from the wind. The agricultural peasants' full trousers always remained at three-quarter length. In the Ukraine and parts of Russia, they early formed a part of the regular costume of peasant and Cossack, and are due to the mixture of nomad and settler.

THE DEVELOPMENT OF THE BASIC GARMENTS

By the fourteenth century all these basic garments of attire, apron or overskirt, over-jacket, smock and trousers were known all over Europe. The women's smock was worn long and was sometimes the only garment, whilst the men's smock was worn short. In some places this male smock grew wider, and it is still worn by peasant farmers in

France and Russia. The smock was the nearest approach to a national costume England has ever known. The wide material was drawn together with intricate embroidery; the more prosperous the farmer the more elaborate did his wife make the embroidery. The rise of a leisured class of people, the importation of wonderful materials from the East, the increasing manufacture of cloth (particularly in England), and above all the need in court circles to be dressed in the latest styles imported first from Italy and then from France, changed the simple smock into an almost unrecognizable article.

It is not possible here to embark upon a history of fashion but it is important to understand how aristocratic costume has influenced national costume. The local conditions under which each costume is worn create its details and make it characteristic of one particular group. The forming of national costume began with the Italian Renaissance, and certain well-known features were established as early as the fourteenth and fifteenth centuries. French costume reached its highest standard during the reign of Louis XV, whilst Dutch costume reached its finest peak in the sixteenth and early seventeenth centuries, Dutch head-dresses deriving from fifteenth century modes.

In most Eastern European countries, the middle areas of the U.S.S.R., and the Eastern parts of Czechoslovakia and Poland, the linen smock is still worn as the basic garment. Over it comes the sleeveless waistcoat. The wealthier men wear tight trousers of hide, but the poorer peasant has the looser trousers made of coarse cloth bound to his legs with strips of leather or material. The women may add an overskirt of felted cloth or pleated linen, with an apron to cover the opening on their overskirt. If wealthy, both man and woman will wear a long, sometimes sleeveless overdress, or coat of fur or felted cloth in winter. The women usually affect a kerchief for the head which is worn in various ways (Plate I, page 8).

The further west one goes, the more the woman's basic smock loses its original form. In the rich areas, particularly in Hungary, northern Yugoslavia, and western Czechoslovakia, the costumes become extremely elaborate (see frontispiece). The upper part or blouse becomes fuller, with large sleeves and many gathers or pleats. The lower part becomes one or several petticoats according to the wealth of the wearer, and over them is worn the overskirt and apron. The sleeveless jacket sometimes retains its original form, as in Russia, but in the Ukraine it becomes a complicated waisted and padded jacket. In the Tyrol it is a tight-fitting knitted garment (Plates IV and V, pages 17 and 20), but in France, Poland, Italy and elsewhere it becomes the corset-like bodice, often made of black velvet and laced up the front. The silhouette of such a costume displays its origin in the fashion of making one garment appear as two, so prevalent in the seventeenth century court dress. The panniers of this court dress were copied from the peasant women's habit of tucking up their overskirts into their waist-bands in order to save them from the mud. The peasant imitation of court fashions has led to some queer extravagances, such as the curious version of the eighteenth-century aristocratic overcoat cut away in front, seen in parts of Poland and France, and the Eton-like "jackanapes" coats, common to many Western European countries, derived from the coats of the time of Louis XIV and Charles II.

HEAD-DRESS

Head-dress shows the influence of court fashion most of all. The exquisite lace caps of France, Holland and elsewhere are often deliberate copies of the elaborate medieval head-dresses worn by court ladies (Plate III, page 16). The heavy gold-embroidered black velvet caps of Denmark, Savoy (Plate V, page 20) and northern Yugoslavia were a fashion brought from Italy when the Italian merchant princes led the world in fashion. Other Danish styles show the influence of Dutch fashions dating from the time when the Netherlands extended farther than it does to-day. The curious black lace top-knots of the women in Bresse are the French peasant versions of the beautiful black lace mantillas, which were worn by Spanish court ladies when this area was under Spanish rule.

In some countries the type of cap worn denotes the woman's status. Usually the unmarried girl wears her hair loose, in plaits or braided over the top of her head, sometimes with a tiny cap. The married woman's hair is hidden by a kerchief or cap, often of black, to which may be attached many types of decoration. The widow often wears a black cap or kerchief with white wings. This custom of wearing a cap to hide the hair has given rise to the charming Danish beaded cap of North Zealand, where beads are so sewn that they look like the braided hair. Another favourite form of head-dress in Slav countries, particularly for festive occasions are wreaths of real flowers, a relic of an old fertility rite, which demanded the picking and wearing of bunches of flowers to ensure a good harvest.

Another interesting head-dress is the "Troubeyetka," the little round cap worn by men and women alike in many Slav countries. This originally belonged to the eastern nomads, who brought it with them on their travels, and, like their leather breeches, it gradually penetrated as far west as the Scandinavian peninsula. In the same way the high boot was introduced to Russia by Genghis Khan and was then copied by other countries. The tiny round hat of Italy and Switzerland, as well as the "beret," has evolved from the the ecclesiastical skull-cap worn to cover the tonsure.

DELIBERATE COSTUME DESIGN

Some national costumes were deliberately designed at a time when nationalistic feeling was running high. Among these are the Greek costume known as the "Amalia," copied from Queen Amalia's own dress with its full flared skirt, tight-fitting bolero bodice and fez-like head-dress. This appeared when Greece regained her freedom from Turkish rule. Another creation is the Austrian "Dirndl" costume (Plate IV, page 17), which acquired its present form after the 1914–18 war, when patriotic upper-class Austrians, disgusted with the division of the Austro-Hungarian Empire, began to revive the long-dead folk dances, customs, and wearing of national costumes. The movement started in the towns and its centre was Salzburg. Coinciding as it did with the revival of the Salzburg Music Festival, the idea soon spread. This accounts for the widespread wearing by the young Nazi girls of the black-knitted jacket with its red, white, and green pattern, and the buttons with the eagles, which are reminders of the colours and emblem of the old Imperial flag.

DECORATIVE MOTIFS

Historical and aristocratic influences are not the only features which help to distinguish between the varied national costumes. Their decorative motifs denote more accurately the specific area to which they belong. These designs are first and foremost dictated by man's beliefs and superstitions. Costume was worn not only as a protection from the elements—its function was also to protect man from evil influences. The most primitive races still paint their naked bodies with red-ochre, woad, saffron, and chalk to keep away evil spirits. These four colours are still used for magic purposes by peasant races and, although it is impossible to say with any certainty why these colours are chosen, it can be said that red is always considered by primitive people to be the colour of the earth and life; therefore if one wears it one has command over the earth and life. Similarly, blue is the colour of the sky or air, yellow of the sun or fire, and white of water.

The invention of clothing did not do away with man's belief in evil spirits. Like his ancestors, he took care that wherever there was an opening through which an evil being could enter his body, he placed a magic charm to prevent this awful happening. This magic charm can be found in the form of the exquisite borders of the Indian sari and other draped garments, the embroidered anklets of the Eastern and other races, the knitted socks of the Scandinavians and Yugoslavs, and the embroidered edges of countless shirts, smocks, dresses, and blouses of Europe. Their elaborate neck and arm bands serve a similar purpose. As time went on superstitions seem to have grown, and it was thought necessary to take precautions with regard to the seams of the clothing. This accounts for the elaborate embroideries up the sides of some garments. Finally the gaps that occur between garments and bodies are protected by elaborately designed belts, neck-cloths which fall from head to blouse, or protect the women's faces, and anklets or footless hose to protect the space between shoe and trousers.

Those parts of the body which remain uncovered are often given protection by magic charms. Blue beads are tied to the hair and round the neck of many Balkan children, particularly those in Serbia; Italian babies wear red coral necklaces. They can be seen in some famous old Italian paintings of the Christ-child. These red bead necklaces are common articles of protection in many parts of the world.

The motifs used in all these elaborately designed precautionary measures vary considerably, and there are no hard and fast rules about their appearance. In countries of the

East where the Moslem or Greek Orthodox faiths predominate, it is usual to find more conventional geometrical patterns. In such countries cross-stitch embroidery is common, and this lends itself to a more rigid type of design. Cross-stitch itself is thought to be a powerful preventive of evil in many countries, as are the beautiful lace designs decorating peasant petticoats, aprons, head-dresses, and blouses everywhere. A Ukrainian blouse or smock has cross-stitch embroidery all round the neck opening, as well as a frill of lace, and down the front, round the sleeves, and usually all round the bottom as well. The introduction of red patches under the arms is intended to prevent one's entrails from being torn out by evil beings. These red patches are occasionally found in other garments besides the smock, such as the Arab "Djibbah."

Flowing floral designs are usually predominant in all fertile lands, such as the Ukraine and the fertile parts of Yugoslavia and Hungary. In such countries there is a wealth of colour because the vegetable dyes used can be so various. In districts with poorer soils, such as the Black Mountains of Serbia, the embroidery is purely conventional in black wool, spun from black goats or sheep, on coarse natural-coloured linen, with an occasional red line and silver, gold, or copper thread, or a particle of such metals. In some other areas where the soil is not rich, such as Scotland, the vegetable and mineral dyes used can still be extremely rich owing to the presence of peat and mineral springs, and one single tartan can show as many as eighty-one gradations of colour.

The introduction of metal thread into the evil-dispelling embroidery is evidence of the primitive belief that all bright metals and stones protect one from the evil-eye, and the amount of jewellery worn is therefore not just an indication of the wealth of the wearer, although a girl does sometimes wear her entire dowry of coins, gold charms, and so on, on her apron and head-dress. The bracelets, necklaces, ear-rings, finger-rings, waist-belts, and anklets made solely of metal and stones show the still powerful belief of the peasants in the protection such materials are supposed to give. The circle is the most important motif of all. According to ancient Greek philosophers, the circle or, better still, the circle within a circle, represented truth and was the most revered of signs. In Christian countries crosses are added to these circles, as an additional protection. Elsewhere they use bells, which certainly help to scare away snakes as well as spirits. In many Catholic countries heart-shaped lozenges worked in scarlet or made of scarlet felt are found not only as ornaments but also as part of the embroidery. Geometrical patterns all with significant meanings, used by ancient Egyptian, Assyrian, and Greek philosophers, as well as magical symbols, have also found their way into peasant design. They are scattered among the glorious designs peasants create for themselves out of the natural elements surrounding them. These natural elements, leaves, flowers, birds, animals and so on, have proved the most fertile source of inspiration of folk artists everywhere, and their use defines the exact locality and regions of the wearers.

CHAPTER VII

The Influence of Costume on Dance

COSTUME is determined by the climatic and geographical conditions, but as some articles of attire, principally footwear, skirts, kilts and trousers, and head-gear do play some part in forming a dancer's movements, the slight differences they can make to the style of dance must be taken into account.

FOOTWEAR

Boots and shoes affect the entire movement of the body, as they determine its stance and carriage. Some tend to restrict the dancer's movements, whilst others lend themselves to very light and quick footwork, or suggest clicking heels and stamping feet.

Bare Feet

It is not surprising that the barefooted dancer possesses the greatest freedom of movement and perfection of carriage. This is particularly noticeable among the gipsies, whose superb carriage is equalled only by that of the poorer peasants in the rich agricultural areas of Eastern and Southern Europe who, during their youth, often work and dance with bare feet. The partly relaxed foot is placed firmly on the ground and immediately contracted in order to maintain balance. The body is held easily erect and responds sensitively to every movement of the feet, swaying gently from the hips, shoulders, or waist.

The Scottish Gillie Shoe, the Georgian Heel-less Boot, and Others

The wonderfully soft elk or doe-skin Gillie shoe, the chamois heel-less boot of the Georgian Cossack and similar footwear, found among mountain people, fit the foot like a glove. (See Plates II and VI, pages 9 and 21.) They protect it from the hard surface, but to some extent control its movement, because they do not allow it to spread to its fullest extent. For this reason there is a certain air of constraint to be noted throughout the entire body. The hips do not sway easily, the head and shoulders are held ready and alert to every change of direction. The spine, particularly among the women, is often straightened to its fullest extent, and breathing is very full, so that the weight of the body does not impede the leaps and springs over mountain obstacles. Yet such footwear also allows tremendous flexibility of ankle and instep; footwork is therefore most intricate, for there are no heels to restrict the full play of the working foot round the ankle or knee of the supporting leg.

The Leather Thonged Sandal of Greece, Yugo-Slavia and parts of Czechoslovakia

This form of footwear (see Plates II, VII and VIII, pages 9, 36 and 37) gives a slight rolling forwards and backwards movement to the foot, which helps the dancer to move easily over the rough or heavy ground. The body responds to the fall of the toe and heel, as can be seen by noting the gentle rise and fall of the head. There is no sideways swaying from the hips and, because the feet are always placed directly towards the constantly changing line of dance, the body movement follows that of the feet, gradually losing impetus as it reaches the shoulders.

The Heavy Hide Shoe, Straw or Reed Sandal of Polish and Russian Peasants and the String Shoe of Spain and Elsewhere

In such shoes (see Plate I, page 8) there is a tendency to place the foot flat on the ground as the dancer travels, which means there is no rising to the highest part of the ball of the foot or pointing of the toes. At the same time, this type of shoe moulds itself to the shape of the wearer's foot and therefore the dancers move freely and easily, if somewhat untidily. The body is held loosely, the arms and head are alert to maintain balance, and there is a great deal of contrary body movement. The feet, although protected, are not restricted.

The Wooden Sabot of France, Holland and Elsewhere

Sabots (see Plate III, page 16) lend a certain stiffness, but do not impede a dancer's movements. The toes cannot be pointed, nor the feet raised very high from the ground. Because sabots do not fit tightly, there is an appreciable danger of their flying off, therefore the dancer thrusts his weight well forwards and down into the ground at each step and the body is held somewhat stiffly. The soles of the sabots have to be kept parallel to the ground, and wherever this is smooth, a tremendous speed can be gained as the wooden shoes glide over the surface.

The Clog of Lancashire, Switzerland and Elsewhere

The clog with the shaped wooden sole and stiff leather upper lends itself to extremely light footwork because it is firmly secured to the foot and thus the ankle has freedom to move, but the weight of the shoe inspires the dancer to indulge in extra beats, taps, and stamps. With this stress on footwork however, the arms, whilst acting as a counter-balance to the weight of the body, are thrown forwards and hang loosely, becoming quite expressionless.

The Heeled Cossack or Russian Boot

This form of footwear is most comfortable for dancing on any type of ground. The foot is supported and protected, but because the sole and upper are flexible the dancer's ankles and insteps can move freely. Such footwear allows the widest possible variety of steps, for the low heels offer a broad base for the erect back and well controlled head and shoulders of the horseman, as well as allowing the stamping of feet, clicking of heels, wide leaps and acrobatic feats of the rider or the agricultural worker with nomadic ancestors.

The High-cut Czech and Hungarian Riding Boot and the Polish High-laced Boot

These boots (see frontispiece) all support the foot in the same way as the Russian boot, but because they come higher up the leg there is a tendency to dance with straighter knees, and although the body is held erect, there is little freedom from the waist. For this reason, the arms and shoulders are kept firmly under control in order to balance the body, compensating for the loss of some elasticity of the knee.

The Heavy, Nailed, Alpine Shoe or Agricultural Boot

Such footwear was more recently introduced into the folk dancers' wardrobe. These boots and shoes restrict foot movements inasmuch as they lack flexibility of sole and upper, and fail to mould themselves to the wearers' feet. This tends to make movements stiff and restrained.

The Ordinary Heeled Slipper, Buckled or Tied Shoe

These again are comparatively recent, but providing the sole and upper are flexible, they have not any special influence on the dancer's movements. They fit firmly, and thus the dancer can move as freely as the rest of the costume allows.

The Portuguese Mule

These light slippers are kept on the feet only by the constant contraction of the foot and pointing of the toes, and the dancer's deliberate placing of the toe first on the ground. This lends a slight forward thrust and a general air of elegance to all movements, because of the nicety of balance required to maintain an erect carriage.

The Spanish High-heeled Slipper

These fit more tightly than the Portuguese slipper, but the higher heels thrust the body further forwards on to the toes; this is compensated by a slight backwards bend from the waist, and by well-controlled shoulders. The forward thrust of the lower half of the leg is also compensated by an incompletely tightened knee, which allows the dancer to use her heels to stress the rhythmic beat; her partner's heels, which are slightly higher and smaller than those of the average male shoe, are used for the same purpose.

SKIRTS, KILTS, AND TROUSERS

The cut and style of skirt, kilt, or trousers firstly affects the position of the hand when placed on hip or waist. Wherever the skirt or trouser is full, it is more usual for the dancer to place the hand with thumb and forefinger firmly on the waist, the outstretched fingers and palm of the hand lying comfortably on the top of the hip. This, to some extent, helps to keep the numerous folds and gathers of the skirt or trousers in place. (See Plate VIII, page 37).

With the tighter skirt or trouser it is more usual to place the back of the hand on the waist in order to avoid displacing the scanty material and thus impeding movement. This position of the hand is usually used with the kilt, as it is essential that the front panels be kept flat. (See Plate VI, page 21.)

Where trousers have an elaborately embroidered pocket or side seam, as in Hungary, the man usually places his hand somewhat lower on the hip, and behind the embroidery. The fingers often lie parallel with the seam, and the thumb rests on the back of the hip. (See frontispiece.)

The width of the skirts never affects the movement a great deal. When at their fullest they are worn with petticoats, which prevent the legs from rising too high, in the same way that the narrow smocks of the Balkans prevent any great upwards thrust of the leg. Moreover, in some Eastern European countries, because of the weight of the dowry sewn on to the apron which is worn over the slit skirt, as well as the fact that knickers are only now coming into use, the dancers tend to keep their legs close together at the knee. (See Plate VII, page 36.)

The cut of the kilt with its flat wrapped-over front makes it important for the legs to be turned out as far as possible, otherwise the material will wrap itself between the dancer's legs. The sporran also acts as a deterrent to a turning-in of the legs. (See Plate VI, page 21.)

It is only the very tight military trouser of parts of Hungary, Poland, and Czecho-slovakia that put any constraint on the dancer's movements (see frontispiece). Elsewhere the tight trouser, as in Greece and Georgia, has extra material grafted into the body part in order to give room for all types of movement. (See Plate II, page 9).

On the other hand, the curious bag-shaped trousers (also Plate II) derived from Turkish fashions and worn by the women in Bosnia, Macedonia, and parts of the Caucasus make the dancers move with a shuffling gait. In such garments it is extremely difficult to raise the feet far from the floor as the centre part of the material is caught into girdle or belt, and any violent movement of foot or knee dislodges this.

HEAD-DRESS

The heavy, festive head-dress of flowers, ribbons, coins, or jewels of the Slav and Finno-Ugrian countries, which are worn especially at weddings, affects the entire carriage of the body, because head movements must be restricted to the absolute minimum if the head-dress is to be kept in place. The dancers surmount this difficulty by using their hands. This accounts for the all-prevailing fashion, where such head-dresses are worn, of placing the hands at the back of the head, or one hand on top of the head, whenever the dance reaches a pitch of excitement. (See frontispiece and Plate VII, page 36.)

The arm movement is also greatly influenced by the use of the veil, which is found principally in the Caucasus. The centre of this is secured to the head and the ends are held between the thumb and finger of each hand. The back of one hand is always placed against the face, thus it is possible to swing the arms to and fro without disclosing the woman's beauty, until that dramatic moment where she stands revealed. (See Plate II, page 9.)

CORSETS

The restrictive influence of the boned corset or tight military coat is noted only in those countries where French court fashions have been widely adapted by the peasants, or where the national costume has been revived after a long period of suppression by church or state, the corset having meanwhile become a common article of attire. This is particularly noticeable in Holland and Sweden. (See Plates III, IV, and V, pages 16, 17 and 20.)

This following of court and military styles accounts for some Hungarian, Polish, and Czech men's customs of wearing their coats slung over one shoulder when dancing. To wear them would entail either a serious bursting of seams or complete loss of arm movements.

PART II

NATIONAL CHARACTERISTICS

CHAPTER VIII

National Differences

IT WOULD be a grave mistake to conclude that the dances of people living under similar climatic conditions look alike in performance. The increasing interest taken by both amateur and professional dancers in the folk dance of the various nations is tending to make all the dances look alike. The amateur acquainted with the English Country Dance evens out all the movements, whilst the professional choreographer and dancer identifies his steps with the technical formulas of classical dance, with the result that *pas-de-bourrées, pas de basques, chassés, pas de valse,* and so on, are not distinguished from each other.

This is not so. There are often very marked differences between the steps of the various nations. These differences can be very subtle, and care must be taken to emphasize them if the dance is to retain its original features and be used for educational or theatrical purposes. This is particularly important with Western European dances, where powerful aristocratic influences and continued wars have tended to spread the English Country Dance and the eighteenth and nineteenth century Polkas, Valses, and Quadrilles at the expense of the ancient Circle, Serpentine, and Processional Dances. These had already suffered suppression and distortion by the church, since they were too closely associated with the dancers' pagan beliefs and practices. Yet it is possible to see subtle differences in the way the now common Valses and Polkas are performed. Like the more genuine folk dance, they too display something of the characteristics of each particular nation's cultural background.

The difficulties facing anyone attempting to explain the reasons for these differences are enormous. Scientists have tried to show that people may be classified as belonging to the same geographical areas, as the Nordic, Mediterranean, and Alpine races; or they may have the same physical characteristics, as the Negro, Mongol, and Caucasian types; belong to the same blood group; have the same head shapes, facial features, hair, and so on. The mass migrations of ethnic groups and their continual intermarriage further complicate the problem, and undoubtedly all these factors play some part in the formation of a dance. Yet it has been discovered by musicologists that music is the most stable art, of any nation. No matter what wars have occurred, what migrations or other disasters, composers of certain groups have always displayed in their music certain features which are apparent in the folk music of their country. This fact makes a dancer's task easier, for a study of the relationship between a folk dance and its music will help to reveal the correct manner of performance. Nearly all the world's leading composers have either consciously or unconsciously been inspired by their own folk music, principally by the mouth music which accompanies the people's festivals, rituals, and dances. They study and consciously make use of its characteristic features, and from them a dancer can learn and borrow much.

The grouping of the European peoples according to the languages they speak is the first definition of their dances (see Map 2, facing this page). Folk dances begin when movements performed together are co-ordinated by common rhythms and sounds. From these rhythms and sounds develop a people's music and language. Therefore wherever the intimate relationship of movement, music and language has been retained, the dance represents a national style.

The European peoples are divided into the following language groups: Greek, Slav, Teuton, Celt, and Latin, which have stemmed from the ancient Aryan tongue; the Finno-Ugrian group, to which Magyars, Finns, and Estonians belong; and the Basques, who have a unique language. Each nation within these language groups has certain features in common with the other members. At the same time, nearly every modern nation has developed some characteristics entirely of its own. These would seem to have been more stressed during the last three hundred years, when the constantly changing political boundaries have made each nation more conscious of its own culture and traditions. It is for this reason that in the following chapters the European countries are grouped according to their languages, before they are dealt with as individual nations.

EXAMPLE I

TABLE OF MUSICAL INTERVALS

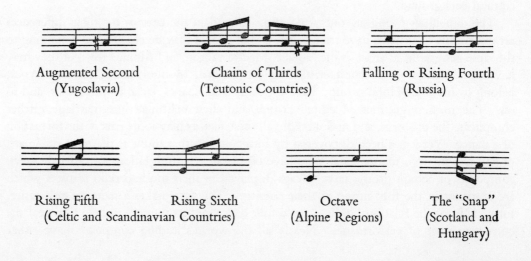

Augmented Second
(Yugoslavia)

Chains of Thirds
(Teutonic Countries)

Falling or Rising Fourth
(Russia)

Rising Fifth   Rising Sixth
(Celtic and Scandinavian Countries)

Octave
(Alpine Regions)

The "Snap"
(Scotland and
Hungary)

KEY TO THE ILLUSTRATIONS

R. side of body is drawn thickly. L. side is drawn finely. Direction of movement is indicated by arrows.

Back to audience	Facing audience	Moving to R. with R. ft.	Moving to L. with L. ft.

N.B. The relationship between step and notes must be observed. The illustration shows on which note the foot is placed in position.

CHAPTER IX

The Middle East and the Turki-Tartars

ALTHOUGH the Middle East is not part of Europe, it is usually accepted as the birthplace of modern civilization. It is here that one must begin to study certain musical and dance characteristics which are strong features of all Spanish music (see page 211) and, to a lesser degree, of Greek, Yugoslav, Russian, and other groups, who at various times have been influenced by Eastern invaders. In Western and Eastern Turkey, Arabia, Egypt, and Persia, tunes are short and often consist of two or three phrases in what can be called free rhythm. By this is meant that there is no regular sequence of bars as understood in the West, for the rhythms are often complex and there is not always a regular number of beats to each bar. This explains why European musicians in transcribing them according to the Western system of notation and time signature, present one with such curiously irregular mixtures of bars in 7/8, 5/4, 9/16, and so on.

In the few dances where a more regular sequence of time signature and bar is followed, such as the favourite 7/8, the performer never takes seven steps to the bar. He normally spaces out each bar by using 3 beats for a long step, followed by two steps lasting 2 beats each. Another favourite device is to dance to complete melodic phrases comprised of an irregular number of beats, often 17, which can be made up of three bars of 4/4 and one of 5/4. This serves as the rhythmic base for a simple yet dignified stepping of two paces to each bar and a lengthening of the seventh step, as the dancer gives a circular swing of his body and touches the floor first with one knee and then with the other.

This irregularity is largely explained by the over-riding importance of the cadences and rhythms of the words which, in many dance-songs, are phrased by the purpose and stress of the movement. Where the words do not dictate the melody and rhythm, the drum beaten by the hand plays an important part.

The uses of the Western drum are vastly different from those of the East. It is a curious but important fact, influencing the music and dance of the Western European nations, that the drum played with the hand was unknown. The Western drum, which is a recent innovation compared with the Eastern gourd and drum, has always been played with sticks. This undoubtedly helps to explain the lack of intricate rhythms in most Western European dances, because before the development of the player's technique and the invention of the modern drum a Western drummer had to lift his sticks very deliberately before hitting his drum, and he had to have time between each accented beat to do this. Thus it often happens that both the strong beat of the drum being hit and the weak beat of the stick being raised are counted by the folk dancers as part of their rhythm. For example, in a 2/4 Polka the drum is only hit twice, but the dancer makes four movements with his feet and therefore accents the first and third steps, while timing his whole movement to fit the regular up-and-down rhythmic gestures of the drummer.

In the East, however, the drummer is subordinate to the dancer. His hands usually rest on the drum and he plays with all his fingers as well as the palm, back, and closed fist of his hand. Very often each hand has a different rhythm, the one marking the comparatively regular pulse dictated by the dancer at the climax of his beat and the other improvising a fascinating pattern of intricate sound, helping the dancer to express his meaning and mood. The rhythms made are thus extremely varied, irregular, and some-times broken, because the dancer does not always mark with his feet alone the complicated rhythms he requires. Sometimes they are marked by the arms and head, while the feet keep to a regular but soundless pulse. Or a movement can start by being marked with the feet, the rhythmic phrase being concluded by arm or hand while the feet rest. Moreover some rhythms are first strongly accented downwards by movements of the feet, then upwards by the hands while the feet keep to a smooth unaccented pulse.

It is essential for the Westerner, before he performs the dances of most Slav countries and of Spain, to understand how rhythms can be distributed to the various parts of the body. People coming from any country influenced by the East undoubtedly hear and feel rhythms in a different way from that of the Westerner, just as most races with negroid blood instinctively syncopate their dances and songs, no matter where these originated.

THE CAUCASUS

(The Soviet Republics of Armenia, Azerbaijan and Georgia)

The dividing of rhythms is seen at its best in some of the dances of the Soviet Republics of Armenia, Azerbaijan, and Georgia, the area lying just north of those Republics, and to some extent amongst the Tartars in the Crimea. The languages spoken by these people belong to the Turki-Tartar group, as do those spoken in Asia Minor, and all these people have been connected by wars, emigrations and immigrations. (See Map 2, facing page 52.)

There is some evidence that the original inhabitants of the Caucasus were of a distinct racial type, and there are still traces of a definite language which bears some relationship to that of the Basques, supposedly the most ancient European people. It is interesting, therefore, that both the Caucasians and the Basques have retained some very ancient rituals and ceremonies, despite the opposition of foreign rulers and the influence of the churches.

Although Armenia, Azerbaijan, and Georgia are within the same geographical area, they have not all had the same history. Georgia has been least influenced by outside events, owing to the inaccessibility of most of the country, which lies among extremely high and precipitous mountains. Here the original Caucasians first merged with Turki tribes coming from the south-east. Later the Greeks, who sailed through the Black Sea to this Land of the Golden Fleece, so-called because of its immense mineral wealth, colonized some of the sea-coast and river areas. This early meeting of eastern and western culture resulted in a fine flowering of the arts during the medieval period. Shot'ha Rust'hveli's famous poem *The Knight in the Tiger's Skin* (written between 1184–1207) is a magnificent example of the Georgian's fine literary skill and imagery. There are also many legends and folk tales of the famous Queen Thamar, which inspired such poets as Lermontov and musicians as Balakirev.

This flourishing period was halted by the Mongol invasion from the north-east in the thirteenth century, and the various Tartar princes held sway until the area was finally annexed by the Russian Tsars from the north during the nineteenth century.

Armenia and Azerbaijan have suffered most from outside influences. Lying at the cross-roads of the great trade routes from east to west, they were swept by the Turki tribes in 1000 B.C., the Persians under Darius in 520 B.C., and the Romans in the first century A.D. Later they became part of the Byzantine Empire (fourth century A.D.) and of the Moslem Empire (seventh century A.D.). This was followed by invasions of Arabs (eleventh century), Mongols (thirteenth century), Turks (sixteenth century), and finally the Russians (nineteenth century).

In addition to the many changes of rulers, all of whom governed either according to an ancient patriarchal code or by the feudal system (each princeling or khan owing his allegiance to the head of some far-away state), the three Republics have also suffered changes of religion according to the will of their masters. These changes have not been the same in each Republic. Georgia was largely converted to Christianity very early and remained faithful to the Greek Orthodox Church in the sea-coast areas even after the invasion of the Mongols. Armenia also became Christian, but the church broke away to form its own particular creed and ritual; even when it became part of the Moslem Empire many of its inhabitants remained faithful to this Armenian Orthodox Church and suffered cruel persecution until Armenia became one of the Soviet Republics. Azerbaijan became principally Mohammedan after the Moslem invasion. The various religious factions have not, however, been able to suppress the old folk dances entirely, although in some instances they have successfully altered their original significance. It is interesting to note also in what way and to what extent the various invasions have affected them.

ARMENIA

Armenia has over three hundred dances which depict every change of mood, from the exaltation of the ancient circular rituals to the wild hilarity of the comic dances based on clownish antics and jokes of old men, travellers, and well-known characters like the marriage-broker, whose jerking fingers, meaning nods, and sideways glances are accurate portrayals of such types. There are sad love and mourning dances which are particularly beautiful, or precise, purposeful dances based on military or work processes. The most outstanding of these is the famous Carpet-weaving Dance derived from one of Armenia's most important industries. Here the girls not only depict the actual work process undertaken by the hands, but also mark the carpet's pattern with their feet. Like the Finns, the Armenians perform a number of dances based on natural phenomena. One is the Willow Dance, in which rows of women sway and bend as the willow-trees wave over a brook, and another is a Wind Dance, in which long scarves and arms billow and blow like clouds across the sky.

No invader or conqueror ever goes into a country without leaving some traces behind him. In Armenia can be found many dances belonging to other people, such as the Persian War Dance in which one man is hurled through the air like a cannon-ball; this dance dates from the Persian invention of this weapon. There is the Turkish Butcher's Dance as well as a Spring Ritual brought by the Turks, and numerous wild Tartar dances. Moreover many foreign elements have crept into the Armenians' own dance, such as Turkish tunes or Tartar steps in a solemn ritual.

AZERBAIJAN

Azerbaijan dance is picturesque and strikingly beautiful. Many women's dances are to be found which are intended only to show off feminine beauty. Both Azerbaijan and Georgian women are still considered the most beautiful in Russia; their hall-mark is the straight black eyebrows meeting in the centre over deep blue eyes, rich black hair worn in pig-tails, and a wonderful carriage. In their dances great play is made with handkerchieves, scarves, and veils. These are so manipulated as gradually to disclose the eyes, nose, face, and breasts. Such dances are relics of the time when the girls had to dance either before the man who was arranging to buy her in marriage or before the overlord. It is from such a dance that the story of Salome's Dance of the Seven Veils must have come.

It must be noted that throughout these dances the girls keep themselves sedately aloof and move the veils with great delicacy and discretion.

GEORGIA

With many Caucasian tribes, agility, swift and daring horsemanship, warlike athletic contests, and courage are still considered the supreme virtues. The Cossack saying, "The dark night, a trusty steed, a blade of steel, and a stout heart are my friends," sums up the feeling that lies behind most Georgian dancing, where the male is supreme. Their dances are exceptional because the man dances on the very tips of his toes in an ever-increasing tempo, like the classically trained ballerina in present-day ballet. But whereas she moves her body in long flowing lines or short staccato movements, the Georgian's body scarcely moves at all and his arms only sway from side to side as if balancing his body.

These extraordinary men's dances are explained by the life and customs of the Georgian people. For centuries these hillmen have lived among the narrow mountain tracks. Hunting or pasturing flocks on the hilly slopes and in steep gorges, they have had to learn how to use the smallest ledge as a foot-hold on the heights, maintain balance over a stream or precipice, and negotiate every kind of mountain obstacle. From this way of life has come their smooth-soled, heel-less tight boots, their habit of balancing on their toes, and their tightly girdled coats.

In the old days the Georgian Cossack worshipped the eagle, whose method of attacking a victim he imitates in the Lezghinka. He circles swiftly round with tiny steps on his toes, hovers for a moment above his prey, often represented by a dagger flung into the ground, and then drops on his knees, seizes the dagger in his teeth, as the eagle seizes his prey, and soars up again.

The Georgian has three other types of dance. The friendly competition Cherouli is similar to the Ukrainian Gopak and the Norwegian Halling, but contains many steps more directly derived from a horse's galloping, leaping, and rearing movements. The Khorumi depicts a battle among the mountains and reflects the history of an area which has never been conquered but which has always had to fight to retain its independence. The men enter as if reconnoitring, hide behind rocks, and bend low listening for the enemy. They build a pyramid to scan the horizon, and advance and form a circle to depict the hilly barrier barring the enemies' path. The enemy, however, arrives and a fight takes place.

The theme of the lyrical Lekouri is quite different and is the only dance performed by men and women together. The day's work is over and the youths are gathered together. They go up to the girl of their choice and invite her to join the circle. The maiden agrees, but during the dance her eyes are kept carefully lowered and only rarely does she turn her glance to his. The man never touches his partner but always follows close behind her. Her arms are the barrier beyond which he must not pass. The grace, smooth quality, and quickly changing pattern of the dance depend entirely on the unexpected turning of the girl. Her partner turns as swiftly, so that they never meet face to face. The dance represents the continual travelling up and down the zig-zag mountain paths, and the single step shows how each section of the path must be tried before any weight is put on to the foot, lest the boulder should fall or the ledge crumble. This dance usually follows a Lezghinka.

The musical characteristics of these Caucasian republics are similar to those of the Middle East, with the addition of extreme contrasts of emotional expression, which in the mountainous areas are achieved by larger intervals between the notes. Certain dance characteristics are also held in common.

The Basic Step

All Caucasians possess the erect carriage of the horseman, which gives great smoothness of movement and is exemplified in their performance of the basic step of a Georgian Lezghinka and Lekouri, Azerbaijan Dyasmaly, Armenian Circle, and other dances. One arm is usually held out to the side, while the other is bent across at chest level for the men and eye-level for the women. It is usually danced to a 2/4 rhythm, but is sometimes found in a 6/8. But no matter in which rhythm, it is essential that the dancer keeps absolutely even and smooth the three steps of which it is comprised (Ex. 3, page 62). At first the step must give the impression that the ground is being tested. Then the speed and space are gradually increased until it looks as if the dancer were skimming over the surface of the ground like a galloping horse.

The Balance

In most Caucasian dances the body must be held delicately balanced on both feet, so that either is ready to commence at any point in the dance. An example is found in the Azerbaijan Dyasmaly (Ex. 2, page 61). In the Lekouri, this balance is very important as the dancers must be prepared to start again with whichever foot happens to be the easier after a sudden turn or twist in the direction of the dance.

Interpretation of Rhythms

A favourite device in a number of Caucasian dances is the doubling of the speed of a step while the musician continues to keep to the same tempo. For example in the Armenian Cradle Dance and the Carpet-weaving Dances and the Georgian Lezghinka, the dancers often performs two basic steps (Ex. 3, page 62) in the first two bars of music, followed by four of them in the next two bars. This happens in other interesting steps (Ex. 4, page 62).

It is important to note that in some Caucasian dances, usually those performed to mouth-music only, the dancers do not accent the first beat of each bar but work across the bar line in order to accent their step with the appropriate word. Occasionally this appears to cut right across the regular pulse of the rhythm, but it will be found that the dancer ultimately accents the first beat of a bar again, and if carefully watched it will be seen that the regular pulse beat has been marked elsewhere than by the feet. This happens most particularly in the work dances and in one or two ancient Armenian rituals. It is also usual when performing certain steps that resemble the classical *pas-de-basque* to alternate the accent, marking it first with the feet and then with the hands (Ex. 5, page 64).

Position of the Hands

In most women's dances, whether with or without a veil, the hands are very carefully poised. The thumb and the first and second fingers are joined in a circle, whilst the others are held lightly apart. The wrist is so turned that when the arm is curved at eye-level, the back of the hand is opposite the face. The man's hands are often clenched at shoulder-level, or held with fingers stretched and palms facing the ground. The arms rarely go directly above the head.

Male Dance

The male dance steps are often very spectacular. There is the great leap in the air as the body is twisted from side to side. This is found in both military and competitive dances; so is the leap with one leg bent up to the other, and the jump-turn with the change of feet in the air (somewhat like the *grand jeté entrelacé*). Among the Georgians there is the swift fall to the ground from the toes on to the knees and the immediate rising again, the running on the toes and the swift turns on two feet. There are very curious jumps performed as the men crouch close to the ground and turn swiftly in the same place. There is also the marvellous goat-like leap, in which the dancer appears to be reining his horse up for a jump over an obstacle or down a mountain (Ex. 6, page 65).

A Unique Feature

Armenian dances have one unique feature in a very swift and deep back bend, performed by both men and women.

The performers usually bend slightly forwards, bringing the hands together in front of the knees, then rise on to the toes at the same time as they throw the body and head backwards and open the arms to the side. This movement is seen at its best in some ancient Armenian rituals and the Carpet-weaving Dance (Ex. 6, page 65).

General Characteristics

There is throughout a remarkable neatness of step coupled with a freedom and speed of movement that come from the nomadic and mountain origins of these peoples. There are very few couple dances, although since 1936 these are gradually increasing in number as the various work processes come to be undertaken by everyone instead of being exclusive to one sex. There are many circular communal dances, which usually start on the right foot and move counter-clockwise. These resemble the hundreds of Kolos found everywhere, and always have some ritual significance. The steps are similar to those found in the Middle East and Slav countries.

EXAMPLE 2

THE GIRL'S STEP FROM DYASMALY

1. Fall on to L. ft., head turned to side, body facing front.

2. Bring R. ft. to L., resting weight on both toes.

3. Fall on to L. ft.

4. Bring R. ft. to L., resting weight on both toes.

1. Fall on to L. ft.

2. Bring R. ft. to L. resting weight on R. toe only.

3. Raise L. ft. in front of R. knee.

4. Drop L. ft in place, both feet resting on toes.

Dyasmaly

EXAMPLE 3

THE LEZGHINKA BASIC STEP

1. Slide R. ft. forwards and then slightly backwards.

and   Bring L. ft. to R.

2. Slide R. ft. forwards

Repeat movement with L. ft.

Lezghinka

EXAMPLE 4

DOUBLING OF RHYTHMS: PIVOT STEP

The first two bars constitute the usual method of performance in other countries.

1. Fall on to L. ft.

2. Bring R. ft. behind L. transfer weight on to R. toe.

Eᴏxᴀᴍᴘʟᴇ 4 *(cont.)*

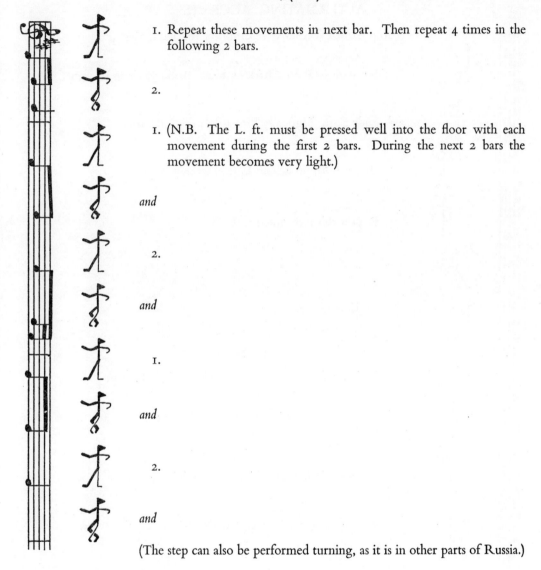

1. Repeat these movements in next bar. Then repeat 4 times in the following 2 bars.

2.

1. (N.B. The L. ft. must be pressed well into the floor with each movement during the first 2 bars. During the next 2 bars the movement becomes very light.)

and

2.

and

1.

and

2.

and

(The step can also be performed turning, as it is in other parts of Russia.)

Lezghinka

etc

EXAMPLE 5

ALTERNATING ACCENTS

A step from Dyasmaly, resembling the *pas de basque*

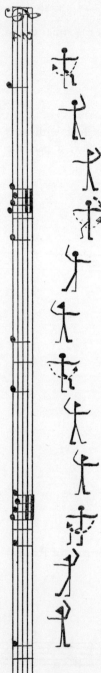

1. Jump on to R. ft., marking beat. Begin to circle R. arm.

and   Slide L. ft. diagonally forwards, raising R. arm.

2. Bring R. ft. up behind L. ft., marking beat.

1. Repeat this movement to L.

1. Spring lightly on to R. ft. Begin to circle L. arm.

and   Step on to L. ft. just in front of R., pressing L. arm upwards on beat.

2. Close R. ft. lightly behind L., remaining on toes.

1. Repeat above movement with L. ft. and moving to left.

From Dyasmaly

ARMENIAN BACK BEND (WOMEN'S)

Bend forwards bringing hands together in front of knees, which are relaxed.

Rise on toes, throw body backwards and open arms sideways and backwards.

Armenian Carpet-weaving Dance

GOAT'S LEAP (MEN'S)

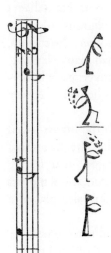

1. Step heavily on to R. ft., raising L. leg behind.

Throw L. leg upwards and forwards and spring off R. ft., throwing body and arms backwards.

and Land on L. ft., bringing arms upwards and round over head.

2. Immediately straighten body and bring R. ft. to L.

Lezghinka

CHAPTER X

The Greeks

GREEK writers from the earliest times have always admitted the Eastern influence in their music. To-day both music and dance still show similar characteristics to those of Asia Minor. The Greeks are of very mixed origins and their history is difficult to trace. Early primitive settlers sailed in from the East, and it is known that before Homer (tenth century B.C.) others came over the mountains from the north and were of the same nomadic peoples who founded other European states. They were later followed by the Northern Dorians, adepts at the art of mime, and by groups sailing in from further east.

Because of the extremely difficult nature of the Greek countryside with its high mountains, narrow passes, and numerous rocky islands, the various groups settled only gradually in the fertile valleys and along the sea coasts, where natural harbours afforded some means of security. These primitive peoples brought with them many dances and rituals, which gradually changed character as some early settlements developed into city states and grew wealthy by trade and by the annexing of small outlying villages whose wares they required. There seems to have been considerable religious tolerance in those days, for although the city states were often at war with one another, the shrines, temples, and groves were held sacred, no doubt because the varied cults had many elements in common and there was as yet no single all-powerful religion. Moreover, each household had its own household gods, whose presence at communal festivals helped to ensure the well-being of all.

By the time that Athens had become the leading city state to which the others owed allegiance, the great age of classical art had begun. Not only do the Greek authors describe how the people everywhere danced in honour of every kind of god on all festive and sorrowful occasions, and in order to acquire physical fitness, but painters and sculptors have left records of these dancing activities on friezes and vases. Dancing also played a large part in the great tragedies enacted in the newly built theatres.

This magnificent flourishing of the arts, which had a remarkable influence wherever the Greek Empire spread, did not cease when Greece became part of the Roman Empire. The Romans assimilated the culture of the conquered and when, in the third and fourth centuries A.D., the Roman Empire itself was split up by the incursions of the Goths, Greek learning continued to lead the field in Alexandria and Constantinople. But Greece itself ceased to have an independent existence and became firstly part of the Eastern Roman Empire (*circa* A.D. 500) and secondly part of the Ottoman Empire (*circa* A.D. 1500), to which it belonged until 1829, when it regained comparative independence by the Treaty of Adrianople.

This classical art and culture affected only the cities, however, for, owing to the difficulties of maintaining communications among the mountains and narrow passes, the remote areas were relatively untouched by this cultural wealth and by changes of government or incursions of raiders. It is well known that in some of the furthest mountain regions the people never acknowledged their allegiance to their Turkish overlords. It is for this reason that so many ancient rituals and dances have come down through the centuries almost unchanged. The Greek Orthodox church, which became the Greek faith during the first period of the Eastern Roman Empire, has certainly attached these people's festivals to the Christian calendar, but it has never banned the dance. In fact, there are many dance-like movements performed by the priests themselves in present-day services. Time has dimmed their meaning and an occasional outside influence may have altered their form, or reinforced early Eastern characteristics shown in the music. Yet because these people continued, unhindered, to practise their ancient dances in the remoter areas, it is still possible to compare the dances to-day with those described by the old Greek authors and depicted on the ancient vases and friezes.

The Relationship of Word and Movement

The most important characteristic of the Greek dance is its intimate relationship to the phrasings of the words which accompany it. These are usually sung by the dancers themselves. This intimate relationship was one of the great features governing the expressive activities of the dancing chorus of the famous Greek tragedies, the secret of which philosophers like Plato, poets like De Baif, and dancing masters like Guido Arena tried to discover. But few have taken the trouble to investigate this peculiar relationship as it has always existed amongst the Greek people's dances.

Many Greek dances have time signatures of 7/8 or 5/4; others of 3/8 and 2/4 are more rare. But the dancer never takes 7, 5, 3, or 2 steps to the bar. Instead the series of steps (or enchaînement) is phrased with varying patterns of slow and quick steps which match the exact rhythm of the words. For example, if the syllable or word occupies 3, $1\frac{1}{2}$, or even a $\frac{1}{2}$ beat, the step will take that amount of time to perform. Whereas in many Western countries it is performed on the first beat, the dancer then pausing until the next word or syllable is commenced. This phenomenon is explained by the fact that whereas all Teutonic languages are languages of hard and soft accents, Greek relies on the varying length of the syllables in order to get the correct inflection and rhythm of the sentences. If the syllable or word is stressed, then the step is correspondingly emphasized.

Épaulement

The second unusual feature is the rapidly changing position of the dancers in relation to the line of dance (épaulement). The dance usually starts with the right foot and moves counter-clockwise. In the slower dances this change usually occurs with every step, as in the Kalamatianos, in which the dancer begins facing the centre, turns his back to the line of dance and then faces it, when performing his first three steps. In quicker dances these changes are not quite so frequent.

To achieve these quick changes of direction, the dancers' bodies are held extremely upright and the weight of the body is moved directly forwards with the foot movement. This gives a very smooth and frieze-like quality to the line of dancers. The slow step is usually large, allowing the dancers to progress, whilst the quick ones are mostly done in place. The foot is held almost flat to the ground; and in hopping steps, the women tend to slide the feet along the ground whilst the men's feet move upwards (Ex. 8, page 70).

Steps

For the most part the steps performed are simple: stepping to the side, followed by a closing of the feet together or a passing of the foot in front or behind the other, hopping, pointing of toes, and occasionally a swing of the legs through the various positions in the air accompanied by a hop or bend and stretch of the supporting leg (Ex. 7, page 69). The leader embroiders these simple steps and works up excitement by increasing either the speed of the dance or the number of turns and jumps.

The ground pattern, like the type of movement, depends entirely on the location of the dancing space. Most Greek dances are simple in structure. Many of them are circles developing into a chain and resolving into a circle again. These are led by one man, who improvises to relieve the monotonously repeated enchaînement of the file and to incite them to further enterprise. As this man tires he often hands his task to another. The enchaînement usually lasts some four bars and is repeated again and again. In those dances usually associated with one particular group in the community, such as the Hassapikos (a butcher's dance originally from Constantinople and found also in Armenia), it can last as long as twenty-four bars.

The very fact that so many dances are Circle Dances rules out much individual movement of hand or arm except from the leader, who often breaks away to express himself with wavings of a handkerchief. In some dances derived from very ancient initiation rites, the dancers are linked by handkerchieves, although usually they hold hands or wrists and very occasionally shoulders.

Male Dance

The Greeks were originally a nation of shepherds, sailors, and fishermen, with grape- and olive-growers in the valleys and on the lower mountain slopes, so that certain dances are connected with these activities. In addition historical events turned many of the young men into fighters, and those dances which were originally performed to encourage physical fitness developed, firstly, into the Pyrrhic or fighting dances found in many areas, and which are the particular property of the Evzones or Royalist soldiers, and then into the more stealthy warriors' dances of the Klephts or Guerrillas in the mountains. The movements of these dances closely resemble the movements performed by the Georgians in their Khorumi, for although the Greeks lack the horse-like movements of the Georgian, their dance represents a similar kind of history.

General Characteristics

Until recently men and women seldom danced together, although chains of men and women danced at the same time, the women's chain often being led and terminated by a man. The few women's dances are very simple and most dignified. The men's dances are often punctuated by feats of strength.

The few couple dances, as distinct from the ancient processionals and chains of men and women standing alternately, are of more recent origin and are similar to those found all over the Balkans. They were probably introduced by the Venetians and other Crusading Knights during the Holy Wars, and particularly at the time of the Fourth Crusade.

EXAMPLE 7

FROM A MACEDONIAN GUERRILLA DANCE

Men are linked in a Chain

1–2. Step on to R. ft., raising L. leg bent behind.

3–4. Rise on R. toe and swing L. leg up in front, toe pointed.

1–4. Sink on R. leg turning to face centre and locking L. leg round behind R.

1–2. Rise on R. toe, leaving L. leg locked behind R.

3–4. Stretch L. leg out and turn on R. ft., to back line of dance.

Teshkoto or Dance of Affliction

EXAMPLE 8

KALAMATIANOS
(Greek National Dance)

Dancers stand in a chain, holding hands, feet together, toes to centre.

1–3. On first beat begin to step to side on R. ft., turning to left, completing step on third beat.

4–5. Step back on L. ft., turning back to line of dance.

6. Step to side on R. ft., turning to face centre.

7. Hop on R. ft., turning to face line of dance.

1–3. Step on L. ft. in front of R.

4–5. Step to side on R. ft., turning towards left.

6–7. Step back on L. ft., turning back to line of dance.

1–3. Step to side on R. ft., turning to face centre.

4–5. Step on L. ft. in front of R., to face line of dance.

6–7. Transfer weight of body back to L. ft.

EXAMPLE 8 *(cont.)*

1–3. Step to side on L. ft., turning to face centre.

4–5. Step on R. ft. in front of L., turning back to line of dance.

6–7. Transfer weight of body back to R. ft.

(N.B. Each first step of each bar takes 3 beats, the others take 2 beats.)

Kalamatianos

CHAPTER XI

The Slavs

PEOPLES speaking a language derived from a common source and having folk dances and arts in common are to be found throughout the Balkans, in the Danubian Plains, and in the vast European-Asiatic Plains and Steppes that stretch from the Pripet Marshes in the west and onwards south of the Urals to the far eastern mountain ranges, and from the White Sea in the north to the Black Sea in the south (Map 2, facing page 52). The ancestors of these Slav peoples were descendants of the nomads who had spread throughout Europe and Asia after the receding of the ice-cap that once covered the entire area. Some came from the northern plains and are usually known as the proto-nordics; others came from the south-east and others again from the eastern Turki and north-eastern Ugrian tribes (Map 1, facing page 32).

Some idea of the mixture of tribes that went to make these Slav peoples can be understood by referring to the *Chronicles of the Ancient Years*, a book written by the priest Nestor (1056–1114), in which he describes how the Grand Prince of Kiev, Vladimir Svyatoslavich (A.D. 978–1015), when wishing to employ religion to strengthen the unity of his state of Rüs, set up a temple for the many gods of his people on the hill outside the town. Amongst these were the ancient animal gods, water nymphs, Rod and Rozhanitsy (the supposed ancestors of the Slavs), Dazborg a sun-god and Volos a cattle-god, all of whom belonged to the original inhabitants of these north-western Russian regions. In addition he erected the statues of Khors, sun-god of the Central Asian people, and of Mokosh, a goddess of the Finnish tribes originating in the far north-east. Over them all ruled Peroun, the god of thunder and creator of lightning, and to this day Holy Week is still called "Thunder Week" in some parts of European Russia.

During the first seven hundred years of the Christian era, there was a tremendous movement of nomadic tribes, which was very much more than the usual summer migration from southern to northern pastures. The domestication and breeding of horses made travel much easier and the multiplication of tribes demanded a greater pasturage for the flocks. With the fall of the Roman Empire, these Slav countries underwent many changes and it was not until about 800 A.D. that a stabilization of tribal conditions was started. It is interesting to find in the above-mentioned *Chronicles* a call for Slavic unity, when other raiding and emigrating peoples, as well as warlike expeditions, had divided the Slavs into three distinct groups; the Southern Slavs in approximately that area now known as Yugoslavia; the Western Slavs of Poland and Czechoslovakia; and the Eastern Slavs or Russians (Map 1, facing page 32).

Yet despite the many changes that took place before the year 800 A.D., and were to take place after it, all these peoples have retained one form of dance in common, the closed Kolo. The outstanding feature of this is the simple basic step consisting of little more than a step-to-the-right followed by a closing of the feet, then a step-to-the-left followed by a similar closing of the feet. There is no progression either clockwise or anti-clockwise. There is sometimes a movement in and out of the centre, or a different way of closing the feet, or movement of the body. In addition, although each Slav country has its own musical characteristics with which some dance movement is particularly associated, all their music shows extreme contrasts of emotional expression. The best known form is the Dumka, a lament, which is interspersed with passages of wild exhilaration. It is the almost violent changes from sorrow to joy, and from slow to fast, that gives these simple Kolos their tremendous expressiveness. To this is added the frequent introduction of the larger musical intervals, which gives the melodies such variety of mood.

It should be noted that the Slav word for these circle dances differs and can also be attached to dances which move from a circle to a chain and vice versa: Kolo in Yugoslavia, Poland, Czechoslovakia and Russia; also Kolomiykas (Ukraine), Kalamajkas (Czechoslovakia), Khorovod (U.S.S.R.), Krizachok (Byelorussia), Horos (Bulgaria), and Hora (Romania).

YUGOSLAVIA

Greece, Italy, Turkey, Hungary and Austria have all played a part in shaping the folk songs and dances of the six Republics which now comprise Yugoslavia. But although the Republics of Serbia, Montenegro, Bosnia, Herzegovina, Macedonia and Croatia each display some distinct feature of their own, their songs and dances prove that the boundary lines are purely arbitrary, for they possess features in common which stand out so strongly that it seems that the pressure of historical events has never been able to break the will of the Yugoslav people. They have created their own national style, and it has been strengthened by long years of oppression.

The Kolo is danced everywhere and is seen at its best among the Serbians, who are the purest of the Southern Slavs. Ten of their Kolos are danced elsewhere in Yugoslavia, together with more intricate forms. The overwhelming impression of these dances is the superb rhythmic control of the dancers, and their ability to convey, through the rhythm, their emotional reactions to the circumstances through which a dance develops.

Yugoslav dances can be roughly divided into two categories: those in which the dancers make and dictate their own rhythm, and those in which they follow the music.

In areas of Montenegro and Macedonia where the Turkish overlords, who conquered the country in A.D. 1566, were unable to subjugate the people completely, the musicians are the servants of the dance. The dance leader, who attains his position after long practice and competition, plays a unique role. Firstly, he must know the basic structure and purpose of the dance. Secondly, he must inspire both dancers and musicians by the force of his own example. By a glance of his eye or nod of his head he commands the dancers' efforts and dictates his rhythms to a drummer, whose heavy drum-stick often marks the duration of the phrase and whose light one marks the rhythm of the steps within the enchaînement. Thirdly, he must be so convinced of the necessity of co-operative effort that he will hand on the leadership to another should his powers fail him. Finally, he must be so sensitive to the mood of the group that he can anticipate that important moment when all are working together as one, and he can work up the dance to a tremendous climax by improvising on the basic step, the other dancers following him.

The rhythm of such dances begins tentatively, becomes insistent, develops unexpected elements, and finally becomes overpoweringly exciting. The often accompanying pipe tune changes gradually from a haunting sadness to triumphant gaiety, therefore such dances, like the Macedonian Teshkoto, are profoundly moving. This dance arises from the period of Turkish domination, when the young men had to earn their living away from home and returned for the annual wedding ceremonies. The grave opening, with its cat-like steps and vigilant attitude, shows how the men remained impervious to outside influences. But as their hearts warm to their native soil and friendly faces, so their movements expand and quicken until they are vigorously leaping and turning to express their joy at the home-coming. Similar dances are performed by the Montenegrins, who have the absolutely uninhibited freedom of movement typical of a nation that has never submitted to a conqueror. Their warrior's Dance with a Rifle is very like the Manx Dirk Dance, in theme, but is completely unrestrained and culminates in the rapid firing of the rifle.

Bosnia and Herzegovina were completely suppressed by the Turks and thus the dances seem nervously restrained. But they appear more determined because the rhythms are more regular and controlled, and therefore more persistent. As in Montenegro, the dancers usually sing their own accompaniment and the steps are allied to the stress of the words. The Turkish prohibition of native song and dance has led to the development of many "silent dances," where the only sound is that of the dancers' feet and the jingle of the coins and medals on their costumes. In one of these "dumb reels," Starobosansko Kolo, the man tests the powers of his girl. The dance-leader incites the men to improvise twists, turns, leaps, and bends, whilst the girls, holding their partners' hands, have to keep up with them continually repeating a simple step which becomes extremely fast, tortuous in pattern, and complex in rhythm.

Everywhere the woman's style of dance is notably different from that of the man. She often performs the same steps as he does, but with modesty, and she usually keeps her eyes lowered. The woman's status in Yugoslav society is often indicated by the position she occupies in the dances. In many wealthy Moslem areas she seldom appears.

The wealthy Bosnians and other princes, in order to retain their estates when overrun by the Turks, swore allegiance to the Ottoman Emperor and adopted his faith and customs. To prevent the Turks from carrying off their women, these princes dressed them in Turkish fashions, so that their beauty would be hidden under the voluminous yashmak and baggy trousers. They forbade them to dance in public, therefore the women developed their own dances in the harems. In poorer Moslem areas and remote mountain villages, the women usually have their own Kolos and dance apart from the men. In areas where the Greek Orthodox church prevails, the women join the communal Kolo as a separate group, or the Kolo is divided into sections, men on one side and women on the other. A man often leads the women's chain, and a woman the men's. In Croatia, Slovenia and North Serbia, where the Catholic church and western influences dominate the social atmosphere, men and women stand alternately in the Kolo, or perform Couple Dances from Austria, Italy and Hungary. An interesting sidelight on the position of the women is also found in some old Serbian Kolos, when the women join in in strict order of precedence.

It is the rich Northern Plains that suffered most from invaders, and this is shown everywhere in the dances. The Plains were overrun by the Ostrogoths in the fourth century A.D., and later became part of the Byzantine Empire. They were then conquered by the Magyars, and in Northern Serbia to-day the Hungarian Czárdás is as popular as the varied Kolos in which typical Hungarian steps are often incorporated. As the Magyars were converted and paid tribute to the Catholic church, they forced their serfs to do likewise. This meant that northern Yugoslav dances were attached to the church calendar, and their content changed. Where these northern areas became part of the Austro-Hungarian Empire a further distortion of the dances took place, for certain elements from western social dances were introduced, such as the hand-clapping and stamping, arming and swinging, and valses and polkas so typical of western Europe.

Owing to the mountainous nature of Yugoslavia, however, no conqueror entered into complete military occupation, and in remote areas the peasants have continued to practise their rituals and Kolos unhindered by church or overlord.

The Basic Step and the Augmented Second

There are fifteen ways of performing the basic step of the Yugoslav Kolos. These steps are fascinating because the stepping to the side followed by a closing of the feet is often allied to the outstanding feature of Yugoslav mouth music, the performers' continual practice of singing in Seconds with an occasional rise to an Augmented Second. In certain dances where the singers closely follow their Second by an Augmented Second, the dancers, who are also the singers and work in two groups one singing a Second higher than the other, mark this difference. As they sing the Second, they step to the side and close neatly, and on the Augmented Second they step to the side but with some extra movement as they bring up the other foot. This relationship of step and sound is found in Bosnia and Herzegovina.

Relaxation

The dramatic persistence of Yugoslav dance rhythms is made more obvious by the dancers' wonderful control. There are very few solos. The dancers are linked in open or closed Kolos, holding one another's hands, shoulders, elbows or fingers, or in Lesa, holding one another's waist-belts. At the beginning of the Kolo, the dancers are curiously tense and alert, but as they proceed they completely relax and submit themselves to the collective rhythm and effort. This relaxation is so complete that sometimes their bodies vibrate until a continuous movement ripples through their encircling arms and from their heads to their feet (Ex. 10, page 80).

These trembling Kolos are often relics of ancient fertility rites, and an old Slav saying tells how the movement of the earth, sun or moon has entered into the dancers and made them dance in tune with the elements.

Movements are all taken from the knee and in some slow dances this leads to a tremendous drive through to the heel, which lends great strength to the movement. It is particularly noticeable in areas under eastern influence, for the dancers suddenly pause and swing their working leg to and fro whilst rising and falling on the toe of the supporting leg, or suddenly crouch down before taking the next step forwards. Such movements can only arise from the need of being constantly alert to an enemy's movements (Ex. 7, page 69).

Rhythms

The rhythms of the enchaînements are often carefully based on the words of the dance-songs, as in Greece. They may last from four up to ten bars of varied time signatures, and the rhythms vary considerably. The complexities usually arise because in some dances the singers or musicians extemporize while the dancers keep to a regular pulse, and in others the dancers break away while the song retains its simple form.

A strong contrasting of rhythms occurs in many Montenegrin dances, when the song sung by the performers often has a different time signature from that of their dance. No attempt is made to alter either rhythm to make the first beats coincide. To some extent this independent functioning of dance and music occurs in Serbia and other areas influenced by western church modes, and where the musician leads the dance. For example the Serbian Vranyanka, in which the dancers' elegant style and proud carriage speak of rich oriental influences, has an enchaînement lasting for five bars, whilst the melodic phrase only lasts for four. Both are in 3/4, the dancers marking 3 beats in each bar, but they always mark the first beat of their enchaînement with an upwards lift of their bodies, and the musicians always mark the first beat of their melodic phrase. This results in a round, the dancers and musicians coming together at only the twenty-first bar. This round is extremely fascinating in many other dances, such as Padushka (Ex. 9, page 78), which is known in Bosnia, Macedonia and Bulgaria.

An accented step usually marks the changing épaulement, which is not so frequent as in Greek dance, but the mixture of slow, quick, and accented step often acquires a syncopated rhythm because of the continual rise and fall of the bodies.

Steps and Patterns

There are three styles of dance; the Shaking, from the most fertile areas, where tiny jumps on both feet rock the body with movement as the dancers move in Lesa as in Troyanats (Ex. 11A, page 81); the Hopping, on the mountain slopes, in which a hop is added to the basic step as in Devojacko Kolo (Ex. 11B); and the Stepping, from the less fertile areas, as in Neda Grivny (Ex. 11C), in which the body sometimes trembles at every step (Ex. 10, page 80). All these Kolos are made up of varying combinations of the basic step with occasional hops, springs, jumps, stamps, and claps.

There are numerous Kolos where the group moves a little to right and then back to the left (Ex. 10), or progresses gradually to the right (Ex. 11C). There are others which open into chains also usually moving to the right, and chains which may make Serpentine Figures, and are from Greek sources. In the northern areas these chains often move into circular or longways sets. There are also northern dances in which a chain of men faces a chain of women, and these may develop into sets or couple dances. Some of these latter may have two parts, one using the simple basic step, and the other using steps from a neighbouring state, such as the Serbian Charlama from near Hungary which uses the *cabriole*, or the numbers of Slovenian dances which break into Austrian polkas and valses. One of these is suspiciously like La Raspa, the so-called Brazilian dance now sweeping Europe.

General Remarks

Until recently the Yugoslavs have largely been shepherds on the mountain slopes and agriculturists in the rich northern plains and narrow river valleys of the south. Many of their dances are old fertility rites, and some Kolos are performed exclusively by the sex to whom the particular work process belongs, the tempo and tonal quality of the work-song being regulated by the appropriate movements of the hands. Sometimes such Kolos are led by a girl holding a snake, an ancient symbol of fertility. In others belonging to a moon-worshipping cult the pattern of the dance appears to wax and wane like the moon. But the most interesting dances are those from the wedding ceremonies, and these vary considerably from district to district. The most varied are those of Montenegro, which show the relatives of the bride and groom exchanging presents, the selling or abduction of the bride, the dressing of the bride, which in some districts includes a dance round the Turkish bath in which she sits as her hair is dyed and plaited, or her nails are painted, and other strange customs.

A handkerchief plays an important part in many Yugoslav Kolos. It is carried by the leader, is carefully twisted and waved to the rhythm of the dance, and is passed on to the next dancer should the leader decide his powers are failing.

EXAMPLE 9

PADUSHKA

(Macedonia and Bosnia)

Girls or men are linked in chains or circles, holding hands

1–2. Fall on to R. ft. in front of L., moving towards left and accenting this beat.

3. Take weight on L. ft., placed just behind R., turning to centre.

1–2. Repeat above movement twice more.

3.

1–2.

3.

1. Step to side on R. ft., facing centre and accent this step.

2–3. Hop on R. ft., raising L. and facing line of dance, accent this step. Pause.

1. Step to side on L. ft., facing centre and accent this step.

2–3. Hop on L. ft., raising R. and back to line of dance, accent this step. Pause.

EXAMPLE 9 *(cont.)*

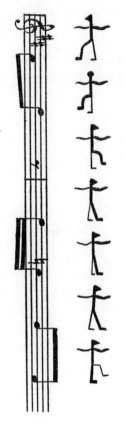

1. Fall on R. ft. in front of L. moving to left and accenting this step.

2. Step back on L. ft., raising R. ft., accenting this step and turning to face centre.

3. Hop on L. ft., accenting this step and turning to face line of dance.

1. Step on to R. ft., moving to right facing line of dance.

and Bring L. ft. to R.

2. Step on to R. ft.

3. Hop on R. ft., raising L. knee forwards.

Repeat this step beginning with L. ft., and then with R. and L. again, making 4 times in all. These steps are like a very smooth polka and are danced without any accent.

Padushka (Macedonia)

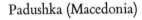

EXAMPLE 10

ZHIKINO'S KOLO
Danced widely in Yugoslavia

Girls are linked by hands on shoulders in a circle, and the dance gradually develops speed as they relax, until they appear to tremble all over.

1. Step to side on R. ft., facing centre.

2–3. Roll L. ft. round and place in front of R. The movement takes 2 beats.

1. Step to side on R. ft.

2–3. Close L. ft. to R. and pause.

1. Step to side on L. ft.

2–3. Close R. ft. to L. and pause.

1. Step to side on R. ft.

2–3. Close L. ft. to R. and pause.

Repeat beginning with L. ft. When speed develops, dancers bounce slightly on ground with each step and in 2–3 develop a tiny *pas-de-basque*. The second beat of bars 2, 3, 4, is accented.

TROYANATS
(From N. Serbia)

The group of men and women, standing alternately, dance in a circle holding one another's shoulders. They take tiny steps and jumps, moving all the time to the right, the entire group seeming to shake. The Kolo is very quick, and the feet are not allowed to leave the floor so that although a hop is mentioned, it is only a movement on the floor.

1st bar. 1. Step sideways on the R. ft.

and Hop on R. ft. turning it slightly outwards and travelling to the right.

2. Place L. ft. beside R., so that both feet are slightly pointed towards the right.

2nd bar. Repeat 1st bar.

3rd bar. Hop lightly 3 times on L. ft., holding R. ft. lightly on ground at side of L. ft., but with R. toe just in front of L. toe.

4th bar. Repeat 3rd bar hopping on R. ft.

5th bar. Repeat 3rd bar.

Repeat these 5 bars *ad lib.*

The dancers' enchaînement lasts 5 bars, therefore it does not always coincide with the melodic phrase.

Troyanats

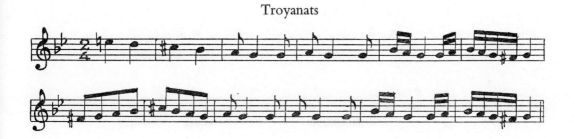

EXAMPLE IIB

DEVOJACKO KOLO
(Serbian mountain regions)

Girls' Kolo, danced either holding hands in a closed circle or opening out into chains and winding through the village and fields.

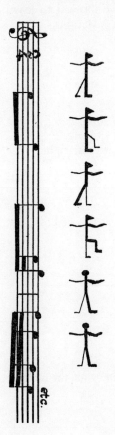

1. Step on to R. ft., facing line of dance.

and Hop on R. ft., raising L. leg slightly in front.

2. Step on to L. ft.

and Hop on L. ft.

1. Step to side on R. ft., facing centre.

and Close L. ft. to R.

Repeat this step to side on R. ft. and close once more.

   3rd bar. Step to side on L. ft., close R. to it.
           Step to side on R. ft., close L. to it.

   4th bar. Stamp 3 times and pause.
Repeat entire sequence *ad lib.*

EXAMPLE IIC

NEDA GRIVNY
(From Schumadina. Now danced elsewhere)

Dancers hold hands in a circle and always face the centre

1st bar.   Step to side on R. ft., close L. to it.

2nd and 3rd bars. Repeat 1st bar.

4th bar.   Step to side on R. ft. accenting this step, close L. ft. to R. ankle.

5th bar.   Step into centre on L. ft., bringing R. ft. to L. ankle.

6th bar.   Repeat 5th bar using R. ft., raise arms slightly.

7th bar.   Step back on L. ft., closing R. to it, drop arms.

8th bar.   Repeat 7th bar.

9th bar.   Step to side on R. ft., close L. ft. to R. ankle.

10th bar. Step to side on L. ft., close R. ft. to L. ankle.

Repeat whole sequence *ad lib*, increasing speed very slightly.

Neda Grivny

RUSSIA

The widest possible variety of dance is found among the Eastern Slavs largely because Russia has no natural boundaries to the east or west; the Ural Mountains have never prevented invasions. Intermarriage and movement from place to place have gone on for so long that folk dance, music, arts, and customs have been intermingled.

The influx of the Turki and Ugrian tribes were not the early Slavs' first contact with an Eastern people. Archaeologists working in the Ukraine, Czechoslovakia, and Hungary are gradually disclosing traces of a highly cultivated art belonging to the Scythians, whose own origins, it is suggested, were in the Middle East. The rich designs, colours, and fine workmanship of Scythian art are still found in the wonderful embroideries, pottery, and mosaics of these areas. The dances, too, show a similar wealth of movement.

During the tenth century A.D., the Viking Rurik and his descendants sailed in from the Baltic and first organized the nomad peoples of European Russia into principalities according to the Feudal system (see Map 2, facing page 52). Each prince was persuaded to recognize Kiev as the sovereign state, but this did not prevent them warring among themselves and with the Finnish tribes to the north and Tartars to the south-east. These raids and warlike expeditions led to a further mixing of tribes and rituals.

At this time (circa A.D. 1100) the ties between Russia and the Eastern Byzantine Empire were strong. Trade, particularly in furs, was the principal object, but there was a constant interchange of scholar-priests, and gradually the Greek Orthodox church was accepted by the Russian princes as their official religion. Nevertheless in the vast plains Christianity was slow in developing; therefore the Russians never gave up their pagan gods entirely—their ancient rituals only gradually became associated with the local saints' days and church festivals. To the small communities living in close contact with their overlords, these ancient rituals and customs had achieved a degree of importance which no foreign influence could break. Thus many dances and customs, particularly those of the wedding ceremonies, were preserved almost intact.

Although the Mongol invasion under Genghis Khan in the thirteenth century A.D. broke the Russians' ties with the Byzantine church culture, this impact with an eastern people served to reinforce certain eastern elements already inherent in Russian folk art.

For some hundred and fifty years the main part of Russia was completely dominated by the Khanate of the Golden Horde (the Slav name for their conquerors), except for the area north-east of Moscow. This city, in the centre of a vast plain, gradually increased its power. First, it gave allegiance to the Great Khan, then, having gained his confidence, began to collect the annual tribute due to him from the other Russian princes. When Moscow's leadership was finally acknowledged by these Slav princes it refused to pay the tribute and was thus able to challenge and ultimately to defeat the Tartars. From then onwards until the nineteenth century, the Russian Tsars continued to expand their frontiers to the east, west and south, and the Russian people have remained almost uninfluenced by any other invasions. Peter the Great's transformation of St. Petersburg into his capital did little to introduce western culture to any but court circles. It is for this reason that no recognized western dance can be found except in those regions where the peasants came into contact with Polish dances influenced by the Teutonic Knights.

It is almost impossible for the untrained eye to differentiate between the dances of the three European Russian Republics, the Ukraine, Byelorussia, and the R.S.F.S.R. The most important are those with movements showing the influence of climate and work process. The Ukraine possesses many dances called Kolomiykas, which arise out of sheer exuberance and are permeated with cheerfulness and hearty humour, and, as it is an agricultural area, other Ukrainian dances are based on the daily work of farm, orchards, and herds. In addition there are wonderful men's dances in which the horse-riders' prowess and movements are shown. These are similar to those found among Cossack tribes in the Caucasus, the Crimea, and further east.

The Gopak is one of the most brilliant of these. In it the dancer, always a man, performs all kinds of spectacular steps, the most prominent being the cobbler's step, scissors, twisting, turning or jumping over one's own foot, and tremendous leaps. The girls are never expected to do such steps. They merely form an admiring background, stamping, clapping, or dancing simple steps. This performance is a relic of the time when the man showed off before the woman of his choice to prove how strong and clever he could be.

The Byelorussians' most prominent dance is the Krizachok, which is performed by couples in processional and then circular forms. It is a comedy dance. The boys and girls dance all kinds of odd and unexpected steps, arranged to make their partner laugh. These consist of peculiar and sudden bendings of the legs, a hop on one leg as if the dancer had suddenly gone lame, or a meaning jerk of the thumb with a corresponding jerk of the leg.

In the European part of the R.S.F.S.R. the Khorovod or closed circle dance prevails, Moonshine being a good example (Ex. 16, page 91). It is like other Slav Kolos, and has a very smooth easy movement. In the most Northern regions among the Samoyeds, Ostyaks, and Karelians, some interesting animal dances are found, in which the performers imitate either the hunting of reindeer, polar bears, seals, and other animals, or the animals themselves. Woodcutters' and Foresters' Dances are found everywhere in the forest regions.

Russian music depends a great deal on harmonization, and the dance-songs are sung by choirs, which to-day are accompanied by musical instruments. But the vast majority of ceremonial dances at weddings, christenings, Christmas and spring are still performed in the old style, with vocal accompaniment only. This dates from the time of the mad Tsar Paul I, who, in his efforts to "germanize" Russia, forbade the national instruments, the Bandura and Balalaika. But music and dance were so much a part of the people's life that they merely banded themselves into choirs and sang the old tunes for the dancers.

The Relationship of the Interval of the Falling Fourth to Certain Movements

Russian music contains many Eastern traits, among which is the continual use of the interval of the Falling Fourth, which occurs in more than 75 per cent of all folk tunes, not only at the end of the melodic phrase, but within the phrases themselves. This peculiarity is to some extent due to the Russian use of the pentatonic scale, which produces only five notes within an octave: the interval of the Fourth is therefore the widest and most significant interval. This is sometimes associated with the outstanding feature of many Russian dances, which is a stretching or leaping upwards on the high note, followed by the holding of a position with the weight of the body directed downwards on the lower note, or on the fourth whole or half-beat of a bar. The actual coincidence of step and interval is found mostly in the slow rituals and the sadder parts of a dance, and stresses their emotional expressiveness.

The best known example of this is the *Promenade* (Ex. 12, page 89), the second basic step of Russian dance, which is always danced very smoothly. (The Slav step-to-the-side and close is the first step.) The same relationship often occurs in the *pas-de-bourrée*, or so-called bell-step, and in the *pas-de-basque* (Exs. 13 and 14, pages 89, 90).

In some sad, ritual dances which begin with a Falling Fourth, or in the Wedding Dances which often begin with a Rising Fourth, an opening and dropping of the leg is also matched to the interval. This can be a most expressive movement, because in the slow or sad ritual the dancer merely sinks downwards, but in a happy one the dancer gives a sliding hop forwards on the supporting leg (Ex. 17, page 92).

Interpretation of Rhythms

As in the dances of the Caucasus, there is a great contrast of rhythms and accents, because of the very different origins of these people. Fluid movements from hot countries interweave with more vigorous ones from cold countries. This often leads to capricious rhythms in which there appear to be too many steps for the regular pulse; it is most noticeable in the Ukrainian Horse-riders' Dances and in the girls' steps of the Gopak. In addition to the steps mentioned in dances of the Caucasus, a good example is a boy's step in which he crouches on the ground with a jump on the first beat, and springs up again twisting one foot in and out very quickly on the next half-beat.

The predominance of vocal accompaniment for the rituals emphasizes the important relationship of word and movement. It also explains the complicated variety of time signatures that some tunes present. Most wedding tunes are based on a 5/4 rhythm, but one consists of the following sequence—*Section A*: one bar each of 5/8, 3/4, 7/8, 3/8, 5/8, 3/4; *Section B*: three bars of 5/8, followed by one each of 3/4, 7/8, 3/8, 5/8, 3/4, and so on. This comes from the central part of the R.S.F.S.R. near Perm and was used by Moussorgsky in Boris Godunov. The dancers do not step to each beat, but with the flow and accent of the words of the songs. Two further examples of contrasts of accent and changing of weight are the girl's step in the Gopak and in Moonshine (Exs. 18 and 15, pages 93, 90).

Freedom of Movement

For the most part, Russian dances are not "set." After a preliminary introduction by singer or musician, which is often very sad in tone, the dancers form a ring and start to move with a simple basic step. Then, as they move, the circle grows larger, more and more join in. Eventually someone feels that the communal step is too tame and breaks into a solo in the centre, to be followed by others vying with each other. The music gets faster until it is no longer possible to do anything else but turn. Everyone turns furiously until they or the musicians are exhausted. There is a short rest and the fun starts again.

There is a considerable swing of the body, head and arms. At the same time there is a smooth quality in the movement, which makes the dancers look as if they were skimming over the surface of the ground. This is particularly interesting in such steps as the *Promenade* (Ex. 12, page 89) done at speed, and the *Pivot step*, in which the dancer never accents the downwards beat but tries to keep an even balance whether it is performed as a travelling or a turning step (Ex. 4, page 62).

The Use of Arms

Many dances contain a powerful element of mime arising from the significance of the dance ritual. The use of arms is therefore of great importance, and some examples are given here. There are three bows—

The first is used in the less serious dances and given either to partner, other members of the group, or to a central point in the circle. The dancer stands straight, swings both arms outwards and upwards and claps them over the head, bends low and swings them down in front and out to the side.

The second bow is used in more serious dances and given to senior members of the community (also found in the Boyars' dances). The right hand is placed palm downwards over the heart, and the arm is then drawn backwards to the right side of the body, as the body bends forwards, this to display that the performer has no weapon and therefore has no evil intention. It is seldom used nowadays.

The third bow is used principally in wedding dances and very ancient rituals, and by everyone. The right hand touches the right side of the brow, then the heart, then the lips, and is drawn sideways as the dancer follows these gestures by a bow. It signifies: "My head, my heart, and myself are before your feet."

One of the loveliest movements is that in which the arms are brought up to the breast and opened as if giving something. It is found in many dances, but most particularly in those of the harvest.

In the wedding dances the girls often run their hands up first one arm and then the other, as if displaying their hands and their beautiful embroidery, for they always push their sleeves up with the movement. The handkerchief also plays a large part in these dances. The bride often dances with the handkerchief and finally presents this to her husband, who ties it over her head. The significance of the movement is obvious (see page 12).

The most important arm movements are found in the many dances based on work processes, such as harvesting, sowing, and hunting, where the gesture made is usually a reproduction of the actual work movement.

Kinds of Dance and Patterns

As has already been stated, all types of dance are found in Russia; Circles which usually start with the right foot and move anti-clockwise, Chains, Processionals, Couple Dances, and even some Figure Dances. These last are found near the western frontiers where the Polish, Scandinavian, and Teutonic peoples have had some influence. A few such elements are found in the Boyars' dances. These are in reality folk dances but, having been performed at the Moscow and Petersburg courts, acquired a few niceties of the court dance from the French, Austrian and Italian dancing-masters employed there. They now exist only in the theatre.

The few "set" dances usually consist of simple variations on the Slav basic step, or of three or four enchaînements each comprising one single step, such as the Promenade. Occasionally a dance will contain several enchaînements in which two or three varieties of step are mixed, but these are rare. The Russian prefers to repeat the same step and establish a good pattern before moving on to another step. He sometimes ends a sequence with a *Break*, not unlike the Hungarian *Bokázó* (Ex. 59, page 178), danced to a 2/4 or 4/4 rhythm.

1. Hop on L. ft., pointing R. toe to side, R. knee turned inwards.
2. Hop on L. ft., rest R. heel on floor, R. knee turned outwards.
3. Hop on L. ft., crossing R. toe over L. ft.
4. Hop on L. ft., swinging R. leg out sideways.

Repeat hopping on R. ft.

Special Notes

Polkas and Mazurkas are found only in the west and are danced in a very free style. There are everywhere a few valse-like dances, mostly in 2/4, as the people prefer a movement in which they turn closely together, like the Czech dances.

It is rare to find any hopping forwards, apart from the single sliding hop forwards as the leg opens (Ex. 17, page 92). Hopping backwards is done frequently with the leg turned outwards (Ex. 15, page 90). This is supposed to be part of a fertility step, as is the boy's step in which he jumps to a crouching position on the floor and then springs up with his legs wide apart.

Stampings are seldom used in any quantity, except to encourage the dancers, although in those parts of the Ukraine which were under Polish rule in the seventeenth century one finds an enchaînement ending in the feminine cadence. This can be stamped, or the feet are jumped apart and brought together with a click (Ex. 20, page 99).

A sharp distinction must be made between the long leaps of the horse-riding peoples of the plains and the high leaps of the horse-riding mountain folk in the Caucasus. The former have a free, widely expansive, and even untidy movement, whilst the latter are extremely precise and neatly moving dancers.

EXAMPLE 12

PROMENADE

Danced very smoothly; the third movement lasts two half-beats

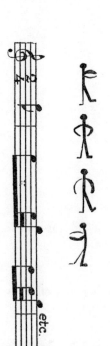

1. Step on to R. ft.

and Bring L. ft. up to R.

2. Step on to R. ft., bending R. knee and sweep L. leg forwards and very slightly upwards. Then bring L. leg backwards to R. before beginning step with L. ft.

From "Moonshine" (Ex. 16)

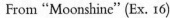

EXAMPLE 13

PAS DE BOURRÉE

(Sometimes called the Bell step)

Prepare by opening R. leg pointed to side, swing both arms over to R. side.

1. Bring R. ft to L. and step on to it. Drop arms in front.

and Step to side on L. ft., moving arms slightly to left.

2. Drop heavily on R. ft., and immediately swing L. leg out to side, moving arms upwards to left side.

From a Gopak

EXAMPLE 14
PAS DE BASQUE

Stand ready facing audience.

Raise R. leg round in a circle, turning sideways and immediately springing off L. ft. Circle L. arm over head.

1. Land on R. ft.

and Bring L. leg round in circle to side of R. Drop arms in front.
2. Stamp R. ft. at side of L.

Wedding Dance, Moscow Region

EXAMPLE 15
HOPPING BACKWARDS

and On last half-beat of bar, hop off R. ft., arms usually opened to the side.

1. Step on to L. ft., just behind R. Continue by hopping off L. ft. and stepping on R. Usually performed 4 or 8 times.

(For complete sequence see Example 16.)

EXAMPLE 16

A VERSION OF MOONSHINE
(Danced in the Ukraine)

An old moon-worshipping dance representing the way in which the workers plough the fields when the moon is full, and plant the seed with the coming of the new moon. They then persuade the seed to sprout and send out many shoots. The final turn represents the corn flourishing.

The girls dance in a circle holding hands.

1. 16 bars. Starting with R. ft., perform 8 *Promenades* (see Ex. 12) to the right; immediately swing R. leg over L. and perform 8 *Promenades* to the left.

2. 8 bars. Gradually raising arms, move into the centre with 2 stamps in the first bar, followed by 3 shorter stamps and a pause in the second bar. Repeat this, lowering arms and moving backwards to places. Repeat whole movement.

3. 16 bars. Repeat first 16 bars.

4. 8 bars. Let go of hands, leaving arms free to close and open with leg movement. Step into centre on R. ft. and perform 2 *développés* (see Ex. 17) first with L. and then R. leg, in first 2 bars. Clasp hands behind head and hop backwards in second 2 bars (see Ex. 15.) Repeat this movement.

5. 8 bars. *Pivot turn* to R. for 4 bars, taking 2 movements to each bar. Repeat movement to L (see Ex. 4).

Repeat *ad lib*

Moonshine

EXAMPLE 17

TWO ASPECTS OF DÉVELOPPÉ

a. Step on R. ft., bending L. knee upwards, arms curved round just below breast.

Sink on R. leg, immediately opening L. leg and arms.

Wedding Dance, Pinnegar

b. Step on to L. leg, bending R. knee upwards, arms curved round just below breast.

Slide-jump forwards on L. ft., immediately opening R. leg and arm throw head and body slightly backwards.

Wedding Dance, near Tambov

EXAMPLE 18

GIRLS' STEP FROM GOPAK

1. Moving to the right. Fall on to L. ft., keeping weight backwards, arms opened in front.

and Step on to R. heel, near to L.

Repeat this movement 3 times (2 bars).

1. Travelling backwards, R. arm bent across chest, L. stretched out behind. Fall on to R. ft.

and Step on to L. toe and take weight of body.

Repeat this movement 3 times (2 bars).

Gopak

POLAND

Although it is often possible to find peasants dancing a simple Kolo in the eastern areas of Poland, very few of the really ancient Slav rituals have been preserved. This has happened because Poland has been swept by many invaders. Like Russia, she has no natural geographical boundaries, except to the south-east, where the Tatra Mountains can afford only a temporary measure of protection. By the eleventh century A.D., with all the other Baltic States, she had yielded to the Teutonic Knights and was already paying tribute to the Roman Catholic church, then in the process of enlarging its powers. The influence of this church never weakened, because the later influx of a Turkish people, coming in behind the Mongols in the thirteenth century, did little to turn the attention of the Polish peasants back to their Eastern ancestors. The Turkish hold was not very strong, and as

Moscow began to beat the Tartars back to the south-east, the Poles, with the help of the Lithuanian princes, also began to reconquer their country and spread southwards to the Black Sea, annexing part of the Ukraine. But this position could not be held for long. As part of the Holy Roman Empire, Austria started to press its claims to the south-west, Russia to the east, and the remnants of the Teutonic Knights in Prussia to the north-west. By 1795, the Kingdom of Poland had been divided between these three nations, and so lost all independence until after the 1914–18 war.

Yet this complete subjugation of a people could not prevent the development of a distinct style of national dance. The conquerors were very little interested in the country. Even to-day Poland is comparatively poor, because her natural resources have yet to be properly developed. Like so many other northern states, in the past she had very little export trade; most of the country was forest or marsh and the rest suitable only for grazing and primitive agriculture. Consequently the Polish landowners were only too willing to be paid for soldiering. They organized themselves and their serfs into cavalry regiments, and their superb horsemanship, inherited from their nomadic ancestors, made them a valuable asset in the many wars fought over this part of Europe.

The allegiance paid by the Polish landowners to first one foreign king and then another did not prevent the Poles, living in the areas east of the Vistula, from retaining their belief in a right to independence. This was particularly the case in the province of Mazowse, in which the capital Warsaw stands. It is from this area that simple dances were developed into the brilliant Mazurs and Kujaviaks seen to-day.

The finish in the performance of these simple folk dances is explained by the fact that they continued to be performed among the Polish cavalry regiments when the country was completely under foreign rule. The officer class was particularly keen to express patriotic feelings at such a time, and to do so in a national dance did not arouse the suspicions of their overlords. By continual practice amongst a particular section of the community, the horse-riding movements, already inherent in the dance, became exaggerated and polished. In addition, other dances like the Krakoviak, which started as a simple Kolo based on the Slav basic step, gradually acquired similar ideas.

The Accenting of the Second Beat

A love and knowledge of the horse may have inspired the most significant feature of Polish folk dance and music, and it does not arise from the relationship of word and movement as it does in other Slav countries. If one listens carefully to a horse galloping or trotting, one realizes that the second beat is the loudest and most heavily accented. This is reflected in the majority of Polish folk dances performed to a 3/4 or 3/2 rhythm, when the Second Beat of the bar is usually heavily accented. Polonaise, Mazurka, and Kujaviak all display this same stressing of accent, and even in the more western parts of Poland, where Teutonic influences have affected the dance, one finds this tendency to stress the Second Beat. It happens in Laura, a valse-like dance from near Danzig, in which the Second Beat of one of the enchaînements is accented. It is even occasionally found in dances of a 2/4 rhythm, such as the clap of the hands on the second half-beat of a curious little dance called Boijko, or the stamp on the second half-beat of the *Break* in the Krakoviak. Moreover, in some Processionals and Kolos performed after a wedding ceremony, the bridegroom always swings his bride towards himself with a heavy stamp on the second step of every enchaînement.

In the Polonaise and the Mazurka, there is a strong outwards or upwards thrust of the working leg as the supporting leg marks the Second Beat. In the Kujaviak, and its after-dances the Oberek or Obertass, the dancer makes a sweeping circular movement on the floor with the second step. In all of these dances, every second step coming on this Second Beat must appear to be twice as long as the first, in both time and space. The third step of a dance in 3/4 time thus often seems like an afterthought. Being usually a preparatory step, it is marked only very lightly and sometimes immediately before the first beat of a new bar. In some turning steps, when the dancers get excited, the third beat may be completely ignored. This happens when the couple spin together, for the man lifts his partner off the floor on the Second Beat and holds her there until the next bar.

Other fascinating uses of this accenting of the Second Beat are those in which the man drops on his knee on the Second Beat, his partner skipping lightly round him, and when he is leading the girl in the Mazurka, turning to and from her on alternating bars as he accents his second step in the enchaînement known as Wibiyany. To get the correct impetus for accenting the Second Beat, the dancers always begin each step from an open position and place the entire foot directly on the floor with a slightly bent knee on the Second Beat. To do this the body has to be held completely under control.

In the very few unaccompanied Polish dances, it is actually possible to hear a similar sound to that of horses galloping as the dancers do the *Cwal* sideways (Ex. 26, page 101), for as their feet glide the heels are very faintly beaten together and a "clip-clop" is heard.

The Feminine Cadence

The accenting of the Second Beat also gives rise to the characteristic ending of many enchaînements in Polish dance, a step-to-the-side and a clip of the heels, which corresponds with the Feminine Cadence, ending the musical phrase. A Feminine Cadence occurs when the melody ends on the second or weak beat of a bar, as opposed to the first or strong beat usually found in Western Europe. Having marked the Second and weaker beat throughout, the Pole does not change this most typical feature at the end of his phrase. Moreover this movement often represents the reining in of his horse, the love of which has inspired the Polish national dance (Ex. 20, page 99).

The Carriage of the Body

The strongly controlled movements and the precise positioning of the Polish dancers are in great contrast to the free-flowing style of the Ukrainians and the neat upwards leaping of the Georgians, who are also great lovers and breeders of horses. This is due no doubt to the more disciplined, militaristic activities of the Poles and their earlier use of horse-trappings and saddles. Every step in the Polonaise, Mazurka, Kujaviak, and Krakoviak, and even in the more modern style Country Dances, displays the erect back, firmly controlled shoulders, head and arms, and swift easy movements of riders on horseback. Arms play an active part in all dances, swinging sensitively with each change of direction, and counterbalancing the feet. They are rarely lifted straight above the head but, if raised, are kept at an angle of roughly 45 degrees to the head. The man often sweeps an arm round in a figure-of-eight, which represents the cracking of a whip, a movement which usually coincides with the Break following a series of *Holubetzs* in the Krakoviak (Ex. 25 and 27, pages 101 and 102). In the progressive figures of most dances, the woman moves a little way behind her partner, whose left hand is held forwards as if he were showing her the way. His right arm may be round her waist, whilst her left hand is on his shoulder, or it may rest lightly in his right. Her free hand often holds her skirt or apron. It is only when the men are dancing alone that their hands are occasionally placed on their hips.

Forms and Patterns

Apart from the ancient Kolos and the more modern valses and polkas of the western areas, most Polish dances are figure dances, a leader ordering the activities of the group, as the "Caller" shouts the figures in American Square dancing or in an Irish Ceilidhe.

The Polonaise is not strictly a folk dance, although it is performed by the townspeople. It is a processional for as many as will. The Mazur is still danced by the peasants as a couple dance for as many as will, but, among the soldiers and in the theatre, where as the Mazurka it retains its enormous popularity, it is usually danced by any number of couples divisible by four. Some versions are "set" for four couples only.

The Krakoviak starts as a processional couple dance, merges into a Kolo, the dancers moving alternately to right and left, then after a Grand Chain or Hey develops into a figure dance. At the conclusion the entire group of dancers glide swiftly away in a procession. There is one version of this dance for four couples which is very old and is peculiar to the outskirts of Cracow whence the dance originated (Ex. 27, page 102).

An enchaînement on the Krakoviak or Mazurka usually lasts for four bars and is repeated four times in all. It can consist of one single step or of a combination of two steps, and is usually concluded with the Break on a Feminine Cadence. The *Cwal* of the Krakoviak and the women's Mazurka steps, however, can be danced for as long as the leader requires to make his patterns, the number of steps always being a multiple of four. If the *Cwal* is divided by changing the leading foot every second step, it develops into the sliding *polka* of the Poles, as opposed to the stepped one of Teutonic origin. This distinction becomes clear in a comparison between the polka dances of Western Poland and the *polka* of the Krakoviak.

The Steps

Because Polish folk dance has been so carefully fostered during the past two hundred years, much time is spent on perfecting the actual steps of a dance, instead of their appearing as a spontaneous outburst of feeling expressed in significant movements, as in other Slav countries. It is for this reason that the steps have to be more clearly defined.

The Polonaise of 3/4 or 3/2 rhythm consists of one step only, which is performed going either forwards or backwards in any pattern dictated by the leader (Ex. 19, page 98).

The Mazurka is in 3/4 broken rhythm and was first described in the sixteenth century. It consists of five steps: *Holubetz*, *Pas Sissone*, *Pas Marché*, *Pas Balayé*, and *Oboroti*, (Exs. 21, 22, 23, 24, 25, pages 99 to 101) which can be performed singly or in varying combinations. With the exception of the *Oboroti* (Ex. 24), all the steps can go forwards, sideways, or backwards. The combinations are known as Obratzani, a mixture of *Holubetz* and *Pas Balayé*, the couple moving alternately face to face and back to back; or Wiybiyany, when the man dances alternately towards and against the line of dance with a *Holubetz* followed by a stamp and three *Pas Sissones*. Movements are often linked by Zaznachania. These consist of risings to the balls of the feet, claps or clipping of heels in various rhythms. The girls perform these while the men do more spectacular steps.

Oboroti (turns or *Pas Boiteux*) are performed with the couple standing side by side, almost touching and facing in opposite directions. The man's left arm is round the woman's waist and her left hand is on his right shoulder. Both right arms are held outstretched and slightly upwards, or the elbows may be linked and the couple can turn either backwards or forwards. Sometimes the partners turn side by side, the man going backwards, the woman forwards. The inside legs, or rather hips, are usually touching in order to gain speed, and occasionally the man lifts his woman right off her feet (Ex. 24, page 100).

Holubetz (*cabriole* or *coup de talon*) is not usually danced by the women; the man always dances it sideways to the line of dance (Ex. 25, page 101).

The Krakoviak is in 2/4 rhythm. It has only three steps and they are usually performed by both men and women. The most important is the *Cwal* (*chassé*), which is a development of the Slav basic step. It can be danced in any direction, the knees always being kept very loose, so that the leading foot can be swiftly changed (Ex. 26, page 101).

The *Oboroti* is the same as in the Mazurka, the hop on the last half-beat of a bar and the two following steps on beats 1 and 2 respectively (Ex. 24). The leg that is raised on the hop usually circles forwards or backwards round the hopping leg before it is placed on the floor on the first beat. The direction of the circling is determined by that of the turn.

The *Holubetz* in the Krakoviak is usually repeated in series, unlike the single one followed by two steps of the Mazurka. An interesting example of the use of this step is where two *Holubetzs* are followed by a Break, which is accompanied by the flicking of an arm in the figure-eight, as if a whip were being cracked (Ex. 27, page 102). This movement is often done by partners moving round each other, alternately meeting face to face and back to back. It is also done by the men alone in the centre in the figure known as Kogucik (Little Cock), who go into the middle pretending to sneer at each other, then out again to their women, raising their hats on the *Break*.

The Kujaviak is a graceful, swinging, valse-like dance in a slow 3/8 rhythm. The girls place their hands on the upper fore-arms of their partners, and the dancers make a circular movement with the working foot on every second step of a valse. Their bodies sway gracefully from side to side. This is usually followed by the Oberek, a very fast dance utilizing the Mazurka steps, the man lifting his partner off the floor in the turns. The Obertass is a wilder version of the Oberek, the man flinging the woman up in the fertility leap and performing low swinging movements, in which his knees often touch the floor. He also indulges in spectacular leaps and turns.

In the Tatra Mountains there are some fascinating male dances depicting the life of the mountain. The men use their ice-axes in somewhat the same way as the Scots use their swords, but at certain times they lift these off the ground for their partners to jump over. At other times they are swung round their own or their partners' heads in wide circling movements. Such dances as these require great skill, and the steps are extremely neat, with upwards leaps. When the peasants in these areas dance, they have not the carriage of the horsemen, but rather the delicately balanced body characteristic of the Georgian Cossacks in their mountain dances.

EXAMPLE 19

THE POLONAISE

The dance consists of one step only, the couples making a procession and then moving into patterns. Man holds his partner by the R. hand. The step must be danced crisply and it starts on the third beat of a bar.

3. Step forwards on to R. ft., man's L. hand on hip, woman's R. hand on her skirt.

1. Close L. ft. just behind R.

2. Drop sharply on R. ft., R. knee slightly bent at the same time as raising L. leg pointed in front. This step is always accented.

3. Repeat beginning with L. ft. and stepping out well forwards.

An Old Polonaise

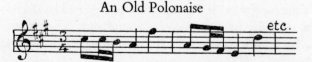

EXAMPLE 20

THE FEMININE CADENCE

1. Step to the side on R. ft., arms open, toes are slightly turned inwards.

2-3. Clip L. heel to R. and close arms across chest, toes are opened. Hold this position for the third beat.

A feminine cadence is found at the end of all phrases in Mazurkas and Polonaises.

EXAMPLE 21

PAS SISSONE

1. Hop slightly forwards on R. ft., raising L. leg behind.

2. Slide L. ft. forwards past R. Accent this step by dropping weight directly on to L. leg as R. leg is lifted behind.

3. Hop lightly forwards on L. ft., keeping R. leg raised. Repeat, hopping first on L. ft.

EXAMPLE 22

PAS MARCHÉ

(A step like the *Pas-de-basque*)

1. Run forwards on to R. ft.

2. Place L. ft. in front of R. with slightly bent knee, and emphasize this step.

3. Step lightly on to R. ft. just in front of L.

EXAMPLE 23

PAS BALAYÉ

(Begins on last half-beat of bar)

and Hop forwards on R. ft., raising L. leg behind.

1. Step forwards on L. ft., bend R. leg slightly behind L. (The R. leg now makes a sweeping movement forward.)

2. Hop forwards on L. ft. at the same time as brushing R. ft. heavily on floor and immediately stretching it out in front. Slight pause.

Repeat whole movement beginning on L. ft.

An Old Mazurka

EXAMPLE 24

OBOROTI

(Can be danced turning to R. or L., and moving forwards or backwards, also with *Holubetz* on beat 1.)

1. Hop on L. ft., bringing R. leg up in front of L., commence turning.

2. Place R. ft., down heavily in front of L.

3. Place L. ft. at side of R. Repeat as often as required, always hopping on L. ft.

In Krakoviak begin on the last half-beat and place R. ft. on 1.

EXAMPLE 25

HOLUBETZ

(Coup de talon or Cabriole)

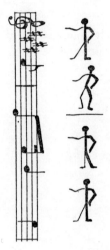

Stand with weight on R. leg and L. leg extended to side.

1. Jump off R. ft. and strike L. heel with R. heel returning on to R. ft.

2. Step sideways on L. ft., slightly accenting this movement.

3. Close R. ft. to L., immediately raising L. leg ready to repeat movement.

EXAMPLE 26

CWAL (GALLOP OR CHASSÉ)

(Can be danced sideways, forwards or backwards)

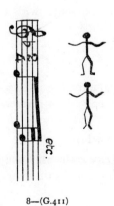

1. Slide R. ft. sideways, keeping weight well over both feet.

and Bring L. ft. up to R., rising on both toes and slightly soaring from floor.

EXAMPLE 27

HOLUBETZ AND BREAK IN THE KRAKOVIAK

Moving to R., and hopping on L. ft.

1. Beat heels together jumping off L. ft.

2. Again beat heels together and then immediately jump as far as possible off L. ft., R. arm begins to describe a figure-of-8.

and Land on R. ft. on last half-beat of bar.

1. Stamp on L. ft. at side of R., arm completes figure-of-8.

and Stamp heavily on R. ft.

2. Raise L. ft. ready to begin movement towards left.

A KRAKOVIAK FOR 4 COUPLES

8 bars.   Men hold R. arms round women's waists, women's L. hands resting on men's shoulders. Outside arms outstretched. *Cwal* round the room in a circle, changing the leading foot every 4 steps (see Ex. 26). Finish in a square.

8 bars.   *Oboroti* (see Ex. 24). Man moving backwards and woman forwards, outside arms raised.

4 bars.   Join hands in large circle and *Cwal* sideways for 7 beats, closing feet together with a click on 8th beat as if reining in horse.

4 bars.   Repeat this movement, travelling to left.

8 bars.   Repeat *Cwal* movement in circle to right and again to left.

8 bars.   Grand chain. Partners give each other their R. hands and begin a grand chain using a sliding polka step (i.e. change leading foot of *Cwal* every two steps). Pass partner at first time of meeting, at second time link R. elbows.

8 bars.   *Oboroti.* Both moving backwards and leaning well away from each other.

16 bars.   Perform *Holubetz* with *Break* (see Ex. 27) in squares, i.e., partners face each other and start on R. ft., on *Break* make a quarter-turn, to finish back to each other. Start again

with L. ft. and on *Break* make a quarter-turn to face each other again. Repeat this movement 8 times in all completing two squares.

8 bars. Men kneel and women perform 8 *polkas* round their own partners.

8 bars. All *Cwal* round in circle as at beginning, changing leading foot every fourth time.

8 bars. Men perform *Holubetz* with *Break* in and out of the centre of the circle. (The figure is known as Kogucik.)

8 bars. *Oboroti.* Men moving backwards and women forwards.

As many bars as required. Couples sweep round the room and off with the *Cwal.*

A Krakoviak

CZECHOSLOVAKIA

Czechoslovakia has existed as an independent nation only since the 1914–18 war. This fact can be explained by referring to its peculiar position on the map of Europe (see Map 2, facing page 52). This area of hills and mountains is penetrated by rivers that run from north to south and vice versa, and it lies on the north bank of the Danube, which flows from east to west. These river valleys have served as valuable routes to early migrating tribes and later conquering armies from many areas. Moreover, as the country is rich in natural resources for both agricultural and mineral exploitation, it has been a valuable settling-point and meeting-ground for eastern and western people. It is for this reason that a mixture of Teutonic and Slav features is visible in its dances. These all reflect something of the particular historical events affecting the areas in which they are found.

Although the population is predominantly Slav, speaking dialects of a common language, in no part of Czechoslovakia are the ancient Kolos preserved so fully as they are in Russia and parts of Yugoslavia, where the Greek Orthodox church only slowly converted the tribes to Christianity. Other religious factions influencing Czechoslovakia have not been so tolerant, and the quarrels for supremacy between the various conquering powers have also had their effect.

Until the provinces of Moravia and Slovakia were overrun by the Magyars in the ninth century A.D., the Slavs were the dominating tribes of Czechoslovakia, with Slav princes acting as feudal lords in every area. Like the Ukrainians, they had assimilated something of the rich culture of the Scythians, who had been earlier inhabitants of this area, and this has given much of their folk art its distinctive richness of colour and design. The new contact with the Magyars from the east, served to reinforce the many decorative and other eastern features still found throughout Czechoslovakian folk art. At the same time, however, it helped to suppress the pagan rituals, for as the Hungarians gradually became converted to Christianity and paid tribute to the Pope, so they insisted that their Moravian and Slovak serfs did likewise. In this way the ancient Slav rituals lost their more inherent features and became attached to the new church.

Some hundred years later (A.D. 936) the western province of Bohemia, in which the Slav tribe known as the Czechs had settled, was annexed by the Teutonic Emperor Otto the Great. Bohemia thus became part of the Holy Roman Empire, and the Catholic church, which by this time had become all-powerful, quickly converted these areas and tried to suppress the ancient Slav ritual more thoroughly than the Catholic priests had done in Hungary, which was not part of the Empire.

In this same area of Bohemia the learned Czech, John Hus, inspired by the teachings of Wycliffe, began in A.D. 1419 to preach against the excesses and beliefs of the Roman Catholic church and the Czech and Teutonic landowners. The Hussite movement was the beginning of the religious wars that culminated in the break-up of the Holy Roman Empire and the rise of the German Protestant church, and this was more successful in suppressing folk dance than any other religious faction had been.

In the seventeenth century, however, these puritanical elements were driven entirely out of the country, or into hiding in remote mountain villages, by the total integration of Bohemia, Moravia, and Slovakia into the Austro-Hungarian Empire. This helped to introduce western-styled Court and Country Dances into the Bohemian ballrooms and to the Bohemian peasants, who were gradually changing into an industrial class.

These many historical events have given Czechoslovak dances a varied look. In the provinces of Moravia and Slovakia, which are still primarily agricultural and pastoral, they are akin to most Slav dances, to which are added Hungarian steps. In addition the Gipsy musicians, usually the only ones available, have made the Hungarian Czárdás almost as popular as it is in its own country. Yet these Slovakian and Moravian dances appear to be performed spontaneously on all festive occasions appointed by the Catholic church and at the wedding ceremonies, when the peasants dance with particular freedom. They are still changing their forms with the changing forms of society and methods of work processes. Many of these latter have strong mimetic elements dealing with forestry and the harvesting of corn and of poppy-seeds.

In Bohemia, which has always been more highly developed and was one of the earliest parts of Central Europe to be industrialized, although dances are performed gaily enough, they have not the same air of spontaneity, because they have been too carefully preserved. The introduction of the valse and polka by Austrian and German landowners, and the earlier introduction of court dances (from which the Cushion and Finger dances are derived) by Italian nobles at the Czech court during the sixteenth and seventeenth centuries, tended to oust the more ancient Kolos. Therefore the older traditional Bohemian dances, like those of Poland, have acquired a polish and air of finality through continuous practice on the part of a patriotic Czech minority. They require from the dancers more concentration on the actual performance of the steps than on the meaning of the movement. The only exceptions to these stylized dances are those found in the Bohemian Forest areas of Chodsko. Here the peasants have never been dominated by Feudal princes. As in certain areas of Russia, they have lived in small free communities and have thus been able to preserve some of their very ancient rituals. Like the rituals found elsewhere among the remote Carpathian mountain villages, they are strongly mimetic in character and relate to the various fertility and other communal rites of the early Slavs.

The Short Melodic Phrase

The most fascinating feature of all national music written by such Czech composers as Smetana, Janáček, Dvořák, and Haydn is the quickly changing melodic phrase. Each section of the melody lasts but two or three bars before it is contrasted with another. This feature is borrowed directly from their native music, and it is this that gives Czech dance its air of great variety. The enchaînements are extremely short and usually in great contrast to each other. A solemn procession-like movement with the feet held close to the floor is followed by a series of swift turns, when the dancer uses a rise to the ball of the foot to give him the necessary impetus, as in Do Kola; or a neatly hopped step is followed by a smooth running figure, as in Kalamajka. Both Eastern and Western versions of this are like the Ukrainian Kolomiykas.

In the western part of Czechoslovakia, these rapidly changing enchaînements become much more complex, because they are based on a series of bars with different time signatures. A comparatively simple form is found in such dances as Salát; three bars of 2/4 followed by one of 3/4, making nine beats in all. The accented step, however, in dances of this type, does not always fall on the first beat of a bar, because one step within the enchaînement often appears to begin in one bar and continue right over the bar line. A much more complex form of mixed time signatures is found in dances like Latovák, in which two rhythmic phrases are used. One (A) consists of one bar of 3/4 and two bars of 2/4, and the other (B) of three bars of 2/4 and two bars of 3/4. These are not used alternately, the melody being made up of a pattern of four sections: *AAB/AAB/BB/AAB*, and the four steps within the two enchaînements making the dance are exactly matched to the rhythmic beats.

A great deal of this complexity results from the accurate relationship of word and movement in the various dance-songs of this type, found in Yugoslavia and Russia. But this quickly changing pattern of melodic and dance phrase can also be explained by the constant friction between Teuton and Slav. This has been strongest in Bohemia, and in some of their dances it is easy to recognize that one section is a variation of the Slav basic step or another typical Slav movement, whilst the other section shows the Teutonic influence in the close-turning valse, running steps or lilting polka with its slide and rise, as opposed to the distinct up and down movement of the Slavs. Janoshka, a Slovak dance, gives some idea of the variety of step to be found (Ex. 31, page 110).

The Interval of the Rising Fourth and the Augmented Second

Czechoslovak music uses the same characteristic intervals as Russian and Yugoslavian, but does not relate to the dance in quite the same way. Although the interval of the Falling Fourth is known with the corresponding step, as in Russian dance, that of the Rising Fourth is more usual. This often corresponds to the step and hop with the working leg raised high in front as the dancers turn in the *Vrták* step (Ex. 29, page 109). This association of larger musical interval and step always lends a more emotional expression to the dance. It is interesting that in Bohemia such "wild" steps in which this particular feature appeared, were banned until recently, in the Western areas, as being too dangerous.

The interval of the Augmented Second also occurs frequently and is occasionally matched to some variation of the Slav basic step, as in Yugoslavia. It is more particularly associated with the extra bounce that appears in many Czech dances, when the performer first slides or places a foot on the floor, and then rises on to the ball of the same foot with the passage of the notes, particularly in the turning dances.

Contrast in Emotional Content

Czechoslovakian dance has the same contrasts of emotional content as other Slav countries. This is much more noticeable in the eastern districts, where dance-songs with modulations in the minor prevail. A sad passage alternates with a gay one, or a solemn phrase depicting some work process breaks into a wildly exuberant enchaînement.

In the west, the dance-songs, influenced by both Catholic and Protestant church modes, are mainly in the major key. This deprives the dances of any really strong contrasting passages of emotional expression. Bohemia, however, has one really exciting and subtle change of expression arising out of a change of rhythm. This is their famous Furiant, where the natural 2/4 rhythm is suddenly converted into two bars of 3/4, and the dancers respond to this by a swift, smooth turn on two feet, just after performing some varied enchaînements of either jumped or stamped steps.

Some Steps

The vast majority of Czechoslovakian steps are variations on the Slav basic step. *Přitukávány* of 2/4 or 4/8 is a typical example—

1, 2, 3, Step on to R. ft., leaving L. leg out at side, hold this position.

4. Close L. ft. to R., clicking heels.

Repeat, commencing L. ft.

This is usually performed facing partners, the couple moving first away and then towards each other. (See Ex. 20, page 99 and Hungarian dance, page 196.)

Danced very quickly, it develops into three *Holubetzs*, while hopping on R. ft. and changing the weight of the body on the fourth beat with a stamp. The couple usually face each other, holding R. hands with the L. hands on the hips, turning half-way round clockwise. They then change hands to dance back counter-clockwise, commencing on L. ft. (See Ex. 25, page 101.)

Přisunný is another variation of the Slav basic step.

1. Step to side on R. ft.
2. Close L. ft. to R., slightly bending the knees.
   Repeat to left. The movement is very soft.

This can be varied by clipping the heels together, and the movement then becomes very abrupt. Partners usually face each other, the man starting with the R. ft. and the woman with the L.

The *Polka* is in 2/4 and has no hop (Ex. 30, page 109). (Polka means half-step.) This is particularly noticeable in a variation where the dancers stamp on beats 1–2. There are several dances where a single *polka* is followed by two hops on the working foot.

Otáčivy (Ex. 28, page 108) is only one of the many turning steps of Czechoslovakian dance. Others are—

Točinky, in which man or woman steps sideways on R. ft., then on L. ft. to complete one turn to the right. They continue these two steps at a tremendous speed with hands held on the hips. This can also be danced on the heels.

Sousedka, a valse-like step with many variations—

1. Step forwards or sideways on R. ft.
2. Slide L. ft. to R., raising heels.
3. Step slightly forwards or sideways on R. ft.
   Repeat beginning on L. ft.

> *First Variation.* 1, 2. Step forwards or sideways on R. ft.
> 3. Close L. ft. to R., turning swiftly.
>
> *Second Variation.* On 2, bring L. ft. up with a stamp.
>
> *Third Variation.* 1. Step forwards on R. ft.
> 2, 3. Hop slightly on R. ft., closing L. to R.

Obročak, in either 2/4 or 3/4—

1. Step forwards on R. ft.
2. Turn on ball of R. ft. turning to right.
   Repeat on L. ft., but still turning to right.
   In 3/4 the dancers usually lower their heels on the third beat.

> *First Variation.* Spring on to R. ft. and then hop on it, repeating movement on L. ft.

The speed of this can be increased so that the couple perform four movements in each bar. They can also increase the size of their spring. Sometimes this turn is hopped, or the foot stamped on the first beat followed by a hop.

Vrták (Ex. 29, page 109) is the most important variation of this movement. A smoother version was known as the *Polka Tremblante*.

In most variations of these steps, beats can be added and sometimes there is an exaggerated sway from side to side from the waist.

Running steps are found in some dances, notably Siva Holubička, as in Holubička, (or the Dove), and are very smooth in contrast to most of the other steps. Occasionally one also finds the Teutonic valses and polkas, and jumps with both feet together.

Male dance is very much akin to that of Hungary and the Ukraine, although it has neither the absolute precision and horsemanlike carriage of the former, nor the complete freedom of the latter. There is a wonderful variety of turning movements, particularly in the west, where Couple Dances predominate. In the east, the Circular Dance is still the most popular. Both areas have longways dance-games, which have developed from the ancient Processionals of fertility rites. All turning dances usually work up to a tremendous speed, particularly in the mountain areas.

Because of the preponderance of western Couple and eastern Circular Dances where the performers are linked, the arms do not play a very prominent part. The couples swing their arms up and down, or twist under the handkerchieves, but the most interesting arm movements are in the really ancient eastern rituals and the mimetic dances of the Bohemian Forests. The dances after wedding ceremonies are particularly attractive and, like those of other Slav nations, describe the work that the bride will have to do.

Interesting arm movements are also found in certain men's dances of the Carpathians. These resemble those of the Polish mountaineers' dances, but there are others which show the felling of trees and other aspects of a forester's work.

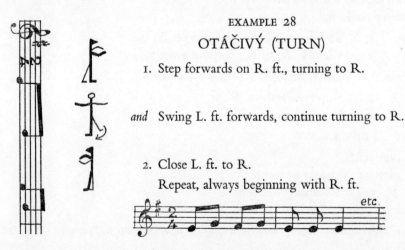

EXAMPLE 28
OTÁČIVÝ (TURN)

1. Step forwards on R. ft., turning to R.

and Swing L. ft. forwards, continue turning to R.

2. Close L. ft. to R.

Repeat, always beginning with R. ft.

EXAMPLE 29

VRTÁK STEP

Man's hands are on woman's waist, hers on his shoulders; couple turns to the right.
If the step is danced smoothly it is called *Polka Tremblante*. Woman commences R. ft.

1. Spring on to L. ft.

2. Hop on L. ft.

1. Give a large hop on L. ft., bringing R. knee higher and turning
as far as possible.

2. Hop on L. ft.
Repeat hopping on R. ft., but still turning to right.

EXAMPLE 30

POLKA WITHOUT A HOP
(Can be danced forwards, sideways or backwards.)

1. Step on to R. ft.

and Close L. ft. to R., raising R. leg quickly forwards.

2. Step on R. ft.
Repeat, starting with L. ft.
Sometimes danced with a stamp on 1st and 3rd steps.

EXAMPLE 31

JANOSHKA, A RECRUITING DANCE
(1st step)

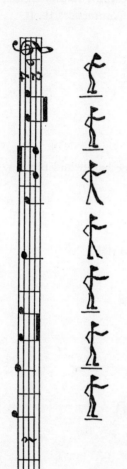

Couple stand side by side, inside arms outstretched and hands on each other's shoulders. She is on his right. Outside arms are on hips.

1. Jump forwards on both feet.

2. Jump on both feet in place.

1. Jump on L. ft. and point R. ft. in front.

2. Jump on R. ft. and point L. ft. in front.

1. Jump both feet together.

2. Jump both feet apart sideways.

1. Jump both feet together.

2. Pause.

First 4 bars.   Perform 1st step as above, looking ahead.

Second 4 bars. Repeat 1st step, but drop arms to side and look at each other.

2 bars. Partners give R. hands and change places with 3 steps and a bow.

2 bars. Repeat these 2 bars moving back to places.

2 bars. Partners facing each other, perform 1 *polka without a hop* to the right, and 1 *polka without a hop* to the left.

2 bars. *Boy.* Beat 1. Hop on L. ft., pointing R. toe to side.

       and   Hop on L. ft., pointing R. toe in front.

2 *and*   Repeat these two movements hopping on R. ft.

1.   Clip heels together and hold position.

Girl. 1–2. Cross R. ft. over L. and make one complete slow turn to face partner again.

1–2. Pause.

Repeat these last 8 bars.

Repeat dance *ad lib*, getting a little faster.

Janoshka

BULGARIA

Bulgaria is one of the few European countries in which a conquering people have almost entirely lost their own identity and assimilated the language and culture of the conquered. This Balkan area was originally occupied by Slav tribes, who became part of the Greek and later of the Roman Empire. The Bulgars, from whom the country gets its name, were comparatively latecomers. They were a nomadic tribe from a Finno-Ugrian group originating in north-east Asia. In search of pasture for their flocks, they had first settled round the Volga, but migrated to the Don Basin, and finally during the seventh century A.D., settled south of the Danube, driven there by other powerful Turki tribes, who annexed the rich areas round the Black Sea.

Although the Bulgars ultimately ousted the Slav princes from this area, they did little to change the ancient Slav rituals, for not only were these akin to their own culture, but the infiltration and settlement of this eastern tribe were so gradual that the newcomers assimilated the customs and language of the earlier Slav inhabitants as they intermarried and worked together. The gradual conversion of the Bulgarian princes and their people to Christianity by the Greek Orthodox Church also did little to change the rituals. The Fall of Constantinople in 1453, followed by the complete subjugation of the Bulgars, who had by this time become entirely Slavonized, served to unite overlords, church and people in attempts to preserve themselves and their ancient rituals from the cruel overlordship of the Ottoman Turks. These attempts became intensified each time the Moslems perpetrated yet another atrocity. Yet some Bulgar princes, like the Bosnians, protected themselves and their women-folk by adopting the religions, customs and fashions of their conquerors. This and the domination of Turkish princes has killed or distorted the older communal rituals and Horos in some parts.

In the remoter mountain regions, however, the invader had little influence. There, the existing dances and rituals are almost identical with those of Yugoslavia and south-east Russia. The dancers are linked in Horos or chains, and there are the three distinct styles, hopping, stepping and shaking, according to the area in which they are found. The Horos are based on some variation of the Slav basic step. The Yugoslav Padushka (Ex. 9, page 78), which has a Bulgarian variant danced in 5/16, is a typical example. The most popular dance is Rachenitsa, also known in Yugoslavia and Romania. It begins as a couple dance and often develops into a communal dance in which a wonderful display of steps is given by the men. As in the Ukrainian Gopak, they are demonstrating their powers before the women, but at the same time they are testing the women's strength, for the woman is expected to keep up with her partner, performing either some form of tiny *pas-de-basque* or hops, or delicate running steps alternated with rockings on the toes. These steps are made interesting because they are danced to a 7/16 rhythm and the first two steps of the bar take 2 beats each, and the third step, 3 beats.

Owing to their long oppression by the Turks, the Bulgarian dancers, however, do not display the same joyousness as the other Slav people. They are often solemn and appear to dance under some kind of strain, as their bodies are held tensely and rarely relax. The rhythms of their dances are usually complex, because many of the melodies are Turkish in origin, and therefore the tune did not originally fit the steps, which have to be adjusted to the appropriate beats of the rhythm. The enchaînements are simple, and there is little embroidery of the basic step of each dance as the group continues to perform.

Some interesting women's Horos are performed during the harvesting of the roses for making the famous Attar of Roses, which forms one of Bulgaria's most important exports. These depict the gathering and pounding of the rose-petals, and the making of the scent, which is followed by a dance describing the beauty of the woman who uses the Attar.

There is little trace of the Bulgar's nomadic ancestry in the male Horos, although horses ar still bred and a hobby-horse plays a part in some rituals. However among certain religious sects, the men have a few ecstatic turning dances, having their origin in the Shamanistic priests' dances of Eastern Siberia, and are possibly the only feature derived from the Bulgarians' original ancestry.

CHAPTER XII

The Alpine People

THE people living in the vast mountain system of the Alps do not belong to the same language group. They speak many different dialects: French in the cantons of the west; Italian in the south and south-east; Romansh, a modified Latin and akin to that spoken in Provence, in the east; and dialects based on old or new German in the north. Common needs and historical circumstances have, however, so united these various people, and their dances have so much in common, that the Swiss and Austrians in the Tyrol will be dealt with as a whole. (See Map 2, facing page 52.)

Ethnologists studying the relics of ancient lake-dwellers in Swiss cantons have discovered that they were of a distinct physical type, still persisting in the central area. They possibly came from Asia Minor and have been called the Alpine Eurasiatics. The river valleys flowing to north and south have been the means by which numerous other types of people have entered and mixed with the earliest broad-headed, dark-skinned inhabitants. Some of the new-comers came in search of fresh pasturage for their flocks of goats, sheep, and swine, and settled round the shores of the lakes and up the river-valleys, where some areas of rich soil allow of excellent agriculture. Others came with such marauding armies as those of Hannibal, Julius Ceasar, Attila, Alaric, Charlemagne, Frederick Barbarossa, and Napoleon. Yet others came in search of refuge from the persecution and oppression of the rulers or of various religious bodies in their own countries.

The almost impossible task of conquering these mountain regions, and the difficulty of communications between the various cantons, prevented most warlike leaders from attempting to add the Alpine area to their own domains, although from time to time the outlying slopes have been annexed by first one king and then another. This lack of an all-powerful king gave the inhabitants an independent form of government early in their history. By the thirteenth century, peasant farmers in the area round Lake Lucerne had formed themselves into a league to stop the Hapsburg family (later rulers of the Austro-Hungarian Empire) from acquiring Alpine territory. Their efforts were so successful that by the sixteenth century this league had been joined by all the other districts in almost the whole of the area now known as Switzerland, and the republican form of government they evolved has remained in existence ever since.

The various European upheavals have had little effect on this government and consequently it might be expected that the varying Alpine dance rituals would remain unchanged. This is not so. There still survive many relics of customs similar to those in the surrounding countries from which the various groups originated. In the central areas there are even traces of rites that possibly belonged to the first lake-dwellers. But the powerful influences exerted by Protestant and Catholic churches have distorted their significance and their forms.

During the eighth century the country came nominally under the jurisdiction of Charlemagne and was gradually converted to Christianity by the Catholic church. This meant that the people's rituals became associated with the church calendar and were shorn of their most pagan elements—not so much as elsewhere, however, because the Catholic priests who acted as missionaries were so often refugees and therefore more tolerant. When, moreover, the peasant-farmers asserted their right to regulate their own affairs they ceased to pay tribute to Rome, and the church's hold was somewhat slackened.

The disgust with which the Swiss League regarded the excesses of the Catholic church and its princes, however, caused many other reformers to seek refuge within its mountains. Among these was the puritanical Calvin, who preached his mission in Zurich, Lucerne, Berne, and Geneva. As his followers grew in strength, so in their zeal and intolerance of Catholic church practices they suppressed, and at times completely destroyed what remained of the ancient rituals in areas they converted. That they were so successful is explained by the fact that Calvin forbade singing in church entirely. Many old tunes, which might have served as an aid to peasant memory when the reformer's zeal had weakened, were in this way completely lost. Moreover, in some cantons the reformers had done their work so well that to-day, in the Protestant parts of Switzerland, only a bare minimum of dance rituals can be found.

The reformers were not able to alter the entire Swiss population. In remote villages the local priests and their flocks remained undisturbed, and when the Austrian Emperor annexed the southern and eastern ranges many were re-converted to the Catholic faith. This meant a revival of certain customs and ceremonies, but owing to the long period of time since their last performance and the loss of tunes that might have kept them alive, these rituals took on new forms as many new social dances gradually found their way into the Alps.

For a long time Switzerland has been a playground for wealthy Europeans as well as a refuge for reformers like Calvin and political refugees like Voltaire. This, together with the arrival of Austrian princes and their courts to take over new estates, and the presence of the Napoleonic armies during the eighteenth and nineteenth centuries, led to the introduction of dances fashionable at the courts of Vienna, Italy, and Paris. These have now become part of the older rituals, such as the few chain dances or Coraule, which begin with a circle and open into a chain, but quickly develop into a polka, valse, or mazurka-like dance, in which figures are occasionally made. The Couple Dances are popular everywhere and hold absolute pride of place. Yet these dances, derived from Austrian, German, and other social sources, when danced in the mountains have acquired features not found in the countries of their origin.

The Preponderance of Stamping and Clapping

Man has always tended to regularize and discipline his communal songs and dances by the stamping of feet and clapping of hands. In this Alpine meeting ground of many peoples, where language is not a common means of communication, this stamping, clapping, and slapping on all parts of the body has developed into a highly complicated performance, and constitutes the most significant feature of the dance. This form of dance is known in Central Switzerland as the Gäuerler, in Appenzell as the Hierig, and in the Bavarian and Austrian Alps as the Schuhplattler. It is notable for the extraordinary way in which the man snaps his fingers, slaps his thighs, buttocks, heels, knees, and cheeks, and claps his hands to achieve an extremely complex syncopated rhythm of sounds as he dances wildly in front of or round his girl. In addition, he punctuates these complex enchaînements of personally made rhythms with high jumps or hops on alternate feet, which make his efforts even more effective and spectacular.

The same love of making rhythms independently of instrumental or vocal accompaniment is found in the herdsmen's dances, in which the men make fascinating rhythms with their clogs. This form of dance originated long before the western drum found its way to these mountainous districts, and no doubt helped to regularize the more primitive dances and customs of the varied inhabitants.

The most interesting Swiss and Austrian dances are those in which this slapping and clapping forms an important part of a more modern polka or valse, when the continually regular movement tends to make them look monotonously alike. Its sudden introduction is exciting, because there is no set method of performance. Each man extemporizes, and the better dancers utilize every possible part of their anatomy, and often that of the other men in the dance, in their efforts to be different.

The Yodel and the Octave Leap

Dance-songs are extremely rare, no doubt because of their suppression by the Protestants and the introduction of instruments by musicians who sailed up the Danube. Solemn processionals are often marched through the villages to the accompaniment of quaint songs sung in the local dialect, but few attempts are made to dance to these. The Alpine people have, nevertheless, a peculiar method of singing, the Yodel, which has developed from their way of calling into the mountains and receiving either an echo or an answering cry, often on a higher or lower note to their own. This form of echoing music is reflected in the curiously echoing sounds made by various ways of holding the hand when clapping and slapping oneself; these sounds are also a feature of the old folk tunes. Many of these melodies are composed of arpeggios and wide leaps of interval, which are often as much as an octave. The dancers often match this peculiarity with upward and downward swings of the body, while in the famous Schuhplattler, the appropriate musical passages are ultimately marked by the girls being flung high in the air as in the fertility leap.

The Swing of the Body

The constant lilting in the older folk music has also given rise to the deep swings and upwards lifts of the body in all the turning dances, from the older type Ländler to the more modern valses. It is found to some extent in the polkas, particularly in Austria, where it often starts with a stamp from the man and then a bounce off both feet as the couple begin to turn.

The tendency to stamp at the beginning of an enchaînement, and the downwards tilt of the body, does not, however, lend the Alpine dance that heaviness found in the more Teutonic countries. In all the mountain areas, movements are always directed upwards and the stamp or the downwards tilt act as a preparation for the lift. They are performed with strength and control, but are only sufficiently heavy to give the proper impetus to the upwards lift of the body.

Arms

Apart from their intricate use in the slapping and clapping movements, arms play a very small part in Alpine Dances. In the Couple Dances, which are preponderant, the men hold their partners' hands or waists. At times, in such valse-like dances as the Steyrisher (Aussee), or A Moléson (Gruyère), the woman pivots or twists under her partner's right hand, whilst the free hands of both are held on the waist or just behind the hip. Nevertheless the man has one peculiarly characteristic movement of his own. It is found in the Schuhplattler, where he imitates the mountain-cock at the mating season. His thumbs are stuck in his braces and he moves his elbows like a bird using its wings.

Occasionally one finds some stylized mime in dances derived from the seventeenth and eighteenth century court dances, when an element of courtship demands that fingers are shaken, heads nodded, kisses blown, and occasionally the couple embrace. In French-speaking Switzerland one finds the Piccoulet, in which the leader in the centre makes gestures to be imitated by the rest of the group, as is done in so many children's games with a ritual origin, such as Louby-Loo (the well-known Hokey-Cokey of modern ballrooms) and When I was a Young Maid.

The Steps

Apart from the complicated Schuhplattler, steps consist of little more than simple variations on the valse and polka.

In Switzerland the polka starts with a step on the first beat of the bar, but in Austria it is more usual to start on the last half-beat of a bar and the hop therefore becomes the most prominent feature. Another polka-like step is called the *Rheinländer* and has an attractive zig-zag pattern which, like the basic step of the Caucasian Lekouri-Lezghinka, is dictated by the narrow mountain paths (Ex. 32, page 117).

The *valse* is always danced with a very full swing of the body. The feet are never placed very accurately and the toes are often turned inwards, giving a much greater degree of turn to each movement.

Many dances are based on the so-called Schottische step, which can be performed sideways and turning. In a 2/4 rhythm this is somewhat like the Scottish step of the same name, but has not its neatness nor turn out of the foot. In a 3/4 rhythm, however, it loses the hop (Ex. 33, page 118).

The *Mazurka step*, which must not be confused with the true Polish dance but has come from the polite ballroom version, is also a favourite (Ex. 34, page 118).

Forms, Patterns and General Characteristics

As Couple Dances prevail the patterns are usually circular or processional, although there are no Longways Dances. But excellent patterns are made by the turning of the woman round her partner, and into the centre and out again. Enchaînements are simple, usually a series of one step followed by a series of another, with an occasional introduction of a single step to change the leading foot or direction of the dance. These enchaînements last a regular number of bars and change with the melodic phrase.

Although the dances of Switzerland and Austria are so much alike, the Austrian dancers are more lively and tend to punctuate their performance with spontaneous passages of leaps, twists, turns, and loud calls and cries. At Carnival time, when relics of the most ancient rituals are performed, much greater licence is taken. There is also the introduction of the clipping of the heels as found in Hungarian dancing. In Switzerland the dancers are much more sedate and nice in their behaviour, and have a more disciplined way of dancing.

EXAMPLE 32

RHEINLÄNDER

(In 4/4 or 2/4). In 3/4 the beats marked are 1 and 2, 3

1. Step sideways on L. ft.

and Close R. ft. to L.

2. Step diagonally forwards on L. ft.

and Hop on L. ft. swinging R. leg across.

etc.

EXAMPLE 33

SCHOTTISCHE STEP IN 3/4

This can be danced forwards, sideways or turning

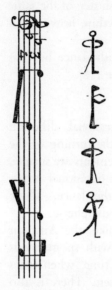

1. Step sideways on L. ft.

and   Close R. ft. to L.

2. Step sideways on L. ft. (When turning this completes a half turn to the right.)

3. Raise R. leg slightly sideways inclining body towards it.
Repeat, starting with R. ft. (Still turning to R. if danced turning to complete one circle.)

EXAMPLE 34

MAZURKA

1. Step forwards on L. ft.

2. Jump on to R. ft. behind L., immediately raising L. leg.

3. Hop on R. ft. Repeat, always starting with L. ft.

Mazurka

CHAPTER XIII

The Teutons

THE nomads of Central Europe, who settled along the shores of the Baltic Sea and in the Scandinavian Peninsula, spoke dialects of a common Teutonic language from which developed the ancient Norse, parent of the German, Dutch, Scandinavian, and English tongues spoken to-day (Map 2, facing page 52). The dances and rituals now remaining have so many features in common that it is often difficult to discover the slight differences distinguishing the dances of one of these countries from those of another. Sparsely scattered through these areas can be found ancient processionals, such as the Seven Springs, which has various forms (Ex. 35, page 123), as well as ancient Chains, Sword Dances, and other rituals.

But French and Italian court dances and the English Country Dances, together with the violent religious wars and final ascendancy of the Protestant church in most of these areas, have all but killed the ancient Teutonic dance forms. England, however, in her most ancient folk dances and arts and their methods of performance, exhibits features more closely akin to those of the Celtic-speaking countries. Her ties with them are older and, despite the almost complete annihilation of the Celt in England herself when overrun by the Teutonic race of Anglo-Saxons, those features still stand out clearly enough to warrant her being included in the Celtic section.

As one enters any of the Teutonic countries from those where a Slavonic language is spoken, or descends the Alps into the Western European Plains, it is immediately noticeable that the dance becomes more sedate and heavier and the melodies less complicated in rhythm, form and tune. That these melodies are so much weaker in tune and rhythms than those of the mountains or of the East can partly be explained by the fact that the Teutonic languages are not characterized by long and short syllables, like Greek, but by strong and weak accents.

In addition, the eastern drum was never known as it was in the Slav countries; therefore, until the invention of the western drum with its sticks, rhythms for dance movements were dictated by the strong or weak accents of the words, or by the stamping of feet and clapping of hands.

Another factor limiting the range of tone in the folk melodies is the lack of larger intervals. The tunes often run in patterns of Thirds and do not move very far from the keynote, to which they are constantly returning. Because of this there are few of the violently contrasted passages of emotional expression found in Slav music and dance, or the range of sound and leaping step found in the mountains.

The lack of these two factors—complicated rhythm and emotional expression—tend to make the dances much more even in style and deportment. They usually have exactly the same number of steps as there are beats or half-beats to the bar: such as the 3/4 valse or 2/4 polka. At the most there is an introduction of an extra step lasting half a beat in an otherwise regularly timed bar, such as the polka-like step to a 3/4 rhythm, or a Ländler or valse-like movement to a 2/4.

Some of the evenness and regularity of Teutonic music and dance is due to the slow and even tempo of the life of pastoral and agricultural workers in many of these flat regions at a time when folk dance was developing. But it is also due to the change in style of official music at the time of the Reformation. Until then the Catholic church music and the music played at court had no part in the people's festivals, which continued to take place. The two forms were quite distinct, since the introduction of folk tunes was of no interest to composers writing specially for the prelates and princes of the Holy Roman Empire. But Luther realized that if he were to re-awaken the people's belief in Christianity and through this obtain their help in reforming the church, he must go back to the simple teachings of the Bible and make these familiar, and as part of his campaign he utilized many of the people's own tunes for his new hymns. This naturally affected their tempos and rhythms, making them more solemn and closely regulated. The identification of tune and religious idea must have affected the dances to which the tunes originally belonged, if ever the dances were performed, as occasionally happened. In the same way, it affected other tunes when newer dances were developed or were introduced from outside after the Protestant church had finally ousted the Catholic from most of these countries.

Another factor that makes the dances of these Teutonic countries look alike is their constant borrowing of each other's tunes for the newer dances. Many of them, such as "Soldier's Joy," come from the British Isles, and are tremendously popular everywhere and were probably introduced by Scottish soldiers during the seventeenth and eighteenth centuries. Continual historical change, however, has given the methods of performance enough variety to justify their being considered separately.

GERMANY

The early history of the varying tribes that were ultimately welded into the German nation is extremely confusing. The first settlers were joined by nomads from South Russia, and there was a return to the mainland by tribes sailing across the Baltic from Scandinavia. Not until A.D. 500 could there be said to be any degree of stabilization; by that time the provinces of Saxony and Denmark, as well as the eastern half of England, had been occupied by the pagan Saxons and Jutes. The main area of Germany was then part of the Frankish kingdom and had been converted to Christianity. France and Germany did not become separate entities until after the death of Charlemagne (A.D. 814), but it was not until the Saxon King Otto was crowned head of the Holy Roman Empire (A.D. 926) that the power both of Germany and of the Western Pope really began to grow. From then until 1871, when the Prussian King became Emperor, the German princes were gradually welding the various Duchies into a whole. This was not done without constant warring between themselves and with the neighbouring states, particularly to the east, where Slav and Magyar often attacked to gain new ground. (See Map 1, facing page 32.)

But although the country as a whole suffered no great invasion or settlement of people, who might have brought fresh elements into the folk arts as happened in the Slav countries, the struggle for supremacy of power between Pope and Emperor affected these arts tremendously. In no other European country has dance been under such periodic bans as in Germany. These were often invoked after the outbreaks of the deficiency disease known as St. Vitus' Dance, which was particularly prevalent during the Middle Ages. One of the worst outbreaks occurred in the Rhine valley during the fourteenth century, when papal wars, plague and starvation had so lowered the peasants' physical resistance that literally thousands of them were seized by what the priests took to be a dance frenzy. A particularly violent decree was passed, by which even those dances hitherto tolerated by the church at certain festivals were completely banned. This was followed by even greater persecutions of the peasants during the wars of the fifteenth century, when the Anabaptists, a group of reformers like the Hussites of Bohemia, attempted to found independent peasant communities.

The bitterness of the German peasants against the Catholic church increased during the sixteenth century, when Luther started his crusade against its excesses, particularly the sale of indulgences. Luther's crusade led to the religious wars, which culminated in the establishment of the German Protestant church.

The new church was as much opposed to the dance as the older one. Following the example of the earlier English Puritans and reformers, it published many pamphlets and decrees against such joyous activities. Yet with all this vigorous banning of the dance which has continued throughout German history, it must not be forgotten that the great German composers, including Bach, Beethoven, Mozart, and Handel, incorporated many old dance tunes in their compositions, as well as writing dance music for social occasions. Such compositions have supplied some of the world's finest dancing music, as many eminent choreographers have realized.

The Close Turning Dance

No German dance came in for so much censure as the turning couple dance peculiar to this part of the world. Curiously enough, the chief feature of that dance is still maintained in the more modern dances, in which the couples rotate round the room. When examining old manuscripts and prints describing the Drehtanz, from which the Ländler and Valse developed, one is amazed to note the extremely close contact maintained between the couple. When turning, both boy's and girl's arms are wrapped closely round each other, and they dance cheek to cheek. If they pass each other back to back they really touch, and if side by side then they dance hip to hip.

In addition there is a rolling movement from side to side, and the first step of an enchaînement is heavily marked. All this matches the regular lilting character of the tunes with their continual return to the keynote, and the heavily accented first beat of the bar. The heavy roll from side to side and plodding nature of the step is also noticeable in the few processionals in the Catholic areas to the north of Cologne and in the south, where dancing is altogether freer.

The Steps

The steps used are unadventurous. There is a great deal of walking and running, punctuated with a stamp or heavier step. This is very noticeable in any valse-like dance in 3/4, which begins with a heavy gliding step on a bent knee followed by a closing of the feet and then another gliding step; and in the stamp on the first beat of a polka, which lacks its usual abandon. The *Pivot step* is used, a *change-step* or *polka-without-a-hop*, in which the heels are loudly clicked together on the first half-beat or the second beat, and the *Two-step Valse* is also used:

1. Spring forwards on to R. ft.

and Transfer weight momentarily to L. ft.

2. Spring forwards again on R. ft.

This completes half a turn. To complete the turn, repeat commencing on L. ft.

There is one interesting step which used to be seen at its best in the famous Echternach processional in Luxemburg (now an independent state). This dance was sanctioned by the Pope because, strangely enough, it was supposed to afford some kind of protection against epilepsy. It was performed over the bones of Saint Willibord, who was said to have cured the disease, and was known as the Pilgrim Step. In it the dancers walk three of five paces forwards and then take one or two paces back, but after reaching a certain point near the Cathedral they take one step forwards, one backwards and then jump onwards three times with feet together. Something similar is found in other rituals when penance is being done, in both Christian and pagan countries.

General Characteristics

In form and pattern most German dances are the same as any Country Dance, Longways Set, Quadrille, or Cotillion. In the predominantly Catholic south, among the forests and the more mountainous regions, dances resemble those of the Alps and Bohemia.

In these areas some interesting rituals are still performed, but in the industrial north and centre real folk dance is almost entirely dead.

Because of the predominance of the Couple Dance the arms play an important part in supporting one's partner. There are also the stereotyped mimetic gestures and claps in the few dances deriving from the old Italian and French court dances.

EXAMPLE 35

SEVEN SPRINGS

The group, for as many as will, walk or hop solemnly round in a circle clockwise, taking 2 steps to each bar. After 16 steps (8 bars), they jump off both feet and then stamp R. ft. heavily on the ground. They repeat the walking round. At the end of each phrase they add one more movement, so that after the seventh round they jump then—

1. Stamp R. ft.

2. Stamp L. ft.

3. Kneel on R. knee.

4. Kneel on L. knee.

5. Place R. elbow on ground.

6. Place L. elbow on ground.

7. Either lie flat, or place forehead on ground.

Seven Springs

After each repeat add one more bar, until the dance is repeated 7 times.

HOLLAND

The people of Holland are mainly Teutonic in origin, although there has been a slight admixture of other nationalities owing to the peculiar part the country has played as a buffer state in western Europe. The complicated system of alliance through marriage, which confused so many historical issues, accounts for many of the difficulties encountered by the Dutch people before they finally achieved independence in 1648. Originally part of the Frankish Kingdom, they then became part of the Holy Roman Empire and were ruled by many different kings. During the thirteenth and fourteenth centuries, the Netherland towns, often with the help of refugee artisans from Italy, France and Germany, began to grow rich through trade, and gradually formed their own municipal governments. These wealthy traders, like their German counterparts, became extremely restive with the excessive demands made for supplies by Philip of Spain (their overlord) for his war against France. By 1567 Holland was in open revolt against the notorious Duke of Alva, who attempted to suppress the people by the most hideous series of murders, sackings of towns, and massacres. These were the more violent because the Protestant doctrines for the Reformation of the church expounded by Calvinistic preachers had also had effect, and the Duke's Jesuit advisers were only too anxious to destroy all trace of their adversaries. But their excesses were in vain. At the famous Siege of Alkmaar (1573), the people's heroic resistance and threat to flood the surrounding countryside by breaking the dykes, led to a withdrawal of the Spanish forces and ultimately, after further struggles, to the declaration of Holland as an independent country.

The almost complete domination of Holland by a Protestant church owing its inception to the strictly puritanical Calvinistic doctrines, and the preponderance of town over country life, led to the complete disappearance of the ancient dance rituals, except in those areas where the Catholic church maintained some hold or where the people's contact with the mainland was difficult. These areas are in the south-east and in the Northern Islands. Here can be found a few processionals common to many nations, which are now danced to old hymn tunes with scriptural words. The same type of song, as well as the more popular types of eighteenth and nineteenth century ballads, often accompanies some of the more modern dances in the same areas, but the words have little or no relationship to the movements, which are similar to those of the European countries where early French and Italian court and later English Country Dance forms and nineteenth century Quadrilles predominate. It is interesting to note, too, that in the lands reclaimed from the sea there are no signs of folk dance at all.

The Downwards Trend of the Musical Phrase

The severe oppression undergone by the Dutch people at a formative period of their history, together with the extreme flatness of the countryside, where many areas lie below sea-level, and the continuously moist atmosphere, have all helped to give Dutch folk music and dance its most characteristic feature, the heavy downwards trend of most melodies and dances. The phrases within a tune show a marked tendency to descend, and almost invariably end on a low note. The dancers continually mark these endings with heavy stamps or claps. Contact with the ground is rarely lost, a mere rise to the ball of the feet usually being the absolute limit. This is most noticeable in the many dances based on the *polka*, which is often danced without a hop and only has a rise or roll of the body to mark the last whole or half-beat of a bar.

The Tendency to Keep the Working Leg Behind the Supporting One

The downwards tendency of the dance movements has resulted in the Dutchman's curious habit of closing his foot or swinging his leg behind the leading foot, or even jumping up very slightly and finishing with one leg crossed behind the other. This movement is best seen amongst the fishermen of Tershelling Island, where dancing still has some fire and spontaneity. It is almost as if the dancers were unwilling to progress at all, except by walking, and this stationary tendency of movement lends a sober and staid character to all the dances.

The backwards swing movement is noticeable in all *polkas*, and in a *hornpipe step*, also found in Denmark. The latter probably originated with the fishermen, because when danced by them it acquires the characteristic rolling quality of all seafaring people's dances. Evidence of this is in Horlepijp, the dance found among the Dutch settlers in South Africa (Ex. 36, page 126).

Steps, Forms and Patterns

Apart from the above-mentioned polka and hornpipe steps, little else is performed except skipping, and even this degenerates into a shuffle or into mere walking, walking itself, and an occasional valse. (See Germany, page 122.)

Many dances begin as a procession, which breaks up to perform the usual figures and patterns of country dance and quadrille.

Arms are seldom used as couple dances predominate, but there is an occasional use of stereotyped mime as in Germany.

General Remarks

Although for the most part Dutch dance seems staid and heavy, it often achieves an air of hearty humour and even vulgarity. The early growth of town-life, the close association of town and country people and the comparatively wealthy state of all, has led to a strange imitation of what the dancers imagine are rustic manners. There is a hoydenish throwing of girls when the men change partners, and a bumping and slapping as well as a heavy clumping of clogs, which are never used to make the intricate beats of the Lancashire dancers.

EXAMPLE 36

HORLEPIJP (HORNPIPE)

Couples hold inside hands or link arms.

1. Step forwards on R. ft.

and   Close L. ft. behind R.

2. Step forwards on R. ft.

and   Step sideways on L. ft.

1. Close R. ft. behind L. ft.

and   Swing L. leg round in a circle behind R.

2. Jump and land on both feet, L. crossed behind R. (Jump is made slightly backwards.)

Repeat above 4 times in all, always beginning with R. ft. Man puts his hands on woman's waist and she puts hers on his shoulders; they then *Polka* fairly heavily for 8 steps, moving round counterclockwise. Repeat a little faster.

Horlepijp

SCANDINAVIA

There are very few differences between the dances of Denmark, Sweden, and Norway, except the slight one dictated by climate, geographical and work conditions. This has happened because during the formative period of their history, they all went through the same process. Originally they were a group of nomadic seafaring peoples, who were long in making any settlement. The Jutes alone in Denmark had made some attempts at permanent settlement by A.D. 500, and had also travelled across the North Sea to England with the Saxons. (See Map 1, facing page 32.)

By the ninth century, all these people had become known to the Christian world as the Vikings, a wild sea-going people engaged in continuous raiding. Some had returned to the European mainland and rejoined their Danish compatriots. Others had sailed to America, Iceland, Greenland, the Faröe and Shetland Isles, and the coasts of Scotland. Rolf the Ganger had journeyed to Normandy, and later Rurik the Viking sailed to Russia, followed the course of the Dnieper to the Black Sea, and crossed to Constantinople. In addition there was a constant movement between the tribesmen themselves. All this was facilitated by the development of shipbuilding and seamanship, which these people had been able to pursue unhindered by the Romans, whose conquest of south-western Europe had cramped any such activity among their victims. Under King Canute and his sons, there seems to have been some unity between the various Viking leaders, who were all in particular opposition to the Christian armies which were then attempting to enlarge the Holy Roman Empire. It was indeed these conflicts of pagans and Christians that gradually sent the Vikings further afield. But the Scandinavian and Danish kings and their serfs did gradually become converted and ultimately paid tribute to the Roman Catholic church.

The valuable forests and the boat-building industry of Norway, Sweden, and Denmark quickly brought these countries into the orbit of the wealthy Dutch and German merchants, and as the Hanseatic League gradually enlarged its activities so these countries grew in strength and power. From then on the history of events which have affected their dances is the same as that of Germany and Holland. There is the increasing influence of the Lutheran Reformation with its elimination of the Catholic church in all but the remote areas, the development of industry and agriculture, and the replacement of all but a few of the ancient rituals by the court dances of the eighteenth and nineteenth centuries.

These few remaining rituals are, however, not quite akin to those of the other Teutonic countries; nor is Scandinavian folk music. The nomadic tribes who first penetrated the Scandinavian peninsula eventually encountered the Lapps and Finns, members of the Finno-Ugrian groups from Asia and living in the Northern tip of this area. There they undoubtedly acquired or reinforced certain Eastern elements, which are still faintly reflected in the folk arts of Sweden and Norway. These also penetrated to Denmark, brought by the tribesmen sailing back to the mainland, and can be traced in the Faröe and Shetland Isles and Scotland. The most important of these features, as far as the dance is concerned, is the presence of the larger interval of the Fifth among the Chains of Thirds found in other Teutonic countries. This allows the dancer greater freedom and length of movement than the closely confined Dutch and German tunes. Moreover, nearly all the oldest tunes for mouth-music are in minor keys and this, coupled with the larger intervals, lends a slightly more emotional air to certain ceremonial dances. It is particularly noticeable in the wedding dances, which contain other features similar to those of the Slav and Finno-Ugrian countries. A most interesting feature of one or two of such dances is that in which the girls kneel as the men swing their legs over their heads, as in the Swedish Daldans (Ex. 42, page 138), an obvious symbol of an old fertility rite, where the woman signifies her subjugation by the man.

There also exist some ancient chain dances, which are found throughout Europe, but instead of merely going forwards or using the pilgrim step as elsewhere (see Germany, page 122), the dancers usually perform some version of the Slav basic step and progress sideways (see page 86). The steps are always carefully allied to the words.

DENMARK

Danish dance is the most akin to Dutch dance. The rich agricultural and pastoral nature of the countryside gives a comfortable but heavy air to most movements. Yet although the dances have hearty humour, they never acquire the supposedly "rustic" air, because Danish towns have not had the same influence as those of Holland, and the dancers are more truly the country-folk and fishermen. There is also more variety of step.

The Downwards Tendency in Dance and Lack of Circling Movements

The downwards tendency of Teutonic dance is particularly noticeable in Denmark, since the dancers immediately draw one's attention to it by their fondness for stamping hard at the beginning of most phrases in a dance. The whole body goes down into the movement of the stamping foot, which is usually placed in front of the supporting leg, not at the side as in other Scandinavian countries. This is called Appel.

The downwards tendency is also more noticeable because most of the steps are performed without any circling movement of the feet. This means that in many turning dances, the dancers take small steps, the feet being picked up and heavily placed at varying angles to achieve the turn, instead of being glided in circular form. In order to gain impetus the couple lean the upper halves of their bodies away from each other.

The only step which has any circling movement is the so-called *French Reel step*, which is exactly like the peculiar hopping backwards of the Russian, with its accompanying

turning out of the knees. The only difference is that the Dane performs this on one spot.
It is very effective when performed by the fisherman in his baggy trousers (Ex. 15, page 90).

Steps, Forms and Patterns

Walking, running, galloping, and skipping are extremely common, as are the *valse* (usually two gliding steps followed by a closing of the feet) and the *polka*, which begins with a tiny hop but does not rise far from the floor. The *polka without a hop* is also used.

The *Hopsa* is a step of the *pas-de-basque* variety and is danced turning or straight, when it is usually called the *Tyroler Hopsa* (Ex. 37, page 130). It is often performed in a series of four travelling and then four turning steps, and is danced in couples.

When danced to a 3/4 rhythm it is known as the *Tyroler Valse*. It then begins with a gliding step instead of the spring and the movement matches the regular beats of the bar.

The *Hurré* or *Old Man's Step* is in reality the *pivot step* known everywhere (Ex. 4, page 62). When the dancer is turning to the right, the weight is held on the right foot, which keeps turning on the same spot, whilst the left foot is used to give the impetus.

Occasionally this is used as a travelling step but, unlike the Slavs, the Danes use the right foot to take the weight when travelling to the left, and keep the left foot just behind the heel of the right foot, reversing this when travelling to the right.

The *Polka Mazurka* is fairly common (Ex. 34, page 118), as are the turn on two feet of the Czechs and the *Hornpipe step* used in Holland (Ex. 36, page 126).

Special Characteristics

The ancient ritual dance exists only in the Faröe Isles. Here can be found the chain dance in which people gradually join, irrespective of sex or status, as they sing a queer, chant-like tune. They perform a variation of the Slav basic step, stepping forwards on the left foot and closing the right to it twice, then stepping forwards on the right foot and closing the left to it once. The arms rock backwards and forwards with increasing excitement until the room rocks with movement. On the mainland this step has degenerated into the so-called pilgrim step, possibly because the music, being newer and semi-religious, does not give the necessary rhythm for the ancient steps. Moreover on the mainland the chains are only a beginning to a more formal couple dance.

A queer relationship of tune and dance is found in the Isle of Fanö in the Sönderho dance. After the promenade the couples perform a valse-like movement to a 2/4 rhythm. This means that in an eight-bar section the valse turn is repeated five times and every second turn begins on the second beat of a bar. This is something like dances in the Moslem parts of Yugoslavia, which are performed to a Turkish tune. Here it seems the tune is old and the dance somewhat newer (Ex. 38, page 130).

The forms and patterns of Danish dances are similar to those of Holland and Germany. Danish men, however, have two important ritual dances, one being a fighting dance and the other, the Millwheel, a relic of sun-worshipping rites.

EXAMPLE 37

HOPSA

(A step like the *pas-de-basque*)

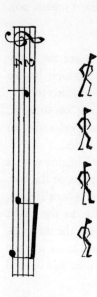

1. Spring on to L. ft., slightly forwards or sideways.

and   Step on to R. toe, just in front of L.

2. Transfer weight back to L. ft.

and   Pause but continue bending L. knee.
     Repeat starting with R. ft.

EXAMPLE 38

SÖNDERHO STEP

Man's Step

1. Step forwards on L. ft., turning to right.

2. Swing R. ft. round behind L., turning on the balls of the feet.

and   Lower both heels.

1. Step forwards on R. ft., to complete turn.
2. Begin with L. ft. again.

Example 38 (continued)

Woman's Step

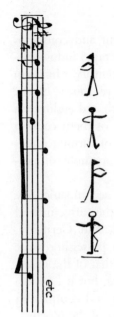

1. Step forwards on R. ft. between partner's feet.

2. Close L. ft. to R.

and Step forwards on R. ft.

1. Spring sideways on L. ft.
2. Begin again with R. ft.

To perform dance—

A. Couple stand side by side with linked arms and promenade counter-clockwise for 8 bars (i.e. walk forwards).

B. The woman's R. hand is held in the man's L. and set on his L. hip; he holds his R. hand high on her back, and she places her L. hand on his R. shoulder. The couple start sideways to the line of dance, and perform the *Sönderho step* 5 times. It must be very smooth, the man gently helping the woman to jump round to complete the turn each time.

Sönderho Dance

SWEDEN

Sweden, like Denmark and Holland, admits to a comparatively recent and conscious revival of the folk dance, which had been completely destroyed by the rapid industrialization and urbanization of the country at the end of the nineteenth century. In form and pattern Swedish dance resembles the couple, longways, and figure dances of the other Teutonic countries, which came into being during the seventeenth and eighteenth centuries, after the subjugation of the Roman Catholic church. Most of them contain long sections of walking or running steps, mixed with enchaînements of turning glides or hops. But despite their similarity of form and tune, the Swedish methods of performance are different.

Firstly, these two different types of movement in one dance are accompanied by two different musical tempos, slow for the walks or runs and fast for the turns, instead of the regular or gradually increasing speed of Denmark, Holland, and Germany. Secondly, the dancers are much more dignified and reserved although possessing some balon, which makes their dancing seem lighter and more buoyant than that of the mainland. Some of this dignity and reserve can be attributed to the climate, but it can also be explained by the fact that the Swedes were at one time a superior and conquering people. During the seventeenth century, their King Gustavus—the Lion of the North— determined to make the Baltic Sea a Swedish Lake, and although he was killed in this attempt, at the time of the Treaty of Westphalia (1648) Sweden was in possession of most of Norway, Finland, and two areas on the mainland to the east and west of the Danish Peninsula.

Their occupation of the mainland areas brought the Swedes into close contact with the Poles, whose ways of dancing they borrowed. The ties with Poland were again strengthened when Poland was divided between Germany, Austria, and Russia, for many Polish aristocrats found refuge in Sweden. It is not surprising therefore that many forms of the *Polska* (which means Polish) are found. These have little resemblance to the real Polish dances perfected by the military, but are based on those elegant movements of the aristocratic court dances, which have been strongly influenced by the modes and manners of the French, Italian and German courts. Nevertheless the Swedes' dislike of any excessive display of emotion in public and their almost puritanical belief in self-restraint has reduced the complicated Polish steps and display of court etiquette to the simplest possible formulas. In the same way they have made more sober the altogether livelier Norwegian dances found in those areas where the political boundaries have never stopped the friendly gathering of people from both sides. The same restraining influence is seen in the very few German folk dances brought back by the farm-workers travelling to the mainland for harvest work. The couples hold each other discreetly apart, feet are not raised high off the floor, even though the dance may contain hopping steps, and there is no rough handling or wild antics. Except for a slight sway from side to side in valse-like steps there is no movement of the body at all. The body is held erect and the head is held somewhat stiffly, the arms serving as links to partners or group but only playing a real part when some clapping movement is to be made, or in some men's comic dances, such as the Oxdansen or the Skobo dance (Ex. 41, page 137). Many of these dances originated among the undergraduates of men's colleges during the last century, and they often degenerate into horse-play. Very occasionally, and usually only in the Daldans (Ex. 42, page 138) when partners divide in a couple dance, arms are held at shoulder-level and the hands are clenched with the thumbs upwards.

Yet despite the strong western aspects of most Swedish dances, some traces of an eastern origin can be found not only in the contrasting of tempos, but also in some ancient chain dances seen principally at country weddings and other festivals in remote districts. They are also found in those queer comic dances where the men caricature well-known local characters or animals, as do the Armenians and other members of the Turki and Ugrian tribes.

The Beginning and Ending of the Melodic Phrase with Stamps or Claps

The unemotional quality of Swedish dancing seems to be stressed by the dancers' particular fondness for reducing to the absolute minimum any extra aids to rhythm. Whilst the Danes often begin their enchaînements with loud stamps and the Dutch conclude theirs with a series of stamps or claps, the Swedes stamp or clap only very discreetly at either the beginning or ending of a phrase. This is often done without any music, as in Huppleken when the couples having danced in a big ring, the woman walking and the men hopping, they then join left hands. The woman places her right hand open on top of the joined hands and her partner claps it with his right before they swing round the room. In other dances the girl stands with arms outstretched and the man swings his arms upwards and outwards before joining his hands to his partner's with a clap. This is called Appel.

The fact that this stamping and clapping has little or no relationship to actual notes of music may be explained by the fact that very few old folk tunes exist, and many Swedish dances to-day are performed to a mixture of tunes, very often from other countries. Moreover there are scarcely any dance-songs. Those that do exist bear little relationship to the actual steps of the dance, although they do indicate in some cases the actions of the dancers.

Steps, Forms, and Patterns

Walking, gliding, or *chassé* form the basic steps of most Swedish dances, and running steps are usually glided along the surface. These are interspersed with *pas-de-basque*, *polka without a hop* (usually called *change-step*), the glided *valse* found in Denmark, the *polska*, and *polka-mazurka* (Ex. 34, page 118). In addition one finds the following—

Bleking Step in 2/4. Jump both feet apart placing L. ft. in front of R., with another jump change position of the feet. This is sometimes known as the Figuré step and is danced with the forward toe pointed on the floor.

Fall-out Step usually occurs at the end of some running steps and is merely a fall on to one foot, the other is then thrust out sideways on the heel, the toe pointed upwards.

Gottland Step in 4/4 is the same as the *Bleking step* but has pauses between each jump.

Hop Step in 3/4—

   1. Jump feet apart.

   2. Step on to R. ft., swinging L. leg upwards and just behind R.

   3. Repeat second movement, stepping on to L. ft.

Ostgota Step in 3/4 or 4/4 rhythm—

   1. Step sideways on L. ft.

   2. Close R. ft. towards L.

 and Step forwards on L. ft.

   3. Step forwards on R. ft.

Repeat this, always starting with the L. ft.

If this is danced to a 4/4 rhythm, the movement is evenly distributed to each beat.

Step-hop Valse in 3/4—

   1. Step forwards on L. heel.

   2. Lift R. ft. and L. heel.

   3. Hop on L. ft. turning to right.

Repeat on R. ft.

Stride-knee Bend or *Jumping Jack* is a large jump forwards with feet open and turned in. Arms are usually swung out sideways with hands closed and knuckles turned backwards. Sometimes the dancer turns round on his right foot after the jump, before jumping again. This version is known as the *Vingaker step*. Both these steps are performed by men only.

There is another interesting *hopping step* found in Huppleken—this is the favourite Wedding Dance of Dalecarlia, which is also only performed by the men. It is in 2/4 rhythm.

1. Jump forwards on both feet.

2. Hop on L. ft. raising the R. knee very high.

Repeat raising L. knee on the hop.

Yet another hopping step is known as the *Dal step* (Ex. 39, below) and is danced to a 3/4 rhythm. It is particularly lovely in the Daldans (Ex. 42, page 138), when the upwards movement is very slight, but in other dances it is sometimes exaggerated.

Finally there is the favourite turning step known as the Swedish *Hambo*, or *Hambo-Polska* in a 3/4 rhythm (Ex. 40, page 136).

Apart from the comic dances mentioned above, no male dances have survived in Sweden, although point and hilt Sword Dances are mentioned in old manuscripts and the men of Dinkelsbühl in Germany perform Guild dances of a Morris-like character brought over by the Swedes in 1632.

The costumes worn for these are those that were in vogue during the Swedish occupation of this area.

EXAMPLE 39

DAL STEP

(N.B. In Daldans mark this very well, otherwise it has only a slight upwards movement.)

1. Step on to R. ft.

2. Rise on R. toe, swinging L. ft. forwards and slightly across to right with toe well pointed.

3. Return L. ft. to side or slightly in front of R., retaining weight on R. ft.

Repeat starting with L. ft.

EXAMPLE 40

HAMBO-POLSKA

Man's Step

1. Bending R. knee, stamp forwards on L. ft.

2. Hop and pivot on L. ft. about $\frac{7}{8}$ of circle to right.

3. Place R. ft. about 12 in. away from side of L. ft.
   Repeat, always starting with L. ft.

Woman's Step

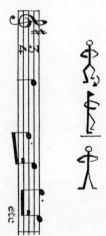

1. Bending L. knee, step backwards on R. ft.

2. Hop and pivot on R. ft.

3. Place L. ft. about 12 in. away from side of R. ft.

   Repeat, always starting with R. ft.
   The step is danced with man's hands on woman's waist, and hers on his shoulders.

EXAMPLE 41

SKOBO DANCE

Danced by men only, with very slow movement

8 bars. Two men, facing each other, take each other's hands and walk 3 steps round to the right commencing with L. ft. Stop with an Appel on R. ft. as if doubtful of continuing, on 1st beat of 2nd bar. Repeat 4 times in all.

8 bars. Repeat above movement circling to left, making Appel very determined.

Bar 17. Men let go of hands, take 3 steps round to R., starting with L. ft., to make one complete turn.

Bar 18. First man quickly kneels on R. knee, whilst second man places R. ft. heavily on floor and swings his L. leg towards the right, over first man's head.

Bars 19 and 20. Repeat bars 17 and 18, second man kneeling, and first man swinging R. leg over his head.

Bars 21 and 22. Both walk round to the right and then bend forwards so that their foreheads touch.

Bars 23 and 24. Both take 3 steps and make a half-turn to the right so that their backs touch and they violently push each other apart.

Bars 25–32. Repeat last 8 bars.

Skobo Dance

EXAMPLE 42

DALDANS

For any number of couples standing in a circle or column. Man folds arms. The woman places her L. hand on his R. shoulder and her R. hand on her hip. Both face front.

Bars 1–8.   Starting with R. ft., couple perform 8 *Dal steps* turning to woman's side and away from front.

Bars 1–8.   Repeat above, returning to starting place.

Bars 9 and 10.   Couple take hands and starting with R. ft., perform 2 *Dal steps* in place.

Bars 11 and 12. Raise arms high and stamping in time to the music, make one complete turn to man's left, woman turns to her R. (They let go of hands—this is known as *Pancake Turning*.)

Bars 13–16.   Repeat bars 9 to 12.

Bars 17 and 18. Man folds arms, his partner places hers on her hips and they run to each other's places, turning to face each other.

Bars 19 and 20. Both take 3 *Bleking steps* and one *stride-knee-bend*.

Bars 21–24.   Repeat bars 17 to 20 changing places.

Bars 17–24.   Repeat bars 17 to 20, twice.

Bars 25–32.   Couple commencing with R. ft., dance 8 *Dal steps* towards each other.

Bar 25.   Man takes woman's hands, steps forward on R. ft. and places L. ft. forward with toe raised and heel on floor. Woman places R. ft. forward in same way. Partners' feet are touching. Both jump replacing outstretched foot, which is raised high with knee bent.

Bars 26–32.   Repeat bar 25 7 times.

Bars 1–8.   Woman dances 8 *step-hop-valse* in place, taking 2 steps to make a complete turn, whilst man dances 8 *Dal steps* round her clapping his hands on the first beat of each bar.

Bars 1 and 2.   Couple perform *Pancake Turning* (see bars 11–12).

Bars 3 and 4.   Woman kneels on R. knee, hands on hip and head inclined and man swings his R. leg towards the left over her head and twists round as she rises. He claps hands on third beat.

Bars 5–16.   Repeat these 4 bars, 3 times more.

Bars 17 and 18. Man takes 3 steps to the left and pauses with arms folded until bar 25. Woman dances 2 *pas-de-basques* forwards.

Bars 19–20.   She continues with 3 *Bleking steps* and 1 *stride-knee-bend*.

Bars 21–24.   Repeat these 4 bars.

Bars 17–24.   She does 8 *step-hop-valse* back to place.

EXAMPLE 42 *(cont.)*

Daldans

Bar 25.	Man with hands folded, her hands on her hips. Both take one step forwards on L. ft., knee slightly bent, body leaning forwards and R. knee stretched out behind (i.e. it is bent upwards and then the toe hits the floor).
Bar 26.	Repeat movement stepping forward on R. ft. and take hands.
Bar 27.	Both place L. ft. on floor slightly behind R.
Bar 28.	With a jump and quick turn to L., both place R. ft. in starting position.
Bars 29–32 and 25–32.	Repeat bars 25–28 3 times.
Bars 1–4.	Couple link R. arms and run round.
Bars 5–8.	Repeat linking L. arms.
Bars 1 and 2.	Man with arms folded, her L. hand on his R. shoulder, both dance 2 *Dal steps* starting with L. ft.
Bars 3 and 4.	Woman places both hands on partner's shoulders. Man with an Appel on L. ft., places both hands on her waist and lifts her over to his L. side.
Bars 5–8.	Repeat bars 1–4 starting with R. ft.
Bars 9–16.	Repeat last 8 bars.

EXAMPLE 42 (cont.)

Bars 17–24.   Woman takes 3 steps to right and pauses. Man dances 8 *Dal steps* forward, starting with R. ft. and swinging arms across chest as he goes. Same arm is across chest as foot is on floor. The other curls round his back.

Bars 17–24.   Man dances backwards 8 *stride-knee-bends* to return to partner.

Bar 25.   Man takes woman's R. hand in his R., her L. hand in his L. and makes an appel with his L. ft. as she jumps across to his L. side.

Bar 26.   Man then jumps across to woman's L. side.

Bars 27 and 28.   Woman jumps again to man's L. side and both wait.

Bars 29–31.   Repeat Bars 25–27, woman first jumping to man's R. side and he following, etc.

Bar 32.   Man stands behind woman, his hands on her waist; her hands are on her hips.

Bars 25–32.   Both dance 8 *Dal steps* swaying in alternate directions. Man starts with R. ft. and woman with L., so that the couple turn towards each other. The swinging leg is only raised in front.

Repeat last 8 bars of music twice more whilst couple dance *Hambo-Polska*. It is usual to make an Appel on the first beat of each bar.

NORWAY

From 1307 to 1814 Norway and Denmark were one nation, and as their previous histories had followed so much the same pattern it is not surprising that there is little difference between the Norwegian dances found in the easily accessible areas and those of the other Scandinavian countries. The Norwegian style of performance is somewhat freer and more spontaneous, as befits the people's more virile and adventurous character. It arises primarily from their love of the mountains and sea, which are the main physical features of the north-west side of the Scandinavian peninsula. These lend some higher leaping and hopping movements and often an attractive gait to the usual Schottisches, Polkas and Mazurkas (Ex. 43, page 142), and Valses. But Norway also possesses a few ancient dances. The difficulty of penetrating a country so cut by deep fjords and high mountains prevented Protestant zealots from suppressing them entirely, and also prevented later dancing masters from introducing new elements into some ancient circles and chains which were once a prominent feature in all Teutonic countries. It is these rituals, sparsely scattered about the interior of the country, which must be studied if one is to understand the two outstanding characteristics of Norwegian folk dance.

The Tendency to Begin Dance Phrases on the Last Beat of a Bar with an Appel

The rhythmic movements of these ancient dances are difficult for any foreigner to capture. The steps are allied to the rhythm and significance of the words, often in a

Norse dialect, which are usually sung by the dancers themselves. These dance-songs are medieval ballads telling of knights and their ladies, or of strange happenings in an earlier age of giants and magic. Like the unique dance of the Faröe Islanders, the basic step of such chains is simple. A typical example is: the left foot is moved forwards twice, the right foot is then drawn up before being placed either to the side or backwards. But this simple basis often becomes a complex enchaînement by the addition of hops; slight stumbles which occasionally denote that the character described in the song is an incomplete person, that is one who has not reached maturity, is wounded or is sick; or quick runs, jumps, or leaps, which are also dictated by significant passages in the words.

The introduction of this apparently spontaneous extemporization into the regular pattern and rhythm of the enchaînement is always unexpected, yet it helps to draw attention to a peculiarity of Norwegian folk tunes, so brilliantly exploited by Grieg—their tendency continually to fall away from the leading note. This peculiar element is possibly what causes the dancer-singers in the oldest rituals to begin each phrase on the last beat of a bar and to accentuate it with a stamp or clap. The Appel (as it is called) usually coincides with the leading note, therefore if the tune falls away and the dance develops unexpected elements the Appel and leading note, by being repeated at the beginning of each new phrase, serve to bring the group once more into accord and give both dance and song a more regular form.

This peculiarity was once noted in some old Scottish dances and is still a common feature of certain eastern male dances, particularly those in which the men are enacting some dramatic scene of war or of a hero's deeds, as a singer tells the story. The element possibly comes from the time when it was customary for a warrior king to employ a bard or singer to chant the great deeds of his ancestors to his newly conquered enemies. The singer often broke away from the straightforward narrative to extemporize on the merits of his own king. When present-day Central Asian Akyns and Bakshys perform similar songs whilst they play old guitar-like instruments, the singer, after extemporizing, strikes the same simple, strong chords with which he started, before recommencing his narrative. This habit of using the Appel is also a feature in more modern dances and is more noticeable than in Sweden or Denmark.

The Halling

Another aspect of the strong relationship of dance and song in Norway possibly accounts for its unique male dance, the Halling, which Sweden has borrowed. To-day this is little more than a magnificent display of male proficiency in complicated steps, in which high kicks, deep knee-bends and leaps take pride of place. Moreover, like the Ukrainian Gopak, it is usually performed for a girl's benefit. Each performer uses his favourite tricks and vies with another for spectacular effect. But the Halling also contains some very significant arm movements, which can be likened to a man honouring his sword, making passes and slashing as if fighting before finally going down on his knees in a salute. The resemblance of these movements to those in certain Scottish dances and the Manx Dirk Dance, recently revived from an old document, in which an explanation is given, is too close to be ignored. (It is important to remember that both Scotland and the Isle of Man were invaded by the Vikings.) The Manx Dirk Dance is supposed to have been danced by the Kings' sword-bearer, who was entrusted with the then precious rarity, a weapon of bronze or iron belonging to his master. The dance perhaps represents his feelings of awe at the amazing deeds it can do. At the same time, if this dance is compared with some performed amongst the Turki and other eastern tribes, it is likely that its origin lies in the practice of the bard having an assistant, who would mime significant passages of his poem. This would be most important when a warrior king conquered a country where his language was unknown, and the bard required the help of a mime to reinforce his words and to strike terror into the hearts of those who might be in opposition.

EXAMPLE 43

NORWEGIAN MAZURKA STEP

1. Step forwards on R. ft. with a stamp.

2. Close L. ft. behind R. ft.

3. Hop on L. ft. raising R. knee well up in front. Repeat always using R. ft. and always drive well down into first beat.

Couple dance using the usual ballroom hold, man with his back to the centre of the circle. He starts with L. ft.

Bars 1 and 2.   2 Mazurka steps moving counter-clockwise in large circle.
Bars 3 and 4.   6 running steps turning clockwise in own circle.
Bars 5—8.   Repeat bars 1—4.
Bars 9—16.   Turn clockwise and progress round the room with man using 2 hops on L. ft. (1st and 2nd beat), 1 step on R. ft. (3rd beat), woman uses opposite foot.

Norwegian Mazurka

CHAPTER XIV

The Celts

TO-DAY there are very few people speaking a purely Celtic language. Nevertheless, descendants of this ancient group of European people do still show similar characteristics in their folk art, music, and dance, despite the many historical events which have obliterated their ancient culture.

The Celts were a people originating somewhere in the Middle East, who travelled south and west through Central Europe to spread across France, Belgium, parts of Spain, and into the British Isles. Their language is said to have an Aryan vocabulary with an Iberian grammar borrowed from the original inhabitants of southern Europe, whom they subjugated. From this are derived the Breton, ancient Cornish, Welsh, Scottish, and Irish Gaelic languages.

The folk arts of all these countries bear some traces of an eastern origin, but at the same time they have also developed certain common features that can be called exclusively Celtic. The most outstanding of these are the fascinating designs found on certain ancient pagan crosses and monuments of Ireland, Scotland and Brittany, which later inspired Christian priests illuminating some of the most famous Irish manuscripts. These are also found in the intricate floor patterns of some of the most ancient dances, as well as the Irish Jig, whose pattern resembles a Tara brooch; the Scottish Eightsome Reel (Ex. 64, page 189), whose pattern reveals an ornamented cross within a circle; the Derbyshire Morris Reel, Sellenger's Round and some of the Breton Rondes and chains. Some authorities who have noted this relationship of dance pattern to intricate ornament believe that the designs on the old Celtic monuments may have been inspired by the dancers' movements in a common ritual, which the artist desired to capture for posterity. The most important feature is the equal value and proportion of each line and form and the even balance of the patterns. This is also found in the dance, where each performer plays an equal part, and his movements are evenly distributed over the dancing floor. If he moves into the centre, he always moves out again an equal pace. If he dances to the left, he returns and dances equally to the right, and in a hey he ultimately returns to his own place, thus equalizing the patterns made by all the other dancers in the Set. No matter what figures may be danced, each performer or each couple does exactly the same amount and type of step. Even in the few solo dances, every movement is balanced to the left and right, forwards and backwards, and up and down.

The most interesting feature of Celtic music is the presence of one of those larger intervals usually associated with the east, the Rising Sixth, although in Brittany, where

143

tunes are of smaller compass, and wherever the pentatonic scale is used, the Rising Fifth is more evident. This introduction of a soaring sound in a tune which is otherwise distributed between the closer musical intervals, has its counterpart in the introduction of a sudden high leap in an otherwise terre-à-terre or low stepping dance; it is a predominant feature of some French and Scottish dancing, and is particularly noticeable in the English Morris.

Another feature shared by these countries is the dancers' preference for moving to the left or clockwise in their ancient circles and chains, instead of to the right as in the Slav countries. Finally Celtic dances often include enchaînements containing a repeated tapping of the feet on one spot, usually with the repetition of the same musical note.

What little is known of Celtic history is derived from the writings of Greek and Roman historians who travelled through the Empire collecting information from the priests of the various cults. The difficulty of learning about the history and rituals of the oak-worshipping Druidical priests of the Celtic tribes who inhabited a great part of the Roman Empire is discussed by Julius Caesar himself. He declares that the Gallic Druids were forbidden to write down knowledge, as they did not wish it to become accessible to the people at large. They preserved their knowledge in verse form, to be sung and repeated by their pupils and descendants, believing that knowledge learnt by way of song is retained in the mind better that that which is written down to be scanned by the eye. This reliance on memorized information of spells to be woven and work to be done is still shown in some of the ancient Celtic dance-songs, and in all probability some of the patterns made in the ancient dances reflect something of the sun-worshipping rituals of these ancient peoples. At the same time it must be remembered that the Celtic people were nearly all overrun by the sea-roving Vikings and Teutons, who also possessed tree and sun-worshipping rituals having similar features to those of the Celts. The intermingling of these Celtic, Viking, and Teutonic tribes served to reinforce certain elements, in the same way that the Mongolian invasion of Russia served to reinforce certain eastern elements in Slav dance. Nevertheless the above-mentioned features are so strongly marked in those countries possessing some Celtic ancestry that they can safely be named Celtic. That they differ in each area is explained by the various historical processes the people have undergone.

FRANCE

France possesses no natural barriers to prevent migrating and raiding people from entering the country. Bounded on three sides by the sea, her northern plains lead directly to the great plains of Europe, and there are mountain passes to the east and west of the Pyrenees, as well as wide river valleys through which the middle plains may be penetrated. It is for this reason that the French nation is of such a mixed ancestry and the relics of her ancient dance-rituals are of so varied a character. She is included in the present group by virtue of certain surviving Celtic rituals.

The Celtic tribes that originally settled in Gaul were joined by Greek settlers sailing to the coastal areas of Provence to establish small colonies. They brought with them rituals from which developed the ever-popular Farandole of the local Saints' Days and Festivals. This peaceful colonization was followed by the total occupation of the country by the Legions of the Roman Emperor (50 B.C.). For some three hundred years the Gauls were completely under their domination, acquiring an organized form of society, a new language, massive theatres and monuments, as well as customs and rituals, such as bull-fighting, and the dances in which sword-play is actually practised. Many of the Celts were converted to Christianity when it became the religion of their Roman leaders.

In the third century A.D. Roman power began to break up under the raids of many barbarian tribes sweeping through Europe from the north and east. Among these were the Franks, founders of modern France. This Germanic tribe had settled in the lower Rhine valley but, under their King Clovis, they started out from Belgium to conquer the Roman Province of Gaul (A.D. 481). During the next four hundred years, until the death of Charlemagne, the Frankish descendants of Clovis, by conquest and wise marriages, had acquired an enormous area of Western Europe, comprising France, Italy and most of Germany. This meant that many other ethnic groups had been incorporated in their kingdom, bringing Teutonic, Alpine, and other rituals which can still be traced in the various regions. These became attached to the Catholic church calendar as more and more people embraced Christianity.

Although this movement of barbarian tribes led to the downfall of the Roman Empire and the complete absorption of the Celtic people in Gaul, it was at the same time, by a curious accident, the means of preserving some of the ancient Celtic rites. Among the many people driven from home by the warring Teutonic tribes were Britons fleeing from the Angles, Saxons, and Jutes. These Celts from Cornwall established themselves as fishermen and husbandmen in the lonely north-western peninsula, which was henceforth called Brittany, and here they retained their ancient language and customs. Owing to its isolated position and the poor quality of its land, Brittany has always been by-passed by the major movements affecting the main body of French people. It is for this reason that the Bretons have developed such a rugged sense of independence and pride in their own achievements, which shows distinctly in their dances.

The Empire of Charlemagne fell apart because of the political differences between those Franks who had learnt to speak the corrupt Latin of Romanized Gaul, which developed into the French language, and those who still spoke the Low German of the Rhineland. In A.D. 843, France and Germany became separate entities, and have remained natural enemies ever since, despite the fact that they have so many cultural elements in common in those areas where their frontiers adjoin.

The history of France, from the ninth century until the accession of Louis XIV, is extremely confusing. It was in a perpetual state of wars of succession between its own princes and with neighbouring states. The situation is not made easier for the historian by the many alliances and conquests made by the intermarriage of ducal and royal houses. The invasion of Normandy by the Viking Rolf the Ganger adds further complication, for his descendants also entered into the struggle for the French throne.

Yet despite the different types of people with their varying rituals found throughout France, historical events have so welded the ethnic groups together in thought and action that similar methods of performance tend to make all their dances look alike. Everywhere they are extremely neat, self-restrained, careful in behaviour, and simple in form.

One explanation of the simplicity and small variety of step in any one dance and of the restrained behaviour of the dancers is that although France has some fertile regions, like the Rhône and Loire valleys, it is by no means everywhere a garden. In the mountains of Savoy, the central massif of Auvergne, Brittany and elsewhere, it is extremely difficult for the peasants to make a living. This difficulty, as well as constant war, has made them very careful husbandmen, using every possible source of material to maintain existence, and always storing enough to tide them over hard times.

Another factor making them careful of their behaviour was the growth of the many petty courts of the Feudal lords, each trying to outvie the other in the building of the magnificent castles and châteaux which are sprinkled throughout France. The best dancers among the local peasants were made to perform at entertainments given by their masters in the halls of these minor palaces to impress visiting princes. This no doubt had a sobering effect on the dancers, as well as serving to show them something of the polite behaviour of the courtiers, whose dances and manners were often imitated.

The tendency to display the folk dances of the country in a form of theatrical entertainment became particularly popular with Catherine de Medici, who used every chance to display the wealth of the French state and court. But this policy ceased when the Cardinals Richelieu, Mazarin, and Colbert, in their attempts to establish the absolute supremacy of Louis XIV, founded the various Academies of Art and Science. Here everything was dedicated to the glory of the King, and the people's folk arts played no part.

This and their masters' absence at the Royal Palaces broke the ties which had hitherto existed between overlord and peasant. For some one hundred and fifty years the peasants were left neglected, therefore few seventeenth and eighteenth century court dances came down to the peasants. The extravagance of Louis XIV and his heirs finally resulted in the Revolution of 1789, and for a time the people danced variations of their old chain and circle dances, which now became known by such names as the Carmagnole, and were accompanied by revolutionary songs. To these were added, for the amusement of the new bourgeoisie in the towns, several dances which were versions of the English Country Dances fashionable among the eighteenth century French aristocracy. These latter are still danced in the Île de France.

The revolutionary government was too short-lived to make any lasting impression on the general tenor of folk arts or the life of the peasants in the outlying areas, and the rise of Napoleon and the campaigns that followed brought further anxieties to discourage the people's own dances. At the same time dances then popular at other European courts, such as the Valse, Mazurka, Polka, Quadrille and Cotillion, were introduced to the officers and wealthy citizens, and occasionally penetrated to the rural areas to which they were brought by returning soldiers. From then (circa 1800) until the rise of the 1940 Resistance movement, old French dances were rapidly disappearing. Then—as happened in other countries at a time of suppression—the people began to practise their folk dances again.

The Small Compass of the Tunes and the Neat but Small Variety of Step

Wherever one goes in France one is struck by the small compass of the folk tunes. Except for the tunes of the Bretons and a few of the mountain regions, they rarely go beyond an octave, those lying within a range of five notes being in the majority. This small range of notes is reflected in the movements of the dancers. Whether they are dancing in couples, threes, fours, or larger groups, they always keep close together, moving neatly and behaving very carefully. There is none of the close couple dancing of the Teutons, or the wild boisterous changing of partners, or the wide sweep of movement of the Slavs. Politesse is observed between the couples and members of a set. The restrained quality of French dance is stressed in that there are usually the same number of steps as there are beats to the bar. Moreover the dancers' single steps never cover very much ground.

The Introduction of the High Leap

What makes some French dances exciting to watch and perform is the introduction of a sudden high leap which appears at the end of a phrase in some Bourrées of Auvergne, La Volta of Provence (in which the man lifts the woman high in the fertility leap), and the Shepherds' and other dances of Brittany. These are the more extraordinary because the jumps performed elsewhere, particularly in the mountain regions and Poitou, never seem to be so much a travelling into the air as a lifting of the legs from the ground, for the legs are usually bent upwards as far as possible (Ex. 45, page 151).

In the high jumps of Auvergne, of Brittany, and occasionally in the mountain areas, the dancer leaves the ground with straight legs, parts them in the air, and returns to the ground with feet together. In Brittany he also leaps up and hits his seat with his feet (Ex. 44, page 150). This is quite different from the curious jump of the Danse Maraîchine of Poitou in which to a 2/4 rhythm the enchaînement takes 2 bars (Ex. 45).

At the end of the phrase in the Bourrée à Quatre of Auvergne, which is danced by two couples round four wine-bottles, the girls jump on one leg and clap their hands under the raised leg. In all mountain districts beats and capers somewhat similar to those of Scottish and Irish dances may be encountered, but they are nowhere brilliantly executed.

Repeated Stampings, Clappings and Tappings

Some of the oldest dance-songs of Provence and Brittany have strange rhythms in which the dancers' movements coincide exactly with the words, and often in these dances there are vestiges of some definite work movement, such as the Provençal Danse Ronde de la Civaia, a harvesting dance; the Breton Piler-Lan (Gorse beating) (Ex. 46, page 152), and Stoupik (Hemp-stripping); and a woodcutters' dance from Champagne, the Soyotte (Ex. 52, page 158). In such dances the regular bar line is often broken so that the dancers wishing to continue an important movement can introduce an odd step or pause in an otherwise regularly formed enchaînement, and finish evenly with the music. But the rhythm is more often evened out by a tapping of the feet or a clapping of the hands two or three times to mark the end of a phrase, which occasionally ends with a feminine cadence.

This repeated tapping and clapping also occurs with the repeat of a musical note, and an alternate heel and toe movement is sometimes used to mark the beginning of an enchaînement when this occurs at the beginning of a melody, as in the Polka Piquée, which is widely danced in a 3/8 rhythm (Ex. 53, page 160).

Steps

A number of old circular dances of France are built up of variations of a step-to-the-side and close, to which is added a neat bend of the knees. This sometimes makes the dancers look as if they were continually bowing. In addition there is often the twisting of one foot in front of and behind the supporting leg, which is very common in Brittany, or a swift tap of the clogs as a foot passes from front to back, as in the Bourrées of Auvergne. Running steps are widely used, as well as *Pas Sautés*, which are light jumps from one foot to the other with the leg raised comparatively high in front, and the usual skips and occasional polkas. Some regions, however, have a basic step for many of their dances, such as the Gavotte of Brittany, and this appears in several dances. It is likened by the Bretons to a wave of the sea and is performed as if the dancers were running neatly over the ground. The movement is always to the left and is in a 4/4 rhythm (Ex. 47, page 152).

Other interesting dances from Brittany are the Ridées, which are usually circular dances consisting of a simple walking movement to which a hop or pointed toe and heel movement is added. The word Ridée signifies a wrinkle! The Ridée of Pontivy has an unusual rhythm and interesting combination of steps, and the arms also swing backwards and forwards evenly with the beats of the bar (Exs. 48, page 154).

There are several Bourrées, that of Bourbonnais in a 2/4 rhythm and that of Auvergne in a 3/8 rhythm being the most interesting. The former is done lazily with a considerable swing of the shoulders and hands on the hips or aprons; the latter is more virile, with hands often held over the head as in Scottish dancing (Exs. 49 and 50, pages 155, 156). The Bourrées of Poitou, whence the Minuet is believed to derive, still contains a step prominent in old charts of this court dance. Its rhythm is 6/8—

1. Drop on R. ft. in front of L.
2. Step on ball of L. ft. behind R.
3. Step to side on R. ft. Repeat, beginning L. ft.

In some areas steps are found in which the legs are flung up sideways alternately, and the feet are clipped together as the weight is transferred. To this is often added a curious turn, in which the step is performed three times as the dancer whisks round (Lou Panliran of Limousin). This step was known as the *Rue de Vache*.

There is also the Farandole, curious, because although usually danced to a 6/8 rhythm, the steps would normally fit a 4/4, for they lack the little hop at the end of each triplet which is usual with the 6/8 rhythm. Probably the Italian love of cantabile, or go-as-you-please, penetrated the regions where this dance is found (Ex. 51, page 156).

Use of Arms

An unusual feature of the dances of Provence, the Vendée, and Brittany, is the regular swinging of the arms to and fro, which is extremely interesting when the dancers occasionally perform two steps to two half-beats, whilst the arms keep to a regular rhythm (Ex. 48, page 154). This arm movement is quite contrary to that of the English Morris.

In Brittany the dancers are very fond of linking their little fingers together. This is supposed to be a magic formula for good, a supposition which is borne out by the fact that in some old witches' dances in the Pyrenees they moved counter-clockwise or "widdershins," and held each other by the thumb!

Apart from the few work dances left, however, the arms play little part in French dance. When standing alone the men usually hold their hands on their hips and the women hold their skirts or aprons, except in Auvergne and regions under Spanish influence, where the arms are often held over the head.

Forms and Patterns

The forms and patterns of French dance are of great variety. Simple and more complex circles in which patterns are made are very common. There are many processional couple dances and a few longways sets, as well as simple couple dances, most of which possess an element of courtship. Simple chains and those with serpentine figures are found mostly in Brittany and Provence. Elsewhere there are dances for groups of threes and fours, as well as sets for four couples, which sometimes involve complicated crossings.

The majority of French dances are based either on one single step, i.e. all *pas sautés*, or skips, or on a mixture of two steps, one walking and the other running, skipping, polka, or a repeated tapping of feet. The enchaînements of the remainder are similar to those of Greece and Yugoslavia, as the Breton and Provençal examples show (Exs. 45, 46, 47, 48, 51.)

Characteristics of the Various Regions

France is more regionally conscious than most nations, each area being very aware of its own particular traditions and customs, so that certain characteristics stand out above the commonly held French features. Brittany is the most strongly individual of all. There is often a jerkiness in the movement, particularly in the backwards swing of the arms in the Ridées. Moreover, owing to its isolated position very few examples of more modern dances are found.

A major element influencing the folk dances of the southern regions of Provence, Savoy, Dauphiné, and parts of Languedoc at a very early period was the emergence of the troubadours. They and their assistant jongleurs from the Provençal courts travelled widely, singing courtly songs, and these had some effect on the peasants' dancing. Some songs actually contained a dancing lesson, and it is notable to-day that dancing in these areas is more courtly than elsewhere in France. In Burgundy, dance displays the more indolent ease of the Italian peasant. Alsace and Lorraine show more Teutonic influences, particularly in the valse-like dances, while the Northern provinces round Paris show in the few dances that exist, the influence of the French court and of English country dancing. In the regions of the Pyrenees are to be found the wonderful Basque male dances which have left traces in the dance of so many adjacent mountain areas. These varied characteristics lend colour to the performance of the simple steps.

EXAMPLE 44

TWO MEN'S JUMPS FROM FRANCE

In Auvergne the step is usually danced on the cry "Holla!"

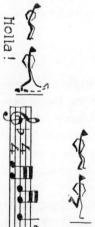

1. Preparation is made by bending both knees. Hands usually on the hips.

2. Leap up and part legs in the air.

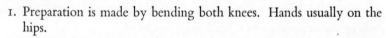

Breton Shepherds usually tuck their fingers into their armholes.

1. Prepare by bending knees.

2. Leap up and hit seat of trousers with R. or L. ft.

From A Breton Shepherd's Dance

EXAMPLE 45

DANSE MARAÎCHINE OF POITOU

The couples stand side by side, either in one long line, which advances and retires, in two long lines facing each other and meeting and retiring, or in a circle moving into the centre and out again. Everyone holding hands.

1. Jump on L. ft. Arms swing forwards and upwards.

and Jump on R. ft.

2. Jump on L. ft. Arms swing backwards

and Pause with both feet on floor.

1. Stamp R. ft. on floor. Swing arms forwards and upwards.

and Jump off both feet (picking them high off floor, but not rising high in the air).

2. Fall on to R. ft. Swing arms backwards. (L. ft. remains bent up in air.)

and Pause on R. ft.

Repeat the dance gradually increasing speed.

Danse Maraîchine

EXAMPLE 46

PILER-LAN (GORSE BEATING)

A chain of women and a chain of men begin this dance facing each other. The men hold hands and do not alter their position. The women have their hands on their hips and on the first beat of each phrase, turn to face the direction they are going.

To begin, the women have the L. heel poised on the ground opposite the men's R. heel, also poised on the ground.

1. Men bring R. ft. to L., women bring L. ft. to R. and turn to face line of dance.

2. Men step sideways on L. ft. Women step forwards on R. ft.

3. Men close R. ft. to L., women step forwards on L. ft.

4. Men step sideways on L. ft., women step sideways on R. ft.

1. Men close R. ft. to L., women close L. ft. to R.

2. Men hop on R. ft. swinging L. ft. in front of R., women step sideways on L. ft.

3. Men bring L. ft. to side of R., marking beat. Women make a quarter turn to face partner and bring R. ft. to L.

4 *and* 5. Men thrust R. heel out in front and hold. Women thrust L. heel out towards partner and hold.

Repeat, getting faster.

Piler-lan

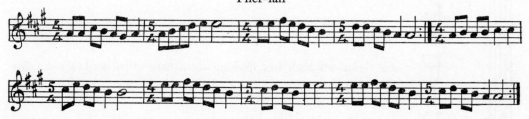

EXAMPLE 47

GAVOTTE

The sequence of steps is the oldest Breton dance and they often appear in other dances. In Le Pays de Quimper it is danced in chains of four, a man at each end and two women in the centre. It can also be danced in circles with little fingers linked or in long chains which weave in and out. In these hands are held, elbows linked or little fingers. The line always moves sideways to the line of dance and the dancers appear to skim over the surface with very light running steps.

EXAMPLE 47 (*cont.*)

1. Step obliquely forwards on to L. ft.

2. Bring R. ft. to side of L.

3. Step obliquely forwards on to L ft.

4. Hop on L. ft raising R. knee straight upwards, R. heel roughly at level of L. knee.

1. Carry R. leg round in a circle and place R. ft. on ground just behind L. ft. (These 2 movements are known as the *Paz Dreo*.)

2. Step obliquely on to L. ft.

3. Bring R. ft. to side of L.

4. Hop on R. ft. raising L. knee upwards and slightly sideways, roughly L. toe is on level with R. knee.

Repeat, always starting with L. ft. Dance gets a little faster.

Gavotte from Quimper

EXAMPLE 48

RIDÉE DE PONTIVY

The dance has a very lively movement, the dancers seeming to whisk over the floor.

Men and women standing alternately, dance holding hands in a circle and facing the centre.

1. Step sideways on L. ft., swing arms forwards.

2. Close R. ft. to L., swing arms backwards.

3. Step sideways on L. ft., swing arms forwards.

4. Clip R. heel on L. heel, swing arms backwards.

and Step sideways on L. ft.

1. Bring R. ft. to L. marking step.

2. Rise on balls of feet raising arms high in front.

3. Rise again on balls of feet, holding arms in position.

4. With a jump on R. ft., cross L. ft. over R., resting L. toe on floor, swing arms backwards.

Repeat *ad lib.*

Ridée de Pontivy

EXAMPLE 49

BOURRÉE FROM BOURBONNAIS

Usually danced by the couples facing each other

1. Step forwards on L. ft.

2. Glide R. toe besides L. ft.

1. Tap R. heel forwards.

2. Jump in place on R. ft., raising L. ft., slightly behind R.

1. Step backwards on L. ft.

2. Glide R. toe backwards to L. ft.

1. Tap R. heel on ground behind L. ft.

2. Jump in place on R. ft., raising L. ft., slightly in front of R.
   Repeat, always stepping forwards on L. ft.

EXAMPLE 50

BOURRÉE OF AUVERGNE

1. Step sideways or forwards on R. ft.

2. Close L. ft. to side of R.

3. Stamp R. ft. on floor at the same time as turning on ball of R. ft. and hitting heel of L. sabot as L. ft is slightly raised from the floor. Repeat step with L. ft.

   This step is done in many different formations.

A Bourrée from Auvergne

EXAMPLE 51

FARANDOLE

(Provençal version from near Nice)

Men and women standing alternately and linked to each other by their handkerchieves. The leader draws them down the dancing space with a long serpentine figure. He then winds them into a tight maze or knot, and leads them directly out of it by going under the arches made by any couple. Having brought the dancers into a straight line, he and his partner make an arch for the others to wind through; or he, followed by his partner and the other dancers may wind in and out the arches made by the others.

    The dancers can perform the usual skipping step throughout by making the step on the first note of each triplet, and the hop on the last (i.e. 2 skips to each bar). Usually the following step is performed. Dance always moves to the right—

EXAMPLE 51 (*cont.*)

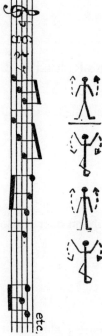

1. Jump both feet apart, swing arms forwards.

2. Cross L. ft. behind R., swing arms backwards.

1. Step to side on R. ft., swing arms forwards.

2. Cross L. ft. in front of R., swing arms backwards.

Alternately a second enchaînement can be used, which occupies 4 bars. This step is often used when the group is getting into and out of the maze figure.

1. Jump feet apart, swing arms forwards.
2. Bring feet together with a jump, swing arms backwards.
1. Jump on L. ft., pointing R. ft. in front, and swinging arms forwards.
2. Touch L. knee with toe of R. ft. at the same time as hopping on L. ft., swing arms backwards.
1. Jump on L ft., pointing R. toe to side, and swinging arms forwards.
2. Touch L. knee with toe of R. ft., at the same time as hopping on L. ft., swing arms backwards.
1. Step sideways on R. ft., swing arms forwards.
2. Step sideways to R. on L. ft., placing it just behind R., swing arms backwards.
    Repeat *ad lib*.

Farandole (Provence)

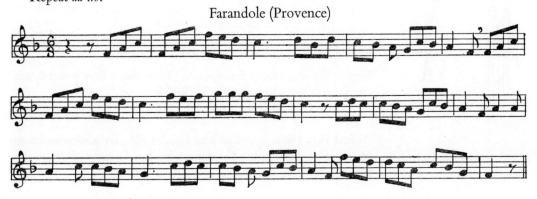

EXAMPLE 52

SOYOTTE

The couple stand together side by side holding hands crossed, i.e. man's R. hand holds woman's R. hand, his L. holds her L.

Bars 1 and 2 and 5 and 6 in each of the 4 verses are always danced the same, bars 1 and 2 starting with the R. ft. and bars 5 and 6 with the L. ft.

Bars 3 and 4 and 7 and 8 are different in each verse.

Bars 1 and 2.

1st Verse

1. Raise R. knee, and immediately hit R. ft. heavily on floor beside L. ft., and raise it again.

2. Step on to R. ft., and raise L. knee.

1. Immediately hit L. ft. heavily on floor beside R. ft., and raise it again.

2. Step on L. ft., and just raise R. ft. from floor.

   For 5 and 6, start with L. ft. During this step the arms are vigorously jerked down and up, as if chopping.

Bars 3 and 4 of 1st verse.

1. Step sideways on R. ft.

and   Close L. to it.

Repeat this side-step 3 times more. Then dance bars 5 and 6, and repeat these side-steps moving to the left.

2nd Verse

Repeat bars 1 and 2, and in bars 3 and 4 man turns woman under his R. arm, then turns himself under her L. arm. Repeat this moving to the L.

EXAMPLE 52 *(cont.)*

Bars 3 and 4,
7 and 8.

3rd Verse

1. Stamp R. ft. across L., toe pointing to left.

2. Stamp R. ft. again twisting it round so that toe points to R. and foot is at side of L.

1. Stamp L. ft. beside R., after raising it slightly from floor.

2. Repeat stamp with L. ft.

Bars 3 and 4,
7 and 8.

4th Verse

Couple now turn to face each other, R. hand holding partner's L. hand, and L. hand in R.

1. Jump on R. ft. pointing L. ft. in front.

2. Jump on L. ft. pointing R. ft. in front.

Repeat these two movements once more. During these 2 bars the arms are pushed to and fro as if sawing logs.

Song

D'avoir dansé la Soyotte, Mon ruban s'envola! Je suis darne et en ri'bott! Mo' cadet le r'trouvra.

2nd verse: *Mon bonnet s'envola!* .... etc.
3rd verse: *Mon sabot s'envola!* .... etc.
4th verse: *Mon doux cœur s'envola!* .... etc.

Soyotte

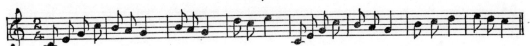

EXAMPLE 53

POLKA PIQUÉE

There are many forms of this dance. In Bresse, the man holds his R. arm round his partner's waist and her L. hand is on his R. shoulder. Other arms are held outstretched. Each polka step makes a half-turn so that the man first faces and then backs the line of dance. Man's steps are given. The woman reverses the movement and begins with R. toe pointed backwards.

The opening 8 bars can also be danced thus: one movement forwards, one movement backwards and then one with the couple moving sideways away from each other and one returning to join arms for 8 *polka-without-a-hop* steps turning.

1, 2, 3. Tap L. heel forwards on 1st beat and hold for the rest of the bar.

1, 2, 3. Tap L. toe backwards and hold position for the rest of the bar.

1. Glide L. ft. obliquely forwards and begin to turn to the right.

2. Bring R. ft. up behind L. ft.

3. Step on L. ft. raising R. knee upwards and completing half-turn very sharply.

1, 2, 3. Hold this position.

    Repeat sequence with R. ft. to complete turn. Continue to progress round counter-clockwise.

Polka Piquée

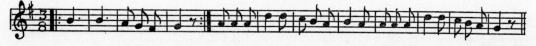

THE BRITISH ISLES

The early history of the British Isles, like that of Europe, reveals a constant shifting of population through migrations and invasions. Scattered over the countryside are the ancient megaliths and long and round barrows constructed by the many different people who lived before the Britons, and in museums may be found their leaf-shaped swords and pottery. Whether such people influenced the dance of later comers it is impossible to say. The Britons, however, who came from North Gaul and spoke a Celtic dialect, undoubtedly danced at the bidding of the Druids in a form of religious ritual in honour of the oak and the sun. Traces of their circular dances are to be found in Ireland, Scotland and Brittany, where the Celts found refuge. The complex patterning of such dances as the Morris Dances and Sellenger's Round (Ex. 56, page 170), whose alternative name At the Beginning of the World is mentioned in very early documents, suggest that they too belong to Celtic history. Moreover the similarity of the designs on Celtic monuments to the floor patterns of many Scottish and Irish dances, and even some more modern Country Dances, as well as the curious lilt in their musical accompaniment, suggest that the Celtic influence was stronger than is generally supposed.

During the Roman occupation (55 B.C.–A.D. 436), the Britons assimilated a great deal of Roman culture, as the relics of great buildings, towns, and roads bear witness. They were also converted to Christianity, but the early priests did not entirely suppress the pagan rites, for traces of the ancient Druidical beliefs, like the magic properties of mistletoe, are found throughout England. Such dances as the Helston Furry Dance, which derived from the Roman custom of dancing through the streets and houses, used to be found in Cornwall, Wales, and Cumberland, where the Romanized Celts found sanctuary from the marauding Teutonic tribes.

ENGLAND

The conquest of Britain by the Angles, Saxons, and Jutes marks the foundation of the English people and language. These new invaders brought with them dances and customs which became a part of the traditional customs. Numbers of these are similar to those found in the northern plains of Europe, from whence these people had come: for example, dancing round the bonfires on St. John's Eve, the Maypoles and Jack-in-the-green, and the Short Sword Dances. The Anglo-Saxons in their turn were invaded by Danes and Northmen, or Vikings, coming from Scandinavia. These people also brought rituals, such as the Long Sword Dances, and possibly the famous Abbot's Bromley Horned Dance, the only counterpart of which is found in the reindeer dances of certain Finno-

Ugrian tribes, with whom the Northmen came into contact during their journey through the Scandinavian Peninsula.

Finally England was conquered by the Normans (1066). This led to the introduction of some form of courtly dance as well as to a revival of certain Roman traditions, for although the Normans were of the same origin as those Northmen who had swept through England, they had settled in France and assimilated the language and culture of Romanized Gaul. It was after the Norman invasion that the well-known figure of Punch, a descendant of the old Roman mimes, appeared in the form in which he is known even to-day. This character represents in some way the Englishman's traditional dislike of official interference with his own private affairs, and is surely the outcome of the continual interference of conquering races, whose customs were often resented and then reluctantly accepted and finally turned into something essentially English.

When Pope Gregory sent Saint Augustine to convert the pagan Anglo-Saxons, the English love of dance was first noted. In letters still existing it will be found that the Pope did not insist on the absolute suppression of pagan ritual (A.D. 597). Instead the priests are ordered "to purify the buildings wherein such rites took place . . . and where the people were wont to sacrifice cattle to demons, thither let them continue to resort on the day of the saint to whom the church is dedicated, and slay their beasts no longer as a sacrifice, but for a social meal in honour of Him they now worship."

This more tolerant attitude ensured the continuance of many rites which were thus brought to the service of the church. It also gave rise to some curious anomalies, because not all the converts were certain of the value of their new religion. Occasionally a king and his serfs would worship both new and old god at the same time; thus Reduald of Anglia worshipped at the altar and then turned to sacrifice to his old demons; and often the congregation danced in the churchyards after the services. In England also there was a widespread use of certain traditional dances in the Miracle and Morality plays staged by the church and later by the guilds, and so was their survival ensured.

The continued struggle between the Roman church and the King and Barons, which was such a feature of early English history, was finally resolved when Henry VIII (1509-47) broke all ties with the Pope and declared himself head of the English church. This had an immediate effect on the dances of all classes of society. People were no longer afraid of the power of the church and everywhere dancing became much gayer and freer, so that foreign ambassadors began to write about "the dancing English." During this period (circa 1520-1640) there was a continual exchange of dance movements between peasants and court, as can be verified by reading the Masques of Ben Jonson and other writers in which folk dancers and courtiers were closely associated.

This gay liveliness was halted by the outbreak of the Civil Wars. The leaders of Cromwell's government were only too anxious to suppress all extravagances, Romish practices, and foreign customs introduced by the Stuart Kings. But it is a mistake to suppose that this was a period of unadulterated gloom. The Commonwealth leaders, including Cromwell himself, were not averse to dancing, provided it was seemly and appropriate to the occasion. Their interest in social dancing led to the publication, by the Printers of many Government orders, of Playford's *The Dancing Master* (First Edition 1650). It contained the music and directions of dances which were performed by the people now ruling the country. Some of these were derived from folk origins, as were some of the tunes, but the largest proportion were specially arranged by dancing masters, so that they would appear decorous in the new society. Such elements as the high jumping of the Morris (Ex. 55, page 168), the fertility leaps of La Volta, gay jigging, and couple dances were eschewed. All permitted dances were longways or circular sets, in which many took part and continually changed partners so that there could be no accusation of flirtatious behaviour. It is important to note that no couple dances exist among these traditional dances of England.

This toleration of a certain form of dance arose from the very varied views of dancing held during the sixteenth and seventeenth centuries. As in every other European country, many tracts were published against "lewd and lascivious dancing," and, in a pamphlet by Christopher Featherstone, the following argument is advanced: "If dancing were a recreation of the body then it should refresh the same being weary, it should make nimble the joints and strengthen the legs, make soft the feet and finally it should bring the body being out of temper into good temperature; but dancing is so far from refreshing the body from being weary that it maketh the same more weary; For I have heard tell of those which have danced one half day for pleasure and have laid in bed for three whole days of pain. . . . How many have been lamed? What incurable diseases have arisen? What agues and shaking? What heaviness, sleepiness and sluggishness ensues after such dancing? How many men's servants being set to work do after their dancing days lie snoring in hedges because they are so weary they cannot work, whereby their masters do reap but small gains."

This statement would seem to prove that the Puritans' violent prohibitions of the May-day revels and similar festivals were not only on religious grounds, but also from the fear that the work-people would be unable to complete their tasks after such revelry. These workers had an important part to play in the industrialization of England, which had started during the Tudor period, and was now proceeding at a tremendously fast pace, as was overseas trading.

Yet, in other pamphlets actually published during the Commonwealth, the arguments advanced earlier by Sir Thomas Elyot (in *The Governour* of 1531), about the value of dance as a method of education, were continually being repeated in favour of an edict to encourage the licensing of reputable dancing masters. Thus Commonwealth leaders tried to have the best of two worlds; to suppress the people's own dance, because it offended against puritanical beliefs and was uneconomic, but to encourage their own sons and daughters to dance because it gave them good carriage, pleasant manners, and a knowledge of how to behave in society.

The Restoration of the monarchy did nothing to restore English folk dance. The new court was made up of foreigners, and the speed with which England was becoming industrialized brought more and more people to the towns, where they found neither time nor space for dancing in the squalid conditions under which they existed. However the prowess of the English dancer-mimes was everywhere noted. John Weaver, the English dancing-master, produced the first complete ballet without words in 1717, and many native dances became popular items in the theatres. Only in the remote areas of the countryside were tiny elements of the real folk dance preserved among the peasants, farmers, fishermen, and miners.

It was not until Cecil Sharp, as a student of folk music, began to realize the great wealth of material lying dormant in some rural areas that a revival of English folk dance became possible. This movement has now gained fresh impetus from the researches into traditional dances kept alive by descendants of the early settlers in America. It is from such sources that a true picture of English folk dance is gradually being built up.

The Constantly Changing Modulation and the Even Quality of English Dance

The real folk dances, the Morris and Sword Dances, as well as the many Country Dances evolved by dancing-masters, possess one characteristic strikingly different from those of other nations that have contributed to English culture. Their outstanding feature is their absolutely even-tempered quality. This is due firstly to the specific quality of English folk music. The majority of English folk tunes, which have been a source of inspiration to English composers since the first days of written music, have a tendency continually to modulate between the major and minor keys throughout the melody. The tunes often run easily up and down the scale known as the Dorian mode (e.g. a scale produced by playing only the white notes on a piano, commencing on D). One of the loveliest examples containing this typically English trait is "Greensleeves." This hesitation between gaiety and sadness (for in folk music one usually finds a happy tune is in a major key, and a sad one is in the minor) seems to reflect the Englishman's traditional reluctance of displaying his deepest emotions in public.

This same reluctance to display any violent emotion appears in the English dance. To the smooth (legato) yet often poignant tune, modulating up and down the scale, the dancers move simply and evenly to the left and back again, into the middle and out, set to their own partners and then to their neighbours in the circle, square, or longways set. They perform Heys and other figures, ultimately returning to their own places, each taking a turn until all have performed. This co-operation and equality among the participants is the outstanding feature of all English traditional dances, as it is in the famous English Madrigal singing, and the influence of both on Continental music and dance is far too often ignored.

The smooth, even-tempered quality of movement which characterizes the performance of the best English folk and ballroom dancers is first achieved by the way in which their bodies are held. They are delicately balanced so that the dancers instinctively incline towards the direction of the whole movement. Thus if the step is directed forwards, the whole body inclines that way, if backwards the weight is adjusted to take the dancer easily back to his starting-point. Nowhere is there any stiffness or tension, for arms swing softly and heads are held easily erect. Moreover, the movements are all softly controlled so that the dancers apparently glide over the ground. They do not sink into it as they would into the rich earth of Teuton or Slav, nor do they rise abruptly off it like the Czech, Polish, or Georgian mountain people.

The even quality is also marked in the complicated Morris and Sword Dances, which are still outstanding examples of the Englishman's love of fine craftsmanship. Unlike the Morris and Sword Dances of other countries, where the leap is either performed at the end of an enchaînement or, in more primitive areas, whenever the dancer feels inspired, in England the regularly balanced jigging movement is punctuated by high leaps that are evenly distributed throughout the dance. In addition, the arms are kept moving evenly throughout, to fit the foot movements. As the dancer jigs, so the handker-chieves flutter gracefully up and down, slings are twirled, or coconuts regularly beaten. With the leap both arms are raised above the head to increase its height, and if the dancer moves sideways, the hand on the same side as the raised foot goes up at the leap. It is in the English Morris, too, that one gets the fascinating "balancing" before a caper. Here the men pose lightly on one toe, the other leg raised in front, and balance their arms delicately sideways before they perform the leap.

In the Sword Dances, whether they use running steps, like the North Skelton men, or complicated beaten movements with feet in clogs like the Grenoside team, the dancers maintain the evenly balanced quality throughout, as arms and bodies are swiftly dropped, twisted, and turned in order to keep the group moving smoothly and easily while it makes its complex patterns with the linked swords. The only pause in such dances is that in the Morris, where the men pause for a caper in a slow movement, and in the Swords, when the leader raises the interlocked swords on high. Incidentally, in some ot these dances, each man takes it in turn to raise the Lock, and this again adds to the even quality of the dance.

Intricacy of Patterns

English folk dance is most interesting choreographically for its floor patterns. These are often extremely complicated, and in absolute contrast to the simple steps of the dancers. They take many different shapes, particularly in the Country Dances such as the Morpeth Rant, a longways set; and Newcastle, a circular set.

But the intricacy of pattern is at its most interesting in the Linked Sword Dances, when every possible way of changing the interweaving figures is exploited, until the swords are linked together in the Lock, and this is held triumphantly aloft. The fascination of these dances is to watch the pattern gradually taking shape, each man moving individually but only in so far as his particular movement affects the group as a whole and helps the group to achieve its purpose, the making of the Lock.

Dances in Three Sections

Another important feature of English dances is that one sometimes finds a dance with three distinct musical sections, instead of the normal two of most western European countries, and although these are not directly contrasted in emotional content they have distinct melodies, and sometimes different rhythms. This gives an unusual aspect to an otherwise evenly balanced form. Gathering Peascods, Rufty-Tufty, Hit and Miss, and Staines Morris from the first edition of Playford's *Dancing Master*, are tunes of this type. It must also be mentioned that there exist some very old folk songs in 5/4 rhythm. Some of these were undoubtedly dance-songs, in which the dancers' movements coincided with the actual rhythm of the words, as they still do in a few of the children's singing games. But these were possibly the first to be suppressed by puritanical zealots because of their significance, and no such dances exist to-day.

Steps

In the folk dances, steps consist of little more than smooth running or walking steps to the regular beats of the bar—that is, two steps are taken in a 2/2 or 6/8 rhythm and three steps in a 3/2 or 9/8 rhythm; or in a skipping or slipping step, the hop or closing of the feet together is performed on the last quarter or last third of a beat.

In the Morris Dances, steps are based on two very simple movements; the first in which the dancer changes feet with a jump, slide, or mere closing, and the second in which he keeps jigging, or leaps off both feet or off the foot on which he has been hopping (Ex. 55, page 168). A tremendous variety of movement can be evolved from this simple beginning, for there are many ways of twisting and swinging the working leg. Moreover, it is important to note that in many movements the dancer appears to hold himself in the air for a single note—this can also be seen in France (Ex. 44, page 150).

In the Sword and Morris Dances when clogs are worn, the rhythms beaten by the feet become extremely complicated, since each beat can be divided into halves, quarters, or triplets by the slick action of the foot moving flexibly from the ankle.

The most complicated steps of English dance appear in the traditional clog dancing among the miners of Lancashire, Yorkshire, Durham, and Northumberland. It was from these that the English tap dancing developed, which has become almost world-famous. In such dances is found the neat footwork, easy movement, and evenly balanced bodies and rhythm that are always notable in English dance.

The English Folk, Country, Morris, and Sword Dances have been fully covered in numerous books by Cecil J. Sharp and published by Novello and Co. Sellenger's Round (Ex. 56, page 170) included here represents a typical circular set. The Morris Jig, Shepherd's Hey, from the Headington group is a solo and gives some idea of the ordinary steps used in a Morris. The hand-clapping is, however, unusual for England (Ex. 55, page 168).

EXAMPLE 54

SWEET KATE

(From *An Introduction to the English Country Dance* by Cecil Sharp)

A Longways Dance for as many as will.

A. Bars 1 to 4. Couples lead up a *double* and fall back a *double* to places. (A *double* is 3 running steps beginning with R. ft., and finished by closing the feet together on 4th step.)

Bars 5 to 8. Repeat this movement.

B. Bar 1. Partners face each other. (1) Spring lightly on L. ft. (4). Hop on L. ft., simultaneously raising R. ft. and swinging it from right to left to hit partner's R. ft.

Bar 2. Repeat, springing on to R. ft.

Bar 3. (1) Each dancer claps own hands. (4) Partner's clap each other's R. hands together.

Bar 4. Repeat bar 3, clapping L. hands together.

Bar 5. (1, 2, 3) Each dancer runs their hands round and round as if winding wool. (4) Shake index finger of R. hand at partner.

Bar 6. Repeat bar 5 shaking L. index fingers.

Bars 7 and 8. Each dancer turns a single on their own (i.e. dance a *double* turning round to right).
Repeat whole of *B.*

Second part. *A.* Partners side with each other, i.e. forward a *double* passing each other by L. shoulder, turn and come back along the same track.

B. Repeat as above.

Third part. *A.* Partners arm with the R., with a running step, and then arm with the L.

B. Repeat as above.

(From Playford's *Dancing Master*, 1670, arranged by Cecil Sharp, by kind permission of Novello and Co.)

EXAMPLE 55

MORRIS JIG

(Headington Tradition)

(From *The Morris Book*, Part II, by Cecil Sharp and Herbert C. Macilwaine)

A man's solo danced with or without handkerchieves, using clapping, which is somewhat unusual. The performer dances facing his audience and makes no movement backwards or forwards. The dance is quiet and restrained.

The first 4 bars (known as "Once to yourself") are played and the dancer waits, feet together, jumping off both feet on the last half-bar. He raises both hands on the jump.

A. Shake-up

1st and 2nd bar. Beginning R. ft., 3 steps on alternate feet and hop on R. ft. Repeat, starting L. ft. The change of foot is made with a slight spring so that it takes place in the air and not on the ground. The dancer alights on the ball of the foot with the supporting leg held straight under the body and at the same time the free leg is swung forward from the hip, the lower leg hanging loosely from the knee. The arms are swung downwards on beat 1 and upwards on beat 2 of each bar.

3rd bar. Cross-back step—

    1. Swing R. ft. behind L. so that big toe touches heel of L. ft.

    2. Twist on both toes and open feet slightly apart. Circle arms inwards during these 2 beats.

    3, 4. Repeat, swinging L. ft. behind and circling arms.

4th bar. 1, 2. Swing R. ft. behind as before and hold position.

    3. Jump feet together. Swing arms upwards.

    4. Step on to L. ft.

Repeat these 4 bars.

EXAMPLE 55 (*cont.*)

B. Hand-clapping

1st bar. 1, 2. Clap hands together twice.

3, 4. Bend down and touch R. calf with fingers of R. hand, open arm, palm of hand facing front.

2nd bar. Repeat 1st bar touching L. calf with L. hand.

3rd bar. 1, 2. Clap hands together twice.

3. Lift R. ft. and clap hands under R. knee.

4. Stamp R. ft.

4th bar. 1. Lift L. ft. and clap hands under L. knee.

2. Clap hands behind back.

3, 4. Clap both hands together and pause.

Bars 5–8. Repeat above 4 bars.

Now continue repeating *A* and *B*, but in the first repetition of *B* instead of touching calf, touch R. breast with R. hand and open arm immediately as if blowing a kiss, then touch L. breast. *B*, second repetition, touch side of cheeks with R. and L. hands. *B*, third repetition, touch side of head with R. and L. hands. Finally repeat *A*, but perform 4 capers, i.e. 4 high springs starting with R. ft. and circling hands in air with each spring during last 2 bars.

For "Once to yourself," play first 4 bars, commence again, repeating 16 bars, 4 times in all. Then repeat first 8 bars for finale.

Shepherd's Hey

(Arranged by Cecil Sharp, by kind permission of Novello and Co.)

EXAMPLE 56

SELLENGER'S ROUND or AT THE BEGINNING OF THE WORLD

Round for as many as will. Men hold partners' R. hands

1st Part

A. Bars 1 to 8.　　All join hands in a circle and perform 8 *chassés* to the left and 8 *chassés* to the right, returning to places.

B. Bars 1 and 2.　　Starting with R. ft., all take 2 *singles* to the centre. (*Single* is, spring lightly on to R. ft., take weight momentarily on L. toe which is placed at side of R. ft., then immediately fall back on to R. ft.)

Bars 3 and 4.　　All fall back a *double* to places.

Bars 5 to 8.　　Partners set and turn single.

Repeat above 8 bars.

2nd Part

A. Bars 1 to 4.　　All join hands and, starting with R. ft., dance a *double* into the centre, and starting with R. ft. dance a *double* back to places.

Bars 5 to 8.　　Repeat bars 1 to 4.

B. Repeat as in first part.

3rd Part

A. Bars 1 to 4.　　Partners side with each other. (See *Sweet Kate*.)

Bars 5 to 8.　　Repeat bars 1 to 4.

B. Repeat as in first part.

4th Part

A. Bars 1 to 4.　　Partners arm with the R.

Bars 5 to 8.　　Partners arm with the L.

B. Repeat as in first part.

(This tune is not in Playford, but is the version used by Byrd, and arranged by Cecil Sharp in *The Country Dance Book*, No. 4. By kind permission of Novello and Co.)

WALES

The Welsh are a nation of singers, whose tunes are echoed by Breton, Scot and Irishman. Yet few Welsh tunes have a dancing rhythm, for they are predominantly solemn and sad, and to-day there are in Wales few traces of the dances that were once shared with other Celtic peoples. This solemnity and lack of dance tradition is explained by the religious influences that have always dominated the lives of the Welsh.

Christianity did not die out with the Roman withdrawal from Britain and the onslaught of Angles, Saxons, and Jutes. These pagan peoples were so busy fighting each other for supremacy over England, that they scarcely penetrated the land of the "mountains and dales." Behind the valuable protection of Offa's Dyke the Christian priests continued to serve their flocks, spreading their missionary work to Ireland, whence later missionaries returned to re-convert the inhabitants of England, who were now pagan again. In manuscripts of this period (eleventh and twelfth centuries) written by monks, descriptions are given of religious processional dances, similar to those found among other Celtic races.

The Welsh finally submitted to the English King in 1282, after many battles had been fought in which the Welsh were always encouraged by their Bards singing songs of heroes and victories, similar to those produced at present-day Eisteddfods. By this time the English had become more tolerant in their attitude to the conquered, and apart from the introduction of new laws, the Welsh were allowed to speak their own language, retain their own customs and live, as before, under the surveillance of their priests; to these were added the English clerics, in attendance at great castles built to keep out fresh invaders.

Because of this connection between the Welsh and English clergy, Wales was always embroiled in the religious troubles of England. From time to time she was swept by Revivalist movements. The most important of these occurred in the eighteenth century when certain Welshmen promoted an educational and religious mission among the illiterate peasants, their aim being to teach them to read the Bible and thereby save their souls. These leaders had a particularly strong influence where dance is concerned, for they gave the Welsh such a puritanical outlook that many old people, whose memory of the dances might have helped research workers, firmly believed that, should they show any dance steps to the outside world, they would be condemned to eternal damnation. This attitude to the dance has so far prevented any attempts at a revival of Welsh folk dance from being successful.

However some traces remain. Lady Llanover tried to preserve something of the old dances. The famous Llanover Reel, which has fifteen figures of an intricate character, has the same step as another Llanover dance, Rhif Wyth. This is a form of polka followed by a jigging in which the feet are thrust out alternately forwards three times at the end of a phrase. The dancers also stamp at the end of every four or eight bars. Both dances have similar forms to those of Scottish and English Country Dances. There is also a vigorous movement to revive what is believed to have been Welsh clog dancing, which resembles Irish step dancing and is quite expressionless.

The Welsh are, however, largely a mountain people and this suggests that their movement would have the gaiety and vitality of the Scots and Irish if they would only let themselves go.

The following story, told by Mrs. Hyllarie Johnston, a great student of Welsh dance, may give some clue to the problems of Welsh dance. After explaining that every booklet on Welsh dance mentions the Wood family of Bala, she continues—

"Now Jim Wood is a gipsy and a very good friend of mine, with whom I often go fishing. Some years ago I had seen him and his brother Llewellyn dance, and had held my own theories about the dances. Perhaps the following conversation which I held with him at the local inn may be of interest.

'Where did you learn your dances, Jim?'

'Well they've been handed down like from my family—in the family for generations, like.'

'Jim, your dances are of Irish origin, aren't they?'

'Yes, ma'am. They is more Irish than anything else.'

'Then, you old bandit, why have you let these writers, etc., quote you as an exponent of old Welsh dance?'

'Well, ma'am (with a very sheepish grin) none of them has had the education to see as they wasn't Welsh, and I never told them as they was—people just takes it for granted that because I lives in Bala, the dances must be Welsh, and why should I tell them as they are not?' "

IRELAND

Irish dance is a perfect reflection of the dual nature of the Irish people, a nation curiously divided in itself—there are two distinct styles. First, there is the gay spontaneous dancing at the village Ceilidhes, which can develop into a most glorious, free-for-all romp, in which all can join, a caller often shouting the figures. Such dances are as invigorating an experience as the brilliant conversation of a loquacious Irishman, and are a true expression of the people's will to live and enjoy themselves in their own way. Secondly, there is the highly professional solo dancing of the competitive Feis held in the towns. This is purely a matter of technical accomplishment in which the legs alone play a part. The upper half of the body is held erect but passive, and the arms hang stiffly to the sides, so that the dancer's whole attitude seems utterly expressionless. He or she never responds to the haunting and emotional tunes that accompany the restless tapping feet. It is as if they were willing themselves to behave in a proper manner according to some rigidly framed command, instead of letting themselves go and allowing the music to guide them into an exciting world of warm, expansive movement.

This striking difference in dance styles can only be explained by studying Ireland's complex historical background, which is full of contradictions. This complicated story cannot be told here. The reader is referred to Sean O'Faolain's brilliant book, *The Irish*, in which he describes the many elements that go to the making of his countrymen's character and mind. Nevertheless, one or two points which are specifically related to the dance must be noted.

When the early Celtic settlers were converted to Christianity in the fourth century A.D., the new priests, in adapting the fantastically imaginative Irish legends into something more in keeping with the new faith, managed to preserve something of their magical properties, by transforming the old gods into saints (Saint Patrick, for example), and used the pagan style of ornamentation in the illumination of their manuscripts. They allowed the peasants to retain those same qualities in their tunes and dances, only banning the more pagan elements of ritual.

These priests were of two types, the one an æsthete who withdrew from the world to contemplate things of the spirit and mortify the flesh, and the other of a more worldly nature who tried to minister to the widely scattered tribes in a country where communications always offered great problems. This gave rise to two distinct forms of Catholicism, which came into conflict with one another. Later they both came into conflict with Protestant reformers when the Tudors extended English Sovereignty over Ireland in the sixteenth century. These religious troubles explain the almost complete lack of ancient ritual which one would expect to find in such a backward country, and also the two types of dance—the professional one concentrating on the feet alone, and the other a warm pulsating stream of life.

The Danish invasion of the ninth century affected only the coastal areas, but the later invasion by Normans had considerable influence on the peasants in the more accessible valleys where roads, towns, and abbeys were built. It taught them better husbandry and craftsmanship of many kinds and helped to give a more stable form to their way of life. It also added a courtly element to the work of Irish poets, who began to adapt the elaborate conventions of Provençal poetry to their own formal traditions, and added an air of sophistication to certain dances which began to be practised in the newly built castles. Some of these dances took the fancy of the sixteenth-century English invaders, and one hears of their being performed at the court of Queen Elizabeth. Trenchmore is an adaptation of the old Irish peasant dance, Rinnce Fada (Long Dance), of which Rinnce Mor (Great Dance) (Ex. 58, page 177) is a modern version. Others can be found in Playford's *Dancing Master*. When such dances were performed at court, the services of dancing masters were required to prune away their crudities, and it is the efforts of these gentlemen that has deprived the professional Irish dancers of their expression.

When the Revolutionary movement to throw off English rule got under way in the early nineteenth century, the attention of all types of Irish artists was drawn to their own national traditions. This gave rise to the founding of such dancing schools as the famous ones of Limerick, Kerry, and Cork. In such an artificial environment, as happened elsewhere, the polishing of steps was vital, and with that came the elaboration of the outstanding feature of all Irish dance: its footwork. Unfortunately, these dancing masters were not interested in the people's dances of the remote countryside, and paid no attention to the occupational gestures, which still remain in a few of them. When the pupils of such dancing masters returned to their homes they began to impose their polished style on that of the peasants, with the result that village dancing lost some of its spontaneity. Moreover, the only thing by way of arm movement that was practised, and this is rarely seen to-day, was a threatening movement with a clenched fist, seen in the Jig danced to what is known as a "Tune of Occupation."

These tunes are interesting because it is difficult to distinguish them from other tunes played in Ireland or Scotland. The constant interchange of population between the Irish and Scots has led to a constant interchange of tune. In addition, certain English characteristics have been acquired by both nations from English regiments during times of war, and by the constant give and take between the sailors of all three countries.

Yet, despite the similarity of tune and pattern between Scottish and Irish dances, Ireland's climate and physical features give their village dances a more downward type of movement, a more fluid style, and sometimes an untidy look. Moreover the Irishman's love of elaborate eloquence and brilliant flights of fancy when conversing seem equally to affect his feet.

The Elaboration of Step

Although most Irish communal dances are based on some five simple steps, it is usually only at the beginning of an evening that one sees them in their original form. As the group gets warmed up and the whisky and Guinness flow, so the dancers add more and more extra taps, stamps, and shuffles. A very good example can be worked out by taking as basis a simple jump on the left foot, simultaneously pointing the right foot in front on the floor. The second stage arrives when the dancer hops on the left foot before pointing the right foot. The third stage finds the dancer hopping on the left foot and then tapping the right foot on the floor twice with the ball of the foot. The fourth stage may involve the dancer hopping on the left foot, tapping twice with the ball of the right foot, stepping again on to the left foot and then swinging the right foot just behind the left and resting the right toe on the floor. This elaboration can be carried out to an amazing length.

A great deal of this elaboration arises from the fact that the Irish now use the same basic steps for dances in either Reel or Jig time, i.e., a 2/4 or 4/4, and a 6/8 or occasionally 9/8 rhythm, and in order to fit the steps more easily some elaboration is needed, otherwise the rhythmic quality of the music is lost or the dancer loses speed, a thing unheard of in Ireland once the fun has started. It is impossible to transcribe the steps of the village dancer fitting himself to the music, for he suits himself. In a similar way it is impossible to transcribe the intricate stepping of the professional at the Feis. The following steps are the base on which all work. It is usual to count the Jig in a 6/8 rhythm as if it were 2/4.

1. The *Promenade* in Jig or Reel, starts on the last sixth or half-beat of a bar—

and Hop forwards on L. ft., raising R. ft., pointed forwards.
1. Step forwards on R. ft.
and Bring L. toe to heel of R. ft.
2. Step forwards on R. ft., raising L. slightly behind R. Repeat commencing with R. ft.

2. The *Seven*, in Jig or Reel, requires two bars of music and is a queer kind of *pivot step* (Ex. 59, page 178).

3. *Two Threes*, in Jig or Reel, requires two bars of music and is a *pas-de-bourrée* type of step (Ex. 57, page 176).

4. *Rising Step*, or *Rise and Grind*, is found only in Jigs. It requires two bars of music and is a good example of the elaboration of a simple step. It is counted as 3 beats to a bar—

The Rise

1. Hop on L. ft., slightly raising R. leg with knee bent and toe pointed downwards.
2. Hop on L. ft. and bring R. to heel of L., without touching ground.
3. Step on R. ft. behind L.

The Grind

1. Hop lightly on R. ft., bring L. behind R. heel.
and Place L. toe behind R. heel, keeping weight of body on R. ft.
2. Beat R. ft. on floor.
and Beat L. ft. on floor.
3. Beat R. ft. on floor and pause.

These beats are done very quickly and the body is kept over the right foot.

5. *Side Step* is found in Reels only, and takes four bars. It combines the *Seven* followed by the *Two Threes*. It is then usually repeated in the opposite direction (Exs. 57, 58).

Other steps are known as *single* and *double shuffles, single* and *double drumming, single* and *double battering, up* and *down tipping, Kerry tipping, ankling,* but these are in the nature of step dancing and are found only in the solo Reels, Jigs and Hornpipes.

Both Reel and Jig are favourite dances and have similar figures to those of Country Dances. The Reel is generally of a smoother character with one accent in the bar. It can be danced by four, six, eight, twelve, or sixteen people. The solo Reel is often in two portions, one simple and the other more complicated. The Jig has an altogether livelier and jerkier movement and can be danced by three, four, or eight people. The solo Jig also has two parts and often has to be specially arranged owing to the irregular form of the music, a phrase of eight bars being followed by one of six. There is also a Hop or Slip Jig in a 9/8 rhythm for two people, which can be particularly lively. It was the Jig that came under so many bans during the sixteenth and seventeenth centuries, because it was believed that the minstrels who sang its accompaniment incited the people to revolt. Its stirring rhythms certainly seem well suited for this purpose, and there was a time when vigorous arm movements and flourishing shillelaghs played a large part in the dance. These have now been all but expurgated, in the same way that all significant arm movements have been eliminated from the Irish Hornpipes. The only thing remaining of its seafaring origin is the rocking movements common to sailors' dances all over the world. An odd result of all this suppression would seem to be the Irish dancers' tendency to keep the weight backwards, and to move backwards more than forwards.

The elimination of significant movement, the ignoring of the rhythmic qualities of the music and the generalizing of the characteristic steps will lead to the complete disappearance of the real Irish dance. For villagers coming into contact with the highly technical footwork of the town-trained dancer become embarrassed when dancing in their own way in public, preferring to take the line of least resistance, and either sit out or wander round to modern ballroom tunes. Moreover there are no Irish regiments to keep the dance alive as national regiments did in Scotland, Poland, and Hungary in times of struggle and serfdom.

EXAMPLE 57

TWO-THREES

In Jig or Reel time, requires 2 bars

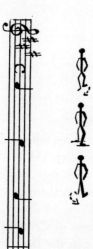

1. With a slight swing of the R. leg bring R. toe behind heel of L. ft.

and Step obliquely forwards on L. ft.

2. Bring R. toe to heel of L. ft. Pause.
Repeat, beginning by swinging L. leg round to bring L. toe behind R. ft.

From "Rakes of Mallow"

EXAMPLE 58

RINNCE MOR

(The Big or Great Dance)

Danced to any good reel tune. There are 2 sections of 8 bars, which are repeated.
Round dance for as many couples as will. Men hold partner's R. hands.

A. Bars 1–4.   All join hands in a circle facing the centre and perform a *side-step* to the left.

Bars 5–8.   Repeat *side-step* moving to the right.

Bars 1–4.   Each man swings woman on his left clockwise.

Bars 5–8.   Both turn and swing round counter-clockwise.

B. Bars 9–12.   Man now swings own partner clockwise.

Bars 13–16.   Partners turn and swing counter-clockwise.

Bars 9 and 10.   Each man links R. arm with woman on his left and turns.

Bars 11 and 12. Partners now link L. arms and turn.

Bars 13 and 14. Each man links R. arm with woman on his left and turns.

Bars 15 and 16. Man goes to his own partner, crosses hands and turns to place partner on his right.

Next 8 or 16 bars. All face counter-clockwise and lead round.

Repeat dance from new position, as often as wished.

(N.B. Swing using *pivot step* and cross hands hold. Lead round with *Promenade*.)

Rakes of Mallow

EXAMPLE 59

THE SEVEN

In Jig or Reel time, requires 2 bars of music

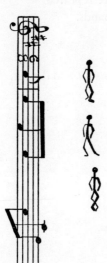

In Jig Time

1. Jump lightly, landing on toes of both feet, R. in front of L. and almost touching.

and Step sideways on toe of R. ft.

2. Step heavily on L. ft., just behind R.

and 1 *and* 2. Repeat last two movements twice more pausing on last half-beat with weight well down.

From "Haste to the Wedding"

SCOTLAND

Although Scotland's history follows as complicated a pattern as that of Ireland, many of her ancient dance forms can still be traced in the extremely lively dances performed throughout the country to-day. This can be explained by the intense pride every Scot has in his race and traditions, and by the fact that nearly every Scot seems to be a potential dancer, despite his reputed dour character and careful nature.

This prowess in dancing is first recorded by the historian Tacitus, who mentions the surprise felt by the Roman legionaries who invaded Scotland in 54 B.C., when they saw the Caledonians indulging in a wild dance round their swords, stuck upright in the ground. This early linking of the dance with the soldiery is one reason why Scotland has managed to preserve so many of her dances. Their continued practice by the Highland

Regiments helped to keep the dances alive when the struggles between Calvinists and Catholics, Royalists and Jacobites, and England and Scotland were at their height. Another reason was the peculiar construction of the clan system, which still plays some part in Scotland's social history. The members of the various clans into which Scotland was early divided were descendants of an actual or mythological ancestor. The chief of these groups, from whom both clan and the territory in which they lived got their names, was in theory the owner of that land and director of the clan's activities. He was not, however, an absolute autocrat. It was an accepted rule that each laird had so to administer his territory that every member of his clan would be suitably provided with food and clothing—no easy task in a land where the natural physical features continually put obstacles in the way of proper agricultural and industrial development. Nevertheless, from this important rule there developed a system by which the members of the clan were deputed to the various tasks, and in time the fulfilment of that particular job became the function of one family.

This was particularly the case with those families who stood closest to the chief and performed such duties as Piper, Sword-bearer, Bodyguard, and Soldiers, and without whom he would have been incapable of withstanding the onslaught of neighbouring chiefs. In addition, the chief always lived in close contact with his clan and was thus kept constantly aware of its needs. Like a father he had to listen to their complaints, their outspoken comments and openly given advice, for a Scotsman, no matter how poor, has never been afraid to speak up for himself, and considers himself as good as anyone else. It is this strongly individualistic trait that has led the Scot to invent so many solo dances.

The close relationship between the chiefs and their followers was not lost when the chiefs began to pay homage to the Kings of Scotland. The fashions and manners they acquired at court gradually influenced the traditional ceremonies and rituals, which had been sedulously maintained, losing only their more pagan elements with the country's conversion to Christianity.

One of the first important elements influencing the dance was undoubtedly the French fashions introduced by Mary Queen of Scots on her return after the death of Francis I. Among her retinue came musicians and dancing masters, who began to organize court entertainments in the manner of those of Catherine de Medici. The chiefs and their bodyguards, all of whom were stalwart young men proficient in sword-play and various Highland pursuits, took part and no doubt tamed and polished their wilder dances to make them more fit for polite society.

The influence of foreign dancing masters continued to be felt for some time for, with the accession of James VI to the throne of England, the King's Scottish bodyguard, composed of chieftains' sons, came into contact with further court fashions and dances, which were now developing an extremely polished technique. Despite the constant religious and political friction between the various Scottish factions and the two countries, and the many Calvinistic edicts banning the dances and old rituals, these continued to be practised, and acquired further polish with the return of the various clansmen from service at court, or from the wars abroad.

The real perfecting of Scottish dance came after the Repeal of the Act of Proscription in 1782. The attempt of Prince Charles Stewart, in alliance with the French, to recapture his kingdom, had been immediately followed by this savage act of 1746, which tried to put an end to the clan system and all Scottish national feelings. Among the things forbidden were the playing of the bagpipes and the wearing of Highland costume, on pain of transportation to the colonies. Strangely enough, as happened in other countries when similar bans were enforced, this had a reverse effect to that which had been desired. It merely drove the Highlanders to wear their dress and to practise their dances and customs with greater intensity, in an "underground" fashion. The first Highland regiment, the Black Watch, had been raised in 1739; it was entirely composed of Scottish clansmen under their own officers, mostly sons of prominent chiefs loyal to the House of Hanover, and their uniform was their own Highland costume. By 1782, when the Act of Proscription was repealed, more than twenty Highland battalions had been raised, all wearing their traditional costume and all keeping up their traditional ceremonies and dances as they travelled abroad to fight the King's battles.

With the repeal of the Act, soldiers from these regiments began to play a prominent part in competitions founded by the various clan chiefs and societies to stimulate interest in Scottish traditions. Hereditary pipers from all the leading clans played against each other, and dancers from the regiments polished, perfected, and enlarged the steps of the solo and male group dances under the eye of a regimental dancing master. Other dancing masters turned their attention to the simple Reels and Strathspeys and encouraged the various chiefs to give grand balls at which clan tartans were worn by all present. They also created special dances based on the ancient Celtic forms in honour of some member of the house. Both Highlanders and Lowlanders joined vigorously in this movement, which travelled further than its native country. The Act of Proscription had broken up the clan system and many Scots emigrated and helped found the British colonies, taking their customs and dances with them. In addition, particularly during the Peninsular and Crimean wars, Scottish Regiments introduced their lively dances to other countries, where they still are practised. Among these is Strip the Willow (Ex. 65, page 190), known as La Boulangère in France and as La Virra Extrapassado in Portugal.

The unbroken history of Scottish dance and its continued performance thus keeps alive Scotland's link with her Celtic ancestry. The similarity of the Sword Dance of Papa Stour in the Hebrides and that of the Baccubert dancers in the Dauphiné has been noted by D. G. MacLennan. The Dirk Dance, now almost forgotten, links the Scots with their Viking ancestors. Scottish Country Dance in form and pattern follows that of the other Celtic and Teutonic countries. But in methods of performance the Scot is very different. In the first place he possesses the characteristics of all mountain people. His extreme lightness, neat footwork, and delicately balanced body are dictated by the country's physical features, and these qualities have been acquired by the Lowlanders, as the Highlanders were driven south by England's deliberate breaking-up of the clans. His movements also are more upwards than along, and this is one important difference between the steps in Scottish and Irish dancing. But there are also other elements to be taken into account.

The Snap

The light, upwards quality of Scottish dance is more particularly notable because of a subtle alliance between certain movements and the peculiar musical feature known as the Snap. This is also found among the Hungarian and Finno-Ugrian groups, and may therefore have been of Finnish origin and brought by the Vikings. This feature consists of a semiquaver immediately followed by a dotted quaver. It usually opens and appears throughout the oldest dance tunes or Strathspeys. The short note is not an anacrusis appearing in the last period of a bar. It is the first note and therefore marks the first beat, although played or sung very lightly. It serves, one might say, to give impetus to the dotted quaver, which always sounds loudly and is stressed but does not mark the actual beat. The best dancers at village festivities, Caledonian balls, and in Army groups instinctively react to this peculiarity. Instead of anticipating a step before the first beat, so that their foot hits the ground as it is sounded, they lift themselves into the air on the first semiquaver or beat with a hop or jump off one or both feet, and arrive on the ground on the dotted quaver or more prominent note which occurs just after the first beat. This means that the dancer's first movement and accent is upwards and not downwards as is usual in European countries. As this subtle alliance of movement and music appears throughout the Strathspeys, Reels, and other dances, it lightens and changes considerably the look of such steps as the basic polka-like *strathspey step*, the *pas-de-basque* and others. It quickens the lilting process of the dance, because the dancer has no time to press his heels firmly into the ground to make the more usual preparation for a jump. The heels, if they ever do touch the ground, only act as an extra springboard to the strength of ankle, knee, and calf muscles to propel the weight of the body into the air. But this rarely happens, as the weight of the body is carried so delicately forwards on the toes that the knees and thighs are kept in a high state of elasticity.

So strong is the urge for a rising movement in the dance that whenever the Snap occurs in the music, even with such simple running steps as those of the Hebridean Weaving Lilt, one sees the dancers raising themselves lightly on the semiquaver or first beat in anticipation, before marking the dotted quaver with a stamp. This reminds one of a spinning-wheel being given a slight swing backwards in order to set it properly in motion.

Bagpipes, which have accompanied the dancers for many generations, have a scale of nine notes. This gives rise to more unusual intervals and thus to the lilting rises and falls in the tunes for dancing. It also helps to account for the Snap, since it is necessary to have a short intake of breath before blowing out the note, and as this intake is not necessarily soundless it has become the semiquaver. But it must be noted that the Snap is also found in mouth music, especially in Hungary, and so great is the urge to make this preparatory sound that the singers often add it to their song as the dancers deliberately add the preparatory jump to their steps.

Elaboration of Step

Like all people with Celtic or Viking ancestors, the Highlanders love ornamentation in their dress. They also love elaboration of step, but it is important to note that, unlike the Irish, who elaborate their steps by beating the floor, the Scot usually beats his feet in the air soundlessly. This again lends an upwards quality to the dance, for if one has to make extra movements in the air one has to stay in the air that fraction of a second longer. It is most noticeable in the *single* and *double shuffles*, *single* and *double high-cuts*, and *shakes*. These are not only difficult to perform without much practice but also to describe. The following is a rough outline.

The Shuffle—spring lightly on to R. ft., throwing L. slightly forwards with toe pointed, brush it on to R. instep and immediately out again. The three movements occupy one beat. Repeat beginning with L. ft.

The High-cut—spring on to R. ft., opening L. leg slightly to side and immediately beat it behind R. calf with knee well opened sideways. This occupies one beat. Repeat beginning on L. ft.

The Shake (as in Seann Triubhas)—spring off both feet, raising R. leg to side and shaking it from knee downwards with toe well pointed. This occupies one beat. It is also performed with the shaking leg pointed obliquely forwards, as in the Fling.

Steps

The most important steps are those of the Strathspey and Reel, for they are the basis of the other dances. Both dances are in 4/4 rhythm, the Strathspey being slower, therefore having smoother and more elegant steps. The names of these steps are at present a source of controversy among the various Scottish organizations. Where any are given here, they are those used by D. G. MacLennan. The dancer always faces front.

Strathspey step or *Figure of* 8, used in figure dancing—

1. Glide forwards on R. ft.
2. Close L. ft. behind R. heel.
3. Glide forwards on R. ft.
4. Hop lightly off R. ft., bringing L. ft. with toe pointed to R. shin.

In Reel time this step usually becomes the *chassé*.

1. Glide forwards on R. ft.

and Close L. ft. behind R.

2. Glide forwards again on R. ft. and pause before repeating with L.

The *Highland Schottische step* requires two bars of music (Ex. 60, page 185). This has a lovely variation in the Seann Triubhas. It should also be compared with the side step of Irish dance (Ex. 59 and 57, pages 178 and 176), and the difference between its upwards and the latter's downwards movement noted.

Another interesting step of the Strathspey also requires two bars (Ex. 61, page 186).

Some Reel steps—

1. *Simple Setting step* or *pas-de-basque* (Ex. 63, page 188).

2. *Swinging step*, requiring two bars—

> 1. Beginning with R. ft. well stretched in front, step on to it in place of L. ft., which is immediately cut (thrust) backwards.
>
> 2. Repeat the cut, stepping on to L. ft. and cutting R. ft. forwards.
>
> 3. Repeat the cut, stepping on to R. ft. and cutting L. ft. backwards.
>
> 4. Hop on R. ft. and stretch L. ft. forwards, beating R. shin as L. ft. passes through.
>
> 1. Cut by stepping on to L. ft. and cutting R. ft. backwards.
>
> 2. Hop on L. ft. and stretch R. ft. forwards, beating L. shin as it passes through.
>
> 3 *and* 4. Repeat these two movements, beginning by cutting L. ft backwards.

In some Country Dances and Reels this step is reduced and mixed with the *pas-de-basque*.

3. A step requiring one bar—

> 1 *and* 2. *Pas-de-basque* to right, beginning on R. ft.
>
> 3 *and* 4. Perform two changes of feet, finishing first change with R. ft. in front and the second with L. ft. in front.

Repeat whole movement to the left.

In the Country Dances, the principal steps are the *pas-de-basque* and a *progressive step*. When this latter is danced to a Strathspey, it is called the *common Schottische step*.

> 1. Step forwards or sideways on R. ft.
>
> 2. Bring L. ft. to R.

3. Step forwards or sideways on R. ft.

4. Hop on R. ft. raising L. ft. well pointed in front.

When danced to Reel time, it is called *Skip-change-of-step* and the hop occurs on the last half-beat of a bar.

Arms

The arm movements in Highland dances are very graceful. Sometimes both arms are raised sideways from the shoulder level, but are not closed above the head. At others, one arm is held aloft, and the other on the hip. Sometimes the arms describe a circle, and they are always used as if to balance the dancer, who often dances on one spot. This makes the footwork very neat.

Dances

The Reels and Strathspeys are the favourite forms of dance at all Scottish festivities. The Three-Handed Reel for one man and two ladies is possibly the oldest form, and the Country Bumpkin, a very old country dance, is a derivation of this. The Four-handed Reels have given rise to other country dance forms, and the Eightsome, now one of the most popular of dances, is founded on a much older Reel and was designed some 85 years ago for one of the balls at Atholl (Ex. 64, page 189).

The men's solo and group dances always take pride of place in all Highland Games and Competitions. The sword dance Gillie Callum is one of the most fascinating, being danced over the sword and its scabbard lying crossed on the ground. In popularity it is closely followed by the Argyll Broad-sword Dance for four men. This is interesting as it retains the clashing of the men's swords as if they were still fighting. It is performed only by Scottish Regiments. The Fling (Ex. 62, page 186) is also very intricate, and requires delicate balance and precision, as it is supposed to be performed on the "targe" or shield of the warrior. The Seann Triubhas is a solo version of a Strathspey, and has wonderful grace and elegance because of the slow tempo at which most of it is performed.

Most of the older dances of Scotland, both solo and group, are in two sections. The one slow and stately, sometimes even sad, and the other quick and vivacious. This gives them an emotional quality like those of more eastern Europeans. The dancers reflect this change by their quick reactions to the change in rhythm and tune, and by the alteration of their dignified and upright carriage into an exciting display of leaps and capers, sometimes punctuated by fervent cries, and even by an occasional outburst of original steps. As long as that spirit is not curbed, Scottish dance will continue to live and to change, although there is danger that the country dancers will lose the lilting quality of their dances through too much concentration on technique.

EXAMPLE 60

HIGHLAND SCHOTTISCHE

Step No. 1 in the Strathspey

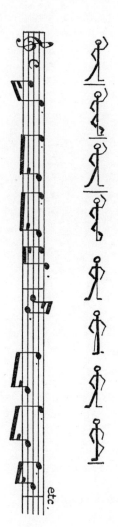

1. Hop off L. ft., pointing R. ft. to side in air.

2. Hop off L. ft. bringing R. toe behind L. calf.

3. Hop off L. ft., pointing R. ft. to side in air.

4. Hop off L. ft., bringing R. toe in front of L. calf.

1. Glide sideways on R. ft.

2. Bring L. ft. behind R. ft.

3. Glide sideways on R. ft.

4. Hop lightly off R. ft., bringing L. ft. behind R. ankle.

From "Braes of Tulimet" Strathspey

EXAMPLE 61

STEP NO. 3 OF STRATHSPEY

1. Glide obliquely forwards on R. ft.

2. Hop off R. ft., bringing L. ft. up to R. ankle.

3. Step back on L. ft.

4. Shake R. leg out to side.

1. Glide R. ft. behind L. ft.

2. Step sideways on L. ft.

3. Pass R. ft. in front of L. ft.

4. Hop off R. ft., bringing L. ft. to front of R. shin.

EXAMPLE 62

THE HIGHLAND FLING

Danced in 4/4 to any good Strathspey. This is D. G. MacLennan's version.

1st step: Round the Leg

1st bar.   1. Spring up and point R. toe to side on floor, raising L. arm over head, R. hand on hip.
       2. Hop on L. ft., bringing R. up behind L. calf.
       3. Hop on L. ft., passing R. ft. forwards so that R. heel rests just below L. knee.
       4. Hop on L. ft., passing R. ft. again behind L. calf.

EXAMPLE 62 *(cont.)*

2nd bar. Repeat "Round the Leg" with L. ft., reversing arms on 1st beat.

3rd bar. Repeat "Round the Leg" with R. ft., reversing arms on 1st beat.

4th bar. Repeat "Round the Leg" with L. ft., reversing arms on beat 1 and making one complete turn to the right on beats 2, 3 and 4.

Repeat these 4 bars, starting with L. toe pointed to side, R. arm raised and L. hand on the hip.

2nd step: Back-stepping

1st bar.   1. Spring up and point R. toe to side on floor, raising L. arm over head, R. hand on hip.
          2. Spring up and bring R. toe behind L. calf.
          3. Spring up and point R. toe to side on floor.
          4. Spring up and bring R. heel in front and under L. knee.

2nd bar. *and* Quickly pass R. ft. behind L. calf.
          1. Spring on to R. ft., raising both hands above head.
  and 2, *and* 3, *and* 4. Repeat this circular movement with the L. and again with the R. and L. ft. (Legs are very close and appear to wrap round each other.)

Repeat these 2 bars starting with L. ft., R. arm raised.
Repeat all 4 bars.

3rd step: Toe and Heel Step

1st bar. "Round the Leg" with R. ft., L. arm raised.

2nd bar. 1. Spring up landing on R. ft. and placing L. toe in front of R. ft. (5th position). Both hands on hips.
          2. Hop off R. ft. and place L. heel in front of R. ft.
          3, 4. Change feet and repeat toe and heel movement with R. ft.

3rd bar. Repeat toe and heel movement with L. and R. feet.

4th bar. "Round the Leg," using L. ft., raising R. arm and making one complete turn to the right on beats 2, 3 and 4.

Repeat these 4 bars, beginning "Round the Leg" with L. ft., raising R. arm and L. hand on hip.

4th step: Rocking Step

1st bar.   1. Spring up and point R. toe to side on floor, raising L. arm, R. hand on hip.
          2. Spring up and bring R. toe behind L. calf.
          3. Spring up and point R. toe in front and at centre of L. ft. (Weight retained on L. ft.)
          4. Hop on L. ft. and shake R. ft. obliquely forwards.

2nd bar. 1. Spring on to R. ft., displacing L. ft., and bringing L. toe on floor behind R. heel. Both hands on hips.
          2. Transfer weight on to L. ft., raising R. heel, so that R. toe is in front of L. ft.
          3, 4. Repeat beats 1 and 2.

3rd and 4th bars. Repeat 1st and 2nd bars, starting with L. ft.

Repeat these 4 bars. (Arms can be raised for the Rocking.)

EXAMPLE 62 (*cont.*)

5th step: Cross-over Step

1st bar. "Round the Leg" with R. ft., L. arm raised, L. hand on hip.

2nd bar. 1. Spring up and point R. toe to side.

      2. Spring up bringing R. toe behind L. calf and turning body slightly to left.

      3. Without moving L. ft., step across L. ft. on to R. ft.

      4. With a slight spring off R. ft., bring L. toe to front of R. (5th position). Change arms.

3rd and 4th bars. Repeat 1st and 2nd bars, starting with L. ft.

Repeat these 4 bars.

6th step

Bars 1 to 4. Repeat "Round the Leg" as in 1st step.

Bars 5 and 6. Repeat "Round the Leg" starting with L. ft., twice.

Bars 7 and 8. Repeat "Round the Leg" starting with R. ft. and making two complete turns to the left, R. arm raised.

The dance often opens and concludes with a bow.

EXAMPLE 63

SIMPLE PAS-DE-BASQUE OR SETTING

Dance in one place

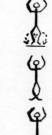

1. Spring off L. ft. and with a circular movement, spring on to R. ft. sideways, knees turned out.

and Bring L. toe in front of R. toe and take weight of body.

2. Beat ball of R. ft. on the spot.

and Pause.

3 *and* 4. Repeat, springing off R. ft.

From "Reel of Tulloch"

EXAMPLE 64

EIGHTSOME REEL

Dance for 4 couples standing in a square, to any good reel tune. Man holds his partner on his R. hand.

Opening

8 bars. All join hands in a circle and perform 8 *chassés* side-ways to the left and return to places with 8 *chassés* to the right.

4 bars. Women give R. hands across (still holding partner's hand) and all wheel forwards with 4 *progressive steps*. Women drop R. hand and step back on last bar.

4 bars. Men give L. hands across (still holding partner's hand) and all wheel forwards 4 *progressive steps*. All returning to places to face own partner on last bar.

4 bars. All set to partners (Ex. 59) with 4 *pas-de-basques* moving to right and left and again to right and left.

4 bars. Swing with partner, using *pas-de-basques*.

16 bars. Grand chain: begin by giving partner R. hand. Take 2 *progressive steps* to each partner, one to greet her and one to leave her. 1st woman goes into the centre during last 4 bars of music.

A. 8 bars. Rest of dancers join hands and perform 8 *chassés* to left and 8 *chassés* to right, whilst 1st woman dances suitable reel step in centre.

B. 4 bars. 1st woman sets to her partner to right and left and swings with him.

4 bars. 1st woman repeats this movement with 3rd man. (He is opposite her own partner.)

8 bars. 1st couple and 3rd man perform a hey for 3, using *progressive steps*.

A. 8 bars. Group reforms and repeats *A*.

B. 16 bars. 1st woman repeats *B* with the man on her right and the man opposite him (i.e. with 2nd and 4th men). She returns to her own place and 2nd woman goes to the centre.

A and *B* are now repeated by the 2nd woman followed by the other women and all 4 men in turn.

After all have danced in the centre, repeat "Opening." After 12 bars of the Grand Chain, partners join hands and turn once. They then bow or curtsey to each other.

EXAMPLE 65

STRIP THE WILLOW

Usually danced to a 9/8 Jig Tune, such as "Hey my Nannie" or "Drops of Brandy" dating from the seventeenth century, or "Frolicksome Paddy." In Jig time a running step of 3 to a bar is used.

Longways Set for as many as will. Men and women stand in two lines facing own partners.

Bars 1–4. 1st couple turn each other by the R. hand one and a half times, finishing so that woman faces 2nd man. (Elbows are also linked instead of hands.)

Bars 5–6. 1st woman turns 2nd man by L. hand.

Bars 7–8. 1st woman turns her own partner by R. hand. She continues thus, alternately turning new man and her own partner until she reaches the bottom of the set.

1st man now repeats this figure up the woman's side, giving bottom woman his L. hand and his partner his R. hand until he reaches the top of the set.

1st couple now turn each other by the R. hands, then both go down the set together, alternately turning each other and a new partner. When they reach the bottom they turn with each other one and a half times and fall back to new places at the bottom of the set.

The dance is now repeated by the 2nd couple and continues until all have danced.

When the couple are dancing down the set together, each couple moves up one pace so that the set always remains in the same place.

Hey My Nannie

La Boulangère (Île de France) is a circular set, each couple taking their turn in the centre.

La Virra Extrapassado (Portugal) is a longways set, couples standing facing each other, but men and women standing alternately in line. The couple dance down the set simultaneously, men always turning women and vice versa. As soon as the 1st couple reach the bottom of the set they start coming up again, for each couple begins to dance as soon as they reach the top.

CHAPTER XV

The Finno-Ugrians

GROUPS of people speaking a language derived from a common source known as the Finno-Ugrian are scattered in isolated pockets throughout Europe and Asia. There are the Asiatic groups known as the Tuvinians in an area of the Altai Mountains, the various Yakut, Samoyed, and Ostyak tribes of Eastern and North Western Siberia, the Voguls living between the Ural Mountains and the River Ob, and the European groups of Finns, Karelians, Estonians, and Hungarians. The ancestors of all these people were of mixed Hunnish-Turki tribes roaming over the vast Asiatic Steppes, who were gradually displaced by other Turki and Mongol tribes pushing in from east, south, and south-west. Yet, despite their varied histories and social development, by some strange accident they have retained the characteristics of their common language, as well as two distinct musical features, which are reflected in their dance.

The first of these features is their curious habit of one set of singers or dancers immediately copying the note or step sung or danced by their opposite partner as they sit or stand opposite each other in song or dance, so that among the best singers and dancers their efforts are all but simultaneous. The second feature is their love of repeating identical notes or bars of music again and again, as one finds in so many passages of Sibelius' music. This has a counterpart in the constant repetition of one particular step throughout a dance, the step only gaining interest because of its varying rhythms.

HUNGARY

Among the European Finno-Ugrian group Hungary is quite unique in being without any direct communication with the other nations speaking a kindred language. Lying at the northern end of the Danube Plain, she is surrounded by Slavs and Austrians (Map 2, facing page 52). But she has never been a buffer state, as was the case with Czechoslovakia. On the contrary, for some seven centuries the Magyars completely controlled this area, and it was this period of domination that helped to preserve many ancient rituals and traditions, despite the Hungarians' later subjugation by Turk and Austrian.

The Hungarians were late-comers to Europe, not entering the Danube valley and penetrating the Carpathians until the ninth century A.D. (Map 1, facing page 32). They were an extremely warlike, fast-moving people, and once established they dominated the Slav tribes, and began to assimilate the polished culture of the land into which they had come. At the same time they kept the Teutons at bay and were strong enough to retain an independent attitude and refuse to be incorporated into the Holy Roman Empire, although paying tribute to the Catholic church on their conversion to Christianity in the eleventh century. Because of their refusal to bow completely to the laws of the Holy Roman Empire, the Catholic church had not the same hold in Hungary as it had elsewhere, and therefore the severe decrees against dancing issued by the priests had little effect on the wild and warlike dances of the herdsmen and soldiers. Certain peculiar, nomadic tribal laws, limiting the power of the King or leader to allow each full member of the tribe a certain freedom, had also been incorporated into the Hungarian Constitution or "Golden Seal" of A.D. 1222, and this helped to preserve the ancient customs and rituals.

Although the Hungarians suffered a temporary set-back when the Mongols swept through the country during their invasion of Europe in 1241, these later invaders soon retired, allowing the Magyars to build up their strength again. For three more centuries they dominated the Plains and were able to withstand the Turks, until the disastrous battle of Mohács' Field in 1526, when their king was slain, and as a result they became part of the Ottoman Empire. But, as happened in other countries overrun by the Turks, many areas were left unoccupied and these continued to be ruled over by Hungarian Khans paying tribute to the Ottoman Emperor, thus maintaining a continuance of traditions. Moreover, some rituals continued to be practised among the famous Hussar regiments composed of Hungarians, which played an important role in the armies of other European nations. It is the link between soldier and dance that has kept some dances alive till to-day.

The particular prowess of the Magyar soldiers in keeping the Turks out of Europe was noted as early as the beginning of the sixteenth century, when Slav and Teutonic Kings began to recruit Hussars from Hungary to bolster up their own armies, and thus withstand the constant attack of other kings. The method of recruitment was unique and arose out of the Hungarians' love of dance, which has always been a strong feature of their communal life.

Many Magyars and the Huns whom they had subjugated, on settlement under more stable conditions, became herdsmen of swine, cattle, and other flocks, the land being particularly suitable for such work. This necessitated their carrying an axe, crook, or other weapon to protect themselves from their own flocks (by no means the tame, domesticated kind of to-day), as well as to protect their flocks from wilder animals and robbers. From this habit there developed the many interesting herdsmen's dances with axes or sticks which became a feature of market-days in Hungary and neighbouring countries when these men came to sell their animals. These dances still exist, and in them the men enact the killing of a boar, or dance with partners twirling axes, or sticks, or cross their weapons on the ground and dance over them. Such dances became associated with more warlike events when the herdsmen—or heyducks—became soldiers during the fifteenth-century Protestant wars of liberation in Bohemia and Northern Hungary. So astounding was the wild heyducks' dance that foreigners began to call it the national dance of Hungary, drawing attention to its peculiarly individual extemporization, its warlike nature with the flashing swords, wild leaps, strange crouchings and clashing weapons, and above all its insistent rhythm stamped out with vigour.

This favourite pastime was used to ensnare the young Magyar herdsmen of the sixteenth century into foreign service. The task was entrusted to Hungarian officers of high rank, who deputed Sergeants with groups of eight to twelve men to tour remote Hungarian villages. All these men were superb dancers, and on arrival they would form a circle and dance, each man accurately copying his opposite partner, or obeying the commands sung by the Sergeant standing in the centre. So strong was the urge to join the dance that any young man onlooker who entered the circle was persuaded to enlist. An important part of the dance was the cunning of the leader, who not only told the young man of the wonderful life he would lead as an officer, but placed the Hussar's shako on his head and buckled a sword round his waist.

The Hungarian overlords' preoccupation with military affairs grew as the Hapsburg Emperors gradually began to drive the Turks out with the help of the Hungarian regiments, and with this movement the popularity of the recruiting dance of Verbunkós grew everywhere. It became more organized in form, and spread to remote villages, where it is now known as the Szekler Legényes (Youth's dance); it is best danced in the areas which are now part of Romania. Here it retains its original circular form, each man standing opposite the man with whom he is most in harmony, and the dance is always begun by the best performer.

The success of the Austro-Hungarian armies in driving the Turks from the country, caused dissension, however, among the Hungarians themselves. One group, called the Kuruc, regarded the Austro-Hungarian union as a threat to their independence, while the landowners, known as the Labanc, felt it was essential. The result of this dissension was a fall in the popularity of the Verbunkós, the Kuruc soldiers feeling that it was being used to recruit men for a foreign army. The failure of the Hungarian War of Independence in 1848 and the Austrian establishment of conscription instead of recruitment nearly killed the Verbunkós, but the patriotic fervour of the Hungarian aristocrats was now aroused, and they immediately turned their attention to a revival of the national folk arts, with the result that dancing masters began to devise ballroom arrangements of the traditional dances. One of these was the Czárdás, derived from peasant dances performed by boys and girls outside the village inns or Czárda after the week's work. It is still danced in the theatres, and contains characteristic Hungarian movements. But it is a pale reflection of the real peasant dances, which began to be revived with particular fervour after the 1914–18 war, when Hungary gained her independence. The Czárdás has few figures, it can be easily learnt, and each dancing master arranges it to suit his own fancy. But real Hungarian dance is extremely difficult, except to the Hungarians themselves.

Improvisation

The principal difficulty encountered in Hungarian dance is the fact that, with few exceptions, it is not "set," but is a spontaneous improvisation. The best dancer leads and the others follow, or each stands opposite the person with whom he or she is most in harmony, and they work with each other. This is most notable in such couple dances as the Kállai Kettös, where the couple first sway opposite each other, advance and retire, embrace and whirl, and then entice each other to further efforts.

A great deal of this improvisation is based on the simple Slav basic step of which most dances are composed. But the rhythm becomes extremely complex and is punctuated by fascinating chains of stamps. The quality and volume of this stamping varies considerably with the type of dance. In the Csürdungölo, danced at balls given to flatten the earth floor of new barns, it is heavy and erratic owing to the uneven quality of the dancing space, and figures seen once may never be repeated. But in the Verbunkós, its derivative Szekler Legényes, and the Borica, a man's set dance of Romanian origin, it is lighter, neater, and more regular because of its militaristic aspect. The dancers clip their heels together, thus complicating the rhythm, and they often wear metal heels, spurs, or plates on their boots, or sometimes even brass rattles or walnuts. These latter derive from the time when serfs were forbidden to wear spurs, as they were a sign of aristocratic rank.

The Snap

In the carriage of the body and use of the arms, Hungarian dance is similar to Polish, for both peoples are great riders and breeders of horses, and have similar military antecedents, but its relationship to the music is different. Hungarian music has some very distinct features which affect the dance tremendously. The first of these is the Snap, which gives a curious stress to many dance steps as it does in Scotland. On the semiquaver or first note of the bar a preparation is made, then on the dotted quaver, which is always strongly accented, one performs the vital part of the step, which often happens to be a clipping of the heels or a stamping on the floor, as in the *Fordulat Bokaveró* (*Holubetz*, Ex. 25, page 101), or *Tetovazo* (Ex. 68, page 199). This feature may have arisen from the curious stress of the Magyar language, for most dances are accompanied by mouth music, and the words often express his feelings or tell the dancer what to do. Or it may come from the sound of horses' hooves, for the rhythm and sound of horses permeates all Magyar dance. The urge for this preparatory movement is so strong that as in Scotland, the dancers make it instinctively at the opening of most phrases, whether the Snap is there or not. But unlike the upwards lift of the Scots, the preparatory movements of the Hungarians are always along or into the ground, and this gives their dance its characteristic swift and abrupt halts and broken rhythm.

Elaboration of Step

This preparatory emphasis of the accented note leads to considerable ornamentation of music and step. Like Hungarian embroidery, it is the most elaborate in Europe—neat, precise, and dainty, demanding concentration on the exact matching of note and step to those of one's partner. A wonderful example of ornamentation is the number of variations made on the Slav basic step, the dancer clicking his heels three, four, or five times as he closes together; or jumping and clicking his heels in the air, dropping with feet apart and then clicking them before closing.

Another interesting form of ornamentation is that accompanying the *Bokázó* or *Break* at the end of most enchaînements in a dance. Its basic form is a simple crossing, opening, and clipping of the heels together, but it can be elaborated by extra pointings of the toe as the feet are crossed, and extra jumps and clippings before the actual Feminine cadence, which marks the final clip, is reached. The ornamentation is particularly difficult because it usually takes only the same time as would the simple version of the step (Exs. 66, 67, pages 198, 199).

Tempo Giusto

Bela Bartók, the famous Hungarian composer, has noted that despite the complicated relationship of movement and music, the structure of his native folk tunes and dances is simple. Phrases are of equal length and therefore the enchaînements are of equal length, and often end in a Feminine Cadence. A typical basis for an enchaînement in a Verbunkós to eight bars of music is: 2 steps to the right, 1 to the left, 2 to the right again, 1 to the left. Then 2 more steps to bring the men back to place. This kind of enchaînement is found in other types of dance.

Bartók also points out that although most dances and tunes are divided into two parts, the slow or Lassu (also Lassan), and the quick or Friss (also Frishka), they are always played in strict rhythm or Tempo Giusto, which is only slightly modified to accommodate the accentuation at beginnings or ends of complete phrases.

The Steps

It is difficult to generalize about the steps of Hungarian dance. The following are but a few samples for, as the dancers improvise, a step seen once may never appear again. Arm movements, too, when dancers are not linked together, are very individual. As a rule arms work in natural complement to the feet, are seldom raised over the head, and are only crossed over the chest when hopping backwards, as in *Kerestezo* (Ex. 15, page 90)

Single steps seldom travel far along the ground, although great leaps upwards are often made and large areas can be covered with many small steps. The dancer never loses control over himself or his partner, so that there is always an air of finality and assurance in everything he does.

The Basic step of most dances is merely—

1. Step forwards or sideways on L. ft.
2. Close R. ft. to L. without changing the weight of the body.

Repeat this movement to the right; this often becomes something like the *Cwal* of Poland (Ex. 26, page 101).

Emelkedo is a woman's variation of this—

1. Step forwards or sideways on L. ft.
2. Close R. ft. to L.
3. Rise on balls of feet.
4. Lower heels.

In the man's variation of this he clicks his heels together on 3.

Fordulat is another variation for men—

1. Step forwards or sideways on L. ft.
2. Bring R. leg round in a circle from back to front of R. ft.
3. Rise on toes.
4. Fall on heels.

Yet another variation is that in which the dancer steps sideways on to the ball of the L. ft., closes R. ft. to L., and then clips the heels together, three, four, or as many times as he wishes.

Ingo is another variation beginning with feet together—

1. Bend knees slightly.
2. Step sideways on R. ft.
3. Close L. ft. to R., bending knees slightly.

This can develop into a sliding movement from side to side.

Bokázó or Break, which ends many enchaînements, has several forms. The simplest is commenced with the feet together (Ex. 66, page 198).

Another interesting *Break* is similar to a step found in Scotland, Spain and Russia (Ex. 67, page 199).

Harang or *Bell step* is the same as in Russia (Ex. 13, page 89), but can also be danced to a 3/4 rhythm, when it is evenly balanced with the beats.

Hegyezö is merely a pointing of heel and toe—

1. Hop on R. ft. pointing L. ft. forwards on heel.
2. Hop on R. ft. pointing L. ft. forwards on toe.

Repeat hopping on L. ft.
Innumerable variations are made of this.

Ugrós is another name for the usual step-hop in which the working leg is always well raised with the toe pointed well downwards on the hop.

Dübbenös Forduló is a variation of the basic step and is found only in couple dances. The man holds his right arm round the girl's waist. Both take two steps, the man transferring the girl to his left arm. They both jump into the air clicking their heels and landing with a strong beat, quickly repeating this jump.

Csápasoló are for men only and consist of a swinging of the leg forwards and backwards, while slapping the thighs with one or both hands. The legs are changed with a large jump upwards whenever the dancer feels inclined.

Tétovázó or the *Promenade* is usually found only in theatrical dances (Ex. 68, page 199).

Fordulat Bokaveró are similar to the Polish *Holubetz* (Ex. 25, page 101) and can be done sideways or turning with a partner. The *holubetz* can be single with two steps in between, but they are usually done in a series of three, followed by a stamp.

Lejtovagas (Lunge) is a prominent step in male dance and finds a place in the Czárdás (Ex. 69, 70, pages 200, 201).

Dances, Forms and Patterns

Most Hungarian dances are still performed in open or closed circles or longways sets, therefore patterns are not made, except by the twisting and turning of the couples. Enchaînements are based on a simple formula as explained above, but one step is seldom repeated more than four times, even in the few set dances. Variety of movement is the principal aim.

There are a number of interesting wedding dances, but these show similar characteristics to any Slav traditional dance, the bride showing her skill in embroidery or weaving, the bridesmaids or mothers showing her the work to be done, and both bridesmaids and groomsmen dancing the couple to bed by candlelight.

There are a number of interesting craftsmen's dances, but most of these emanate from the various Trade Guilds of workmen brought in from Bohemia and other areas to build up the various metal and furriers' industries started in very ancient times by the Scythians, who first inhabited this area. The most interesting of these craftsmen's dances are perhaps those of the coopers, who use the hoops of their barrels, as the English long sword dancers use their various instruments. The unique part of this and several other Hungarian dances for men and women, particularly the dance of the cooks, is the balancing and dancing with glasses of wine. This kind of feat is found elsewhere only among the Basques and Caucasians, and seems to prove some ancient link between these peoples.

The curious link between the Hungarian and Scot by way of the common musical feature of the Snap is so far impossible to explain, except that the Scot may have acquired this from his Viking ancestor, who in turn acquired it from some Finno-Ugrian source. Both races being particularly independent, they have retained it with their own exhilarating dance characteristics, despite all that has been done by other nations to suppress them.

EXAMPLE 66

BREAK OR BOKÁZÓ No. 1

Man's Version

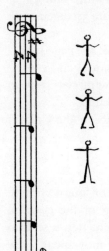

1. Step slightly sideways on R. toe, turning R. heel outwards.

2. Raise L. heel outwards, keeping weight on both toes.

3. Clip heels together and hold position on toes.
4. Pause.

Woman's Version

1. Hop lightly on L. ft., pointing R. toe to side or in front.

2. Hop lightly on R. ft., pointing L. toe to side or in front.

3. Click heels together and hold position on toes.
4. Pause.

EXAMPLE 67

BREAK OR BOKÁZÓ, No. 2

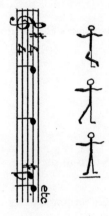

1. Hop on L. ft., crossing R. ft. over L. and resting R. toe on floor.

2. Hop on L. ft., swinging R. leg outwards with a circular movement touching floor and then opening at side.

3. Clip heels together with a jump and hold position on toes.
4. Pause.

EXAMPLE 68

TÉTOVÁZÓ OR PROMENADE

(The counting is not evenly marked, but follows the music. Numbers given are *not* beats)

1. Step forwards on R. ft., bending L. knee upwards, L. toe pointed on R. knee.

2. Slide-jump forwards on R. ft., marking step heavily and immediately open L. leg.

3. Step forwards on L. ft.

4. Step forwards on R. ft.

Repeat starting with L. ft. if necessary.

EXAMPLE 69

A CZÁRDÁS

A dancing master's arrangement, seen in the annual Festival of Dance.

Couple stand side by side, arms crossed over in front. Man holds woman's R. hand in his R. and her L. in his L.

Tempo is very brisk and gets quicker.

1st bar.	2 *Ugros*, starting by stepping on to R. ft., and moving forwards.
2nd bar.	Both perform *Bokázó* No. 2.
3rd and 4th bars.	Repeat bars 1 and 2, moving slightly backwards.
5th bar.	Step and click heels together 4 times, both making a half-turn to the right.
6th bar.	*Bokázó* No. 2.
7th and 8th bars.	Repeat bars 5 and 6, man remaining in place and woman turning to face him.
9th bar.	Woman turns rapidly on both feet twice to right. Man dances 2 *Fordulat Bokaveró* opposite her to left.
10th bar.	Both do *Bokázó* No. 1.
11th and 12th bars.	Repeat bars 9 and 10, moving in opposite direction.
Bars 13–16.	Both perform 8 *Fordulat Bokaveró* turning with each other, L. arms round each other's waists and R. arms raised at side.

Repeat whole dance as often as required.

Tune Probably a Gipsy Version

EXAMPLE 70

LEJTOVAGAS OR LUNGE

(Note position of arms)

Preparation

1. Spring on to R. ft., dropping L. knee on floor. R. hand is behind head, L. hand on hip.

2. Jump upwards on R. ft., swinging L. leg upwards and forwards as high as possible.

3–4. Take 2 walking steps forwards, or stamp twice.

Repeat in opposite direction.

An Old Czárdás Tune

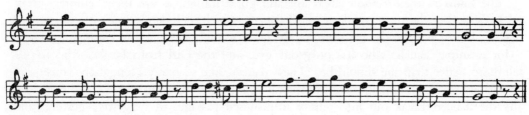

FINLAND

(With reference to Estonia, Lithuania and Latvia)

Tribes of Finno-Ugrian origin entered Europe very early and are known to have settled in Finland and Estonia as early as 500 B.C. They soon mixed with other tribes arriving from other European areas, and since the first century A.D. these two countries have constantly changed hands between the Poles, Swedes, Lithuanians, Germans, and Russians. For this reason most of their dances are similar in form and pattern to the seventeenth, eighteenth, and nineteenth century social dances of Poland and Sweden. The Swedish Protestant church had suppressed most of the ancient rituals, and therefore when dancing was looked on with a more tolerant eye it was the dances which had been through the refining hand of King Gustav's dancing masters, or had been brought in by foreign regiments, that began to be practised. Their very names suggest the countries of their origin: England, France, Sweden, Poland, Scotland, and Russia. The steps and many of the tunes are also borrowed, those from Scotland being very popular.

Yet, in the remote areas of the Karelian lakes and forests, and along the sea-coasts where the ancient language of Suomi (Finland) is still spoken, a few traces of old dances and rituals are to be found. They are not identical with those of Hungary, although having a few elements in common. The climate and geographical situation do not result in the same kinds of work and the horse-riding elements have been completely eliminated. Moreover in these areas, Finno-Ugrian culture seems to have mingled with another ancient tribe, whose worship of nature gods have left many traces on their dances. These are akin to those of Latvia and Lithuania, where the language, Balto-Slav, is thought to be the only relic of the ancient Aryan tongue, the mother of most European languages. They are always danced to mouth music, and very often are imitative of natural things such as seals, bears or swallows, and there are queer ritual dances with very interesting arm movements. Some of these are like the nature dances of Armenia or even further east, a particular instance being the use of the hands and the formation of the Lithuanian Swallow Dance and a similar ancient bird-worshipping dance of the Bashkirian women in the Ural Mountains.

The Finns in these remote areas are also good mimes, as are their remote eastern relatives, and in the more modern social dances, which include elements of courting or making fun of people, the gestures are always extremely clear and to the point. There is for example Taneli, who has only one eye, and the Girl from Forssa, who is certainly no better than she should be. These dances, like so many Hungarian dances, are performed to the accompaniment of satirical verse, sometimes improvised, and occasionally the dancers break out into purely improvised passages of suggestive gestures and movements.

The most important dances of Finland, Estonia, Latvia, and Lithuania are those performed at weddings, but these again are similar to those performed elsewhere, where Slav or other eastern ancestors can be traced.

Among the oldest Finnish dances one finds, as in Hungary, the slight preparation for a step, which is always made to correspond with the occasional appearance of the Snap. This gives old Finnish dance an abrupt quality not found in the more modern dances. These latter, however, have acquired the absolutely regular rhythm, or tempo guisto of the older dances, and whether they be fast or slow the dancers show a finer tension and keener sense of rhythm than the Swedish performers of the same styles of country and social dances. This lends the Finnish dancers a slightly more emotional movement than those of the well-behaved Swedes, and although faces may be expressionless, bodies are more relaxed and respond more easily to changes in direction, step, and rhythm.

Repetition of Musical Notes and of Tapping of Feet

A study of Sibelius's music gives a clue to a peculiarly Finnish characteristic, which was surely derived from his own folk tunes. This is the constant repetition of one single note. It often appears that the accented note is followed by its echo again and again. This feature is reflected in a very few ancient songs and dances, where one set of singers or dancers sing a note or dance a step, which is immediately copied by another set. The step is often a repeated tapping of one toe, or tiny jumps on both feet, and as the performers face one another or are immediately behind one another, this gives a curious see-saw effect to their movements. It is particularly noticeable in certain ritual songs accompanied by the national instrument, the kantele, when the singers rock to and fro as they sing. This rocking to and fro and immediate copying of another's example is a feature of some games played by Finnish children.

Dances, Steps, Forms and Patterns

The most common dances of Finland now seem to be the Purpuri, which are exactly what their name suggests, a mixture of figure dances including the steps of many countries. Although the figures do not always resemble what their names suggest (Polska, Quadrille, Mazurka and Cossack), steps like walking, running, galloping, hopping, valse in 3/4 and 2/4 (see also Sweden for *step-hop-valse*), *polka* and *polka mazurka* (Ex. 43, page 142), *schottische* and jumps on two feet are easily recognized.

The *Polska Reel step*, a *pivot step* in 2/4 or 3/4 (Ex. 4, page 62), is just like the English swinging of partners. Gliding hops in a 3/8 rhythm, where the hopping foot is slid rather than jumped along the floor three times, whilst the other foot trails after it, are found in some of the animal dances, such as Sjalaskuttan (Seal's Jump). Two other steps can be more clearly defined as being Finnish.

The *Polska Change step* in 3/4 is a turning step—

　　1. Step on to L. ft. towards left.
　and Close R. ft. to L.
　　2. Step on L. ft.
　　3. Jump on to R. ft. in front of L.

Repeat beginning with L. ft. To turn to the right, begin sequence with the R. ft.

Polka Heel step in a 4/4 rhythm—

　　1. Step forwards on R. heel. (The step is usually anticipated on the last half-beat of the bar by the R. leg being swung backwards.)
　and Close L. ft behind R.
　　2. Step forwards on R. ft.
　and Hop on R. ft., immediately kicking L. ft. backwards in order to begin the next movement by stepping on L. heel.

In parts of Karelia nearest Russia, certain Russian characteristics appear, especially steps borrowed from Cossack Dances.

All further information about Finnish dance can be gathered by studying Teutonic, Scandinavian, and English country dance forms. This is also true of the dances of Estonia, Latvia, and Lithuania. Only those dances which are still associated with the ancient language of these people and danced in remote places retain their ancient characteristics, and show the close links with the Hungarians and other Finno-Ugrian groups.

CHAPTER XVI

The Latins

THE Italians, Portuguese, French, Romanians, and small groups of people in Switzerland speak a language derived from a common Latin source, although they are not descended from the same tribal ancestors. That they should do so is proof of the power of the Roman Emperors, who ruled large areas of Europe for nearly four centuries, and made Latin the official language of their provinces. During that period derivatives of Latin became firmly established among the different tribes and were adopted by later barbarian invaders. The use of the Latin tongue by the Roman Catholic church also spread it further when the pagan kings embraced Christianity.

The Romans introduced into their provinces a love of spectacle, which was further enhanced as the church brought the people's dance rituals into its own orbit by staging magnificent pageants through the streets. Roman influence is still to be found in the spectacular elements of the rituals that survive in these countries, although these rituals really belong to the common European heritage left by Celtic, Slav, Teutonic, and other tribes. However, as each country has gone through a different historical process since the downfall of the Roman Empire, it is wise to study them individually.

ITALY

It has often been remarked that it is characteristic of the Italians, as it was of the ancient Roman leaders, that they assimilate the arts of the people they conquer. This is certainly true of their dances, for all over Italy one finds dances similar to those of other nations.

The original speakers of a Latin dialect were primitive farming tribes living north and east of the Tiber, descendants of early Aryan groups who had invaded Italy from the north in the ninth century B.C. A fierce warlike people, they began to acquire more land by conquering the highly cultured Etruscans living in northern Italy, who had distinctive art forms of Asiatic origin, and gave the Romans their first incentive to aim at grandeur in building. After many battles against the Gauls, who captured Rome in 390 B.C., the Romans began to establish themselves as rulers of all Italy, and gradually extended further, until by A.D. 98 their Emperor Trajan was in possession of what are now known as Spain, Portugal, France, Germany (as far as the Rhine), England (to Offa's Dyke and Hadrian's Wall), Yugoslavia, Greece, Turkey, Armenia, Palestine, Egypt, and large areas of the North African coast.

For the next two hundred and fifty years the Romans utilized, assimilated, and developed the valuable laws and artistic enterprises of the earlier Greek Empire, which they had subjugated. They also helped to spread some of the rituals of the Greeks and other Eastern Slavs, for such people, having a highly developed popular and classic drama, were in much demand to provide for the Roman's love of entertainment and spectacle. It was from the plays of these people that the Commedia dell'Arte characters (who became such a feature of theatrical art in Renaissance Italy) were descended, and they still appear in their traditional costumes in many Italian festival dances and processions.

Under Theodosius (A.D. 379–393), however, these pagan rituals were rigorously banned by the early Christian church, Christianity having become the official religion of the Roman Emperors after the death of Constantine (A.D. 337). There was terrible suffering at this time, for Theodosius was also fighting for his Empire, which finally broke up under the barbarian invaders entering from Asia, Northern Europe, and Africa. Italy itself was overrun first by the Goths and then by the Lombards.

It is impossible here to cover Italy's confusing history from this break-up until its re-unification under one king in 1861. Its geographical situation made it particularly susceptible to invasion and, after the rise of the Holy Roman Empire, when Charlemagne became the Pope's champion (A.D. 800), it was continually being split into different sections by the interests of warring kings, merchant princes, and political and religious parties. The remaining rituals reflect these many events, and the styles of dance vary from province to province according to the influence exerted by other nations.

In Sicily, Sardinia, and Corsica can be found certain Eastern elements, brought in first by the Vandals of the fifth century A.D., later by the Arabs, and again re-inforced over the whole of southern Italy, when the Kings of Spain possessed these areas. Here are to be found the stronger rhythmic forms, occasional broken cadences, and sudden halts for a pose, as well as numerous attitudes and steps and the use of castanets belonging to Spain. The erotic elements of the couple dances are more exaggerated, although some solemn rituals, versions of the Farandole dating from the earlier Greek occupation, are still danced. In Central Italy dances are more circumspect, no doubt because of the leavening influence of the church in Rome. In the north-eastern and eastern areas there are similar movements to those found in Central Europe, such as the *spunta piedi* (tiny jumps on both feet) of the peasants in Marche, where the body rocks from head to toe as in Yugoslavia. Some dances originated in the latter country because some of the Adriatic Islands with a Croatian population were in the possession of the seafaring republics of Genoa and Venice; therefore an interchange of dances was effected. The Franks entered Italy through the Vale d'Aosta, and throughout the north-western regions are to be found dances akin to those of other Teutonic and Celtic people, particularly the sword dances of many kinds, which are occasionally found elsewhere.

The overwhelming influence of the Catholic church has led to the exaggeration of the spectacular side of these rituals to such an extent that their outer trappings tend to make all Italian dances look alike. It is also possible that the climate in the south and the extreme poverty of the villagers elsewhere have helped to mould them on similar lines.

The Italian Love of Cantabile

The Western European lack of strongly accented rhythms found further East is most noticeable in Italy, except in those parts influenced by Spain. This is possibly owing to the fact that the Italians are great singers and their love of cantabile, or "go-as-you-please," to show off the voice and its emotional capacity seems to lead to a great untidiness in the dance. Although to-day few dances are performed to mouth music, the musicians who accompany the dancers on ancient types of pipes, mandolines, and guitars, or on the now common accordion, also tend to display their virtuosity. The dances are therefore exuberant in feeling but careless of rhythm. The Italian's fondness for singing and dancing in triplets is not accurately matched by the simple steps constituting most of the dances. The dancers often mark only one beat of a 3/8 measure or two beats of their favourite 6/8 time signature. Even in the Saltarello, where the triplets are reduced to a dotted quaver and a semi-quaver, the dancer moves his feet evenly. It is interesting to note that even when mouth music accompanies the dance, the steps and gestures rarely match the words, which are often onomatopœic syllables of unknown significance.

Courtship Dances

Although many ancient chains and circles are still found and are similar to other European forms, for example the Ballo Tondo of Sardinia with its two steps to the left and one to the right, it is the couple dance that now seems to predominate. These are often very fiery and contain much flirtation and bargaining between the couple. These erotic dances, originating in fertility rites, developed with the growth of the medieval Provençal courts. Throughout northern Italy are to be found examples of dances acquired by the peasants from their masters, who followed the example of the Provençal nobles. In the north, these dances have a dignity and even a courtly air and often develop into elementary figure dances for four or more couples. But such dances as the Trescone, Bergamasca, Pavane, Monferrina and the Furlana dissolve into the gayer and freer Saltarello of central Italy, which again gives place to the fiery Tarantella of the south with its passionate love-making. The implications of all these dances have become more exaggerated owing to their inclusion in opera and other theatrical enterprises during the eighteenth and nineteenth centuries, when nationalistic feelings for a unified Italy arose, for the poor peasants found that by copying the professional dancers they could earn money from the tourists flocking to see the famous Italian antiquities.

Steps, Forms, and Patterns

Except in the mountain areas, where movements have the tension and neatness found among all mountain people, most Italians dance easily and almost lazily. Bodies are held loosely and there is a good deal of sway from the waist, except in the traditional Sword and Morris dances which are more rigidly controlled. Unless the dancers are linked in chains or circles, it is more usual for the boy to hold his hands upwards, whilst the girl's are on her apron or held akimbo. There are occasional outbursts of vigorous and impetuous clappings, stampings and heel tappings, particularly when the boy displays himself before his girl. There are also wonderful passages of impassioned mime, notably in Sicily, the home of some of the most famous mime-actors. But for the most part in the purer folk dances, steps are very simple. There is a good deal of skipping, valsing (see Alpine Areas, page 116), pivoting (Ex. 4, page 62), turning by crossing one foot over the other and twisting round on the balls of the feet, and enchaînements of walking steps as found in Greece and Yugoslavia.

The *Balancé* is used principally in the Saltarello (Exs. 71, 72) in addition to the springs and step-hops of this popular dance, although in Ciociaria it becomes a dignified couple or circle dance, performed by uneven numbers of people stepping with feet held close to the floor, bodies inclined forwards and heads nearly touching.

Other steps used by Italians, principally in the Tarantella, are—

High Hops, taking two steps to each bar of 6/8, the couple usually facing each other—

    1. Stamp on R. ft., raising L. knee upwards and forwards.
    2. Hop on R. ft. holding L. knee in position, commence turning to left.
    1, 2. Hop twice on R. ft., completing turn.
    Repeat hopping on L. ft. and turning to the right.

Long Hops, taking two steps to each bar of 6/8, the couple usually back to back, holding each other with their R. arms, L. arms stretched out in front—

    Hop for as many times as wished (usually multiples of 4), travelling forwards or turning to the right on the R. ft. with L. leg raised and pointed backwards, body well inclined forwards.
    Repeat hopping on L. ft.

Heel and toe steps, taking two steps to each bar of 6/8—

    Hop twice on L. ft., placing R. ft. first forwards on heel and then on toe, just in front of L. toe.
    Repeat hopping on R. ft.

There is also another interesting hopping step in which the dancer hops on the R. ft. as he swings the L. ft. diagonally forwards and backwards with the body inclined forwards. This movement is occasionally reversed, the swinging foot then moving across the front of the hopping foot, and the body being inclined backwards.

As a rule Italian dances are simple in form and pattern.

They are made up for four to six enchaînements, each of which consists of single steps used in multiples of four. But the tendency to theatricalize is making them increasingly elaborate. A delightfully illustrated description of a Neapolitan Tarantella of 1830 contains no less than eighteen enchaînements, each of which melts into the next with the couples facing, backing and turning round each other whilst playing castanets. The famous Bournonville ballet *Napoli* has more than forty different enchaînements containing steps still performed in southern Italy, where the peasants improvise and often use tambourines.

The northern figure dances use patterns similar in style to any other Country Dance, often using the usual setting of partners to each other and to the corners.

Other Characteristics

The close interest taken by the Catholic church in the people's rituals can be seen in the many dances forming part of the actual religious ceremonies, such as the Dance of the Flagellants in Calabria, or the Sword Dance performed in Casteltermini at the Festival of the Invention of the Holy Cross. Fighting Sword Dances depict incidents in which the Crusaders fought Moslems, Moors, or Turks, but even in these some theatrical elements have appeared, such as the Moresca of Lagosta, in which Moors and Turks fight for a lovely slave.

The deliberate fostering of the folk dance, started by the organization "Dopolavoro" in Mussolini's Italy as a means to attract the tourist and to further the state's imperialist policy, did much damage to folk dance, for it stressed the spectacular side of the demonstration. It is now possible to find original forms only in very remote villages; even these are losing their character because the extreme poverty and uncertain state of the country is driving the peasants to the towns or else to emigrate.

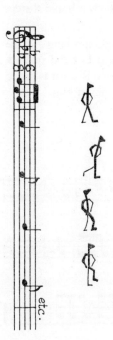

EXAMPLE 71

BALANCÉ
Can be danced in 2/4 or in 6/8

1. Step forwards on to R. ft., bending body slightly forwards.

and
(*or last beat of triplet*) Hop on R. ft., picking L. ft. up at rear and bending still further forwards.

2. Step backwards on L. ft., recovering erect position.

and
(*or last beat of triplet*) Hop on L. ft., picking up R. ft. in front.

Repeat *ad lib.*

The body always rocks well to and fro.

EXAMPLE 72

A SALTARELLO

Probably a dancing master's version

Danced by as many couples as will, or by a solitary pair. The partners take their places with the first long note of the music, which is repeated over and over again. They stand with their arms interlaced round each other's shoulders. Man's R. arm is round woman's L. shoulder.

16 bars. Spring round in a circle taking 2 steps to each bar.

4 bars. Facing each other and both starting with R. ft., perform 2 *balancés* (i.e. go forwards and backwards twice). Then spring round in a circle to change places.

4 bars. Repeat *balancé* and changing movement, returning to own places.

8 bars. Repeat last 8 bars once only.

8 bars. Man kneels and claps his hands on the first beat of each bar, whilst woman skips round him, flirting. She should lift her legs well up.

8 bars. Woman kneels, whilst man skips round her, holding his R. arm over his head and pretending at times to chuck her under the chin.

8 bars. Partners take inside hands with arms held high and spring 8 steps forwards and 8 steps backwards.

8 bars. Partners take R. hands and turn round each other with 16 springs, finishing on the last beat with the man kneeling on his R. knee, R. arm raised and L. hand on hip. Woman stands with her R. toe resting on ground behind L. ft. Her R. arm is raised with elbow turned towards her partner and L. hand on hip. She looks at him.

A Saltarello

SPAIN

To understand the diverse quality of Spanish dance requires a lifetime of study. All that can be given here is a brief outline of the many influences that have gone to its making. Moreover, Spanish dance is now becoming little more than a spectacle for an audience, performed by professionals who care little for the traditional aspect of their work, their main object being to draw attention to their virtuosity and their technical ability to display what the foreigner believes is the Spanish temperament.

Nevertheless, three forms of dance can still be defined: the folk dance with its dignified simplicity or spontaneous gaiety as it is found in remote villages; the classical style, learnt at the dancing schools and seen on the stage, utilizing the technique of the court and later eighteenth-century ballet dancers; and the Flamenco, which is Spanish folk dance as seen through the eyes of the gipsy, with his love of exaggeration, improvisation, and sudden bursts of dramatic energy. All these forms are first and foremost a matter of rhythmic complications, requiring absolute control of every part of the body, which can thrill with movement. Eyes may flash, the head toss, arms flow, and fingers click like pistol-shots or tap out subtle rhythms on castanets, adding to the fascinating cascade of sound beaten out by the toes and heels. Rhythms are often broken and enhanced by dramatic pauses or silent passages, when the dancers make beautifully undulating or abrupt movements with their bodies as if echoing their own previously made dance patterns. Such dances are the result of the enormous influence exercised by the Arab and the gipsy, the eastern peoples who have made Spanish dance unique in western Europe.

Some early inhabitants of Spain, the Celto-Iberians, had their first cultural contact with an eastern people when the southern areas were colonized in 1000 B.C. by the Carthaginians, who were swept away by the conquering Roman Legions in 236 B.C. From the Romans the Spaniards gained their love of spectacle. Roughly five hundred years later there followed two waves of barbarians entering from the north, the Vandals (*circa* A.D. 420) and the Visigoths (A.D. 500), who possibly brought the Sword Dances found elsewhere in Europe. By A.D. 750 however, the whole of Spain had been incorporated into the Moslem Empire, and the southern areas of Spain remained under Moorish domination for seven hundred years. In Andalusia one finds the strongest Eastern traits in both dance and music. The women as they dance make great play with shawl, fan, mantilla, or skirt to display their attractions—in every Moslem country the woman was considered as a chattel to be bought and sold, or to be kept in seclusion to entertain her lord and master. The man's solos are a matter of complicated footwork coupled with strange sinuous twistings of the leg and body. From the Moors has come the peculiar phrasing of much Spanish music, which often cannot be confined to the ordinary western time signatures or regular bar lines. There are long phrases of widely differing note values and rhythms, and the dancer often dictates the rhythms and is followed by the musicians, as in the east. The castanets with which the dancers accompany themselves are like the Kayrak of metal plates and pebbles used by the Uzbeks, and both are relics of Arab invasions to east and west, as are certain arm movements and ways of performing steps.

These rhythmic traits can also be noted where Moorish domination was not so prolonged, particularly in the rhythmic qualities of the many circles and chains in the northern areas such as Catalonia, which retains a great pride in its national traditions. The opening of its Sardana is a perfect example of the solemn ritual chain common to Europe, another valuable ritual is the Asturian Danza Prima. It is in the northern areas that male dance is outstanding, as in all areas where Celtic and Teutonic tribes have settled, or where crusading armies have passed in their efforts to drive the infidel from Europe.

Between the eleventh and thirteenth centuries, Christian kings entered Spain from the North and as they reconquered large areas of northern and central Spain they restored the peasants to the Catholic church. The priests rapidly brought the people's rituals under surveillance and, realizing their passionate love of dance, even allowed certain groups to dance in the churches. To-day the Seises, a group of highly trained boys, dance several times a year in Seville cathedral. Dancing occurs nearly every day somewhere in Spain in honour of some saint or on some other festive occasion. Sometimes this is little more than a solemn procession, but usually the dancing is spectacular and vigorous, and after the religious ceremonies are over the fun waxes fast and furious.

By A.D. 1492, the Kings of Castille had driven the Moslems out of Spain, thus earning the gratitude of the Pope, who designated this dynasty "The Kings of the World" when they became enormously wealthy with the discovery and ruthless exploitation of the Americas during the sixteenth century. By virtue of their wealth these Kings dominated the world for nearly a century, during which the Spanish court dance developed; the peasants, following the examples of their masters, cultivated the couple dance, in which man and woman perform as equals. Each incites the other to further efforts, as well as expressing their love for one another. The finest example is perhaps the Jota, with fascinating leaps and capers, originally a mountain dance from Aragon, which seems to have spread all over Spain and now has many different forms.

The wealth of Spain attracted some of the great ballet dancers of the eighteenth century and their technicalities influenced Spanish professionals, and later the peasants, to copy the dainty batterie and other stylish elements. This led to the establishment of many dancing schools, to which flocked the sons and daughters of wealthy families during the Napoleonic Wars, when it became fashionable to perform one's own national dances. Although these schools fell into disrepute with the relegation of Spain to a very secondary place among the nations, their influence on technique is still visible.

The strangest and, at the same time, the strongest influence on present-day Spanish dance is that of the gipsies. Driven out of country after country by the Mongolian hordes, large groups of them invaded southern Spain in the seventeenth century. Endowed with enviable powers of movement and readily acquiring other people's music and dance, they adapt the latter to their own methods of performance and then utilize them as a means of making money. Taking over the rich heritage of Moorish-influenced Andalusian dance, they exaggerated its rhythmic and erotic qualities, adding to it their own uninhibited freedom of expression and making it even more exciting by their unexpected bursts of tragic sorrow, fiery enthusiasm, or nostalgic melancholy. The couple may improvise for each other until they tremble in an ecstasy of dance, or perhaps the woman with her long, frilled train parades round like a dignified peacock until the moment when her partner, or the singer, the accompanist, or other members of the group, have incited her to a wild tornado of foot-beats or shaking shoulders. The men, too, may vie with each other in displaying their beats, twists, and strange leaps.

As they travelled through Spain, not only did the gipsies acquire the dances and steps of the other provinces, changing and adding to these to suit their own whims, but they also influenced the folk dancers themselves. Being often the only musicians available, they imposed their favourite broken rhythms and cadences on to the peasants' tunes, and thus reinforced their inherent eastern traits.

Many of the gipsies became the professional dancers in the numerous cabarets set up to attract the nineteenth and twentieth century tourists, so that when dancing fell into disrepute amongst the wealthy, it was the gipsy who kept alive the essence of many dances as a spontaneous expression of life. Acknowledging no king but their own, bowing to no political party, they have continued to dance unregulated by church, court, or state, whilst the Spanish peasant, tired of his endless struggle against poverty and authority, is quite content to let others exert themselves to afford him some pleasure.

Those wishing to perform Spanish dance in its original form must first seek it in the remote villages, or study the repertoire of the Sección Feminina de Fet. y Jons, the organization which is fostering and doing research into the genuine folk dance of Spain. Their work has uncovered many valuable dances linking Spain to the rest of Europe by way of Sword, Morris, Handkerchief and Maypole dances. Those who wish to perform classical dances and dances that are interpretations of the music by Spanish composers must go to the schools of Seville and Madrid. But only a Spaniard, and better a gipsy, can dance the Flamenco, because only a gipsy can be so free in rhythm, feeling and movements. His steps, forms and patterns cannot be confined to verbal descriptions, for once danced they may never be repeated. Like the Spanish dances from which they have come, they are endless in their variety.

A recent visit to Spain has led to the inclusion here of two different folk dances. The Mateixas of Mallorca has an easy grace and simple charm with a flowing movement. The Jota de Alcañiz has all the vigorous life of the Aragonese. The author's grateful thanks must be given to Señorita Dolores Pedroso y Sturdza and Señorita María Esparza for their great help in collecting these dances.

EXAMPLE 73

MATEIXAS

A vintage dance from Mallorca—the couple are supposed to be carrying large baskets and at times to pluck and eat the figs. They dance close together and open the dance facing each other.

1st Estribillo (a phrase of 8 followed by a phrase of 7 bars)

On the last beat of the bar, both raise and lower heels twisting slightly to right, hands are on hips.

Bar 1.	Again raise and lower heels completing ¼-turn to right.
2.	Pause.
3.	Raise and lower heels, twisting slightly to left.
Bar 2.	Raise and lower heels completing ½-turn to left.
2.	Pause.
3.	Repeat movement as at beginning.
Bars 3–8.	Continue this movement, twisting slightly to right and left as indicated.
Bars 9, 10, 11.	Both using L. leg as pivot and R. ft. pointed to side as lever, turn slowly to left, finish facing partner. During this the arms are outstretched and bodies slightly inclined to right.
Bars 12–15.	Place R. ft. on floor opposite partner's R. ft. Bend forwards bringing both arms down to knee, raise L. arm to waist level and curve R. arm over head. Both straighten and close feet together. Woman now faces forwards and man backwards. L. shoulders towards each other.

1st Copla (3 phrases of 8 bars each)

A. Bar 1.	Both starting on R. ft.
	1. Step sideways on R. ft.
	2. Bring L. toe behind R.
	3. Rock back on to R. ft. Both arms are curved slightly upwards and sway to right. The dancers make ¼-turn to left during this step.
Bars 2, 3, 4.	Repeat this valse-like step with L., R., and L. feet, swaying arms from side to side and completing one turn. (Dancers turn in own circle.)
Bar 5.	1. Place R. heel out to side, arms sway to right.
	2. Pause.
	3. Bring R. toe up to L. ft., arms sway to left.
Bar 6.	Repeat bar 5.
Bars 7, 8.	Repeat bars 1 and 2, but do not turn. Couple's L. shoulders are towards each other.

EXAMPLE 73 *(cont.)*

B. **Bars 1, 2, 3, 4.** Repeat bars 1, 2, 3, 4 of *A*, but make ¼-turn only to face partner on 1st bar.

   Bar 5. 1. With a little jump bring R. toe in front of L. ft., R. arm curved across waist, L. arm raised over head.
   2. Pause.
   3. With a hop on L. ft. raise R. leg slightly upwards and obliquely forwards.

   Bar 6. *Pas de bourrée.*
   1. Place R. ft. behind L.
   2. Step sideways on L. ft.
   3. Bring R. ft to L., during this the arms are gently rolled round each other.

   Bars 7, 8. Repeat bars 5 and 6 using opposite arms and legs.

C. **Bar 1.** Repeat bar 5 of *B*.

   Bar 2. Moving away from partner, take 3 steps backwards, rolling arms round each other.

   Bar 3. 1. Jump feet together.
   2. Pause.
   3. Jump forwards on L. ft. (this is like a running step), L. arm forwards.

   Bar 4. Jump forward on to R. ft., L. leg stretched out behind, R. arm stretched downwards towards partner, bodies inclined slightly to right.

EXAMPLE 73 *(cont.)*

Bars 5, 6, 7.	Repeat bars 1, 2, 3, of *A*, making ½-turn to left so that woman faces forwards and man backwards. The arms sway over head during this.
Bar 8.	1. Place R. heel out to side swaying arms to right.
	2. Pause.
	3. Bring R. toe to L. ft. swaying arms to left.

2nd Estribillo (First 8 bars)

Bar 1.	Repeat bar 8 of *C* above.
Bar 2.	1. Jump both feet together.
	2. Pause.
	3. Hop sideways to left on R. ft. with L. leg raised. (Partners change places.)
Bar 3.	1. Jump both feet together bending towards partner, R. arm curved across waist, L. arm over head.
	2. Pause.
	3. Hop to right on R. ft., back to original place, raising L. leg sideways.
Bar 4.	As bar 1 above but with jump bend towards partner raising R. arm over head and curving L. arm round waist. Repeat 3rd beat of bar 2.
Bars 5–8.	Repeat bars 3 and 4 twice.
Bars 9–15.	Repeat bars 9–15 of 1st Estribillo.

2nd Copla

A. Repeat *A* as in 1st Copla.

B. Bars 1–8.   Man pivots round twice on own axis to his left, and in each bar.

      1. Places R. heel out to side.

      2. Pause.

      3. Brings R. toe to L. ft. He opens and closes his R. arm to the same rhythm. The woman dances twice round the man to her left, using 8 *running valse steps*, as in 1st Copla, swaying arms as before.

C. Repeat *C* of 1st Copla, followed by Estribillo following 2nd Copla.

3rd Copla

A. Repeat *A* as in 1st Copla.

B. 1st bar.   1. Hop on L. ft. and place R. ft. over L., turning to left, R. arm across waist, L. arm over head.

      2. Pause.

      3. Step back on L. ft. (Couple face each other.)

    2nd bar.   1. Hop on L. ft. and place R. ft. behind L., turning to right, L. arm across waist, R. arm over head.

      2. Pause.

      3. Step forward on L. ft.

3rd bar.   1. Hop on L. ft. bringing R. toe to L. ft., R. arm across waist, L. arm over head and turning towards left.

2. Pause.

3. Hop on L. ft. immediately raising R. leg and turning to right.

4th bar.   *Pas de bourrée* as Bar 6 of Section *B* in 1st Copla.

Bars 5-8.   Repeat these 4 bars, starting with opposite foot.

C. Repeat *C* and Estribillo following 2nd Copla, but this time in bars 13, 14, 15 the man kneels slowly on R. knee and the woman slowly draws herself erect on R. ft., L. toe behind R. ft., arms as before.

EXAMPLE 74

JOTAS ARAGONESAS DE BAILE (ALCANIZ)

An example of one of the many Jotas, showing the difficulties of cross rhythms. The couple play the castanets, the L. hand usually marks each beat with a clip and the R. hand marks beat 1 with a clip and beat 3 with a roll, but this rhythm often varies.

During the first 10 bars of the introduction the couple stand waiting. They then run forward for 4 bars and, having arrived, the man turns the woman under his R. arm to her right. Both finish facing each other, hands on hips. Hands are then raised roughly at shoulder level, where they are held easily.

Estribillo

A. Bar 1.   1. Step forwards on L. ft.
2. Hop on L. ft.
3. Place R. heel forwards.

Bar 2.   1. Step back on L. ft.
2. Hop on L. ft.
3. Place R. toe backwards.

Bar 3.   1. Step forwards on L. ft.
2. Hop on L. ft.
3. Place R. heel forwards.

Bar 4.   1. Place L. heel forwards.
2. Step back on R. toe.
3. Step back on L. toe.

Bar 5.   1. Step forwards on R. ft.
2. Hop on R. ft.
3. Place L. heel forwards.

Jotas Aragonesas de Baile (Alcaniz)

EXAMPLE 74 (*cont.*)

Bar 6.   1. Step back on R. ft.
                2. Hop on R. ft.
                3. Place L. toe backwards.

Bar 7.   1. Step on R. ft.
                2. Swing L. ft. up, knee bent and make one complete turn to the right, finish facing partner.

Bars 8, 9.   Pause.

1st Copla

B. Bar 1.   1. Step on L. ft.
                2. Pause.
                3. Beat L. heel on R. heel (an easy *cabriole*).

Bar 2.   *Pas de bourrée* moving sideways:
                1. Place R. ft. behind L.
                2. Step sideways on L. ft.
                3. Close R. ft. to L.

Bar 3.   1. Hop on R. ft. pointing L. toe with knee turned inwards to side.
                2. Pause.
                3. Hop on R. ft. and place L. heel on floor with knee turned outwards (movement is from hip).

Bar 4.   Repeat bar 3.

Bars 5–8.   Repeat bars 1–4, starting with R. ft.

Bars 9–20.   Repeat this step three times with R., L. and R. feet.

Bar 21.   Partners both kneel on R. knee resting R. arm across waist, with L. arm raised. Man faces forwards and woman faces backwards.

Bar 22.   Partners reverse this movement, kneeling on L. knee.

Bars 23, 24.   Both step on L. ft., raise R. knee and make one complete turn to left, finish facing partner.

Bar 25.   Pause.

Estribillo

C. During the next 8 bars the couple make one complete turn anti-clockwise, facing each other in a small circle. Their knees are almost touching.

Bar 1.   1. Fall on R. ft. bringing L. toe up to side of R. ft., L. knee bent up and forwards.
                2. Pause.
                3. Fall on L. ft. resting R. toe by side of L. heel. R. knee well bent up.

Bars 2–7.   Repeat this movement 6 times.

Bar 8.   Pause. Couple are facing each other in original place.

EXAMPLE 74 (*cont.*)

2nd Copla

D. Bar 1.
  1. Stamp on L. ft. to left.
  2. Place R. toe at side of L. with R. knee turned in.
  3. Place R. heel slightly out to right and turn R. knee outwards.

Bar 2. Repeat bar 1.

Bar 3.
  1. Step back on L. ft.
  2. Hop on L. ft. and swing R. leg with knee well bent up behind L. knee.
  3. Step back on R. ft.

Bar 4.
  1. Hop on R. ft. and swing L. leg with knee well bent up behind R. knee.
  2. Step back on L. ft.
  3. Pause.

Bars 5–8. Repeat bars 1–4, starting with stamp on R. ft.

Bars 9–16. Repeat bars 1–8.

E. Still facing partner, but using opposite feet.

Bar 1.
  1. Jump both feet apart.
  2. Pause.
  3. Man hops on L. ft. raising R. leg upwards and sideways. Woman hops on R. ft. raising L. leg upwards and sideways.

Bar 2. *Pas-de-bourrée* as in bar 2 of B (1st Copla).

Bar 3. Repeat bar 1, man hopping on R. ft., and lifting L., woman hopping on L. ft. and raising R. leg.

Bar 4. Repeat *pas-de-bourrée*, making one complete turn to face partner again, man turning to his left and woman to her right.

Bars 5–20. Repeat bars 1–4, four times.

Bars 21–24. Repeat bars 21–24 of 1st Copla.

Estribillo

F. Partners still using opposite feet, man turning to his left, woman to her right, they make one complete turn in own circle and finish facing each other.

Bar 1.
  1. Jump on both feet slightly apart.
  2. Man hops on R. ft. and swings L. toe in front of R. knee. Woman hops on L. ft.
  3. Man hops on R. ft. and swings L. toe behind R. knee. Woman hops on L. and swings R. toe behind.

Bar 2. Repeat bar 1, using opposite feet. Man hops on L., woman on R.

Bars 3–7. Repeat bars 1 and 2 alternately.

Bar 8.
  1. Man steps on L. ft. and closes R. to it. Woman steps on R. ft. and closes L. to it.

EXAMPLE 74 (cont.)

3rd Copla

G. Duringthe first 4 bars couples make one complete turn, man to his left and woman to her right.

Bars 1–4.   Repeat bar 1 of D (2nd Copla) 4 times, man stamping on L. ft., woman on R. ft. Finish facing each other.

Bar 5.   1. Man steps back on L. ft. woman on R.
2. Man hops on L. ft. swinging R. leg out sideways and well raised; woman hops on her R. and swings out L. leg.
3. Man steps back on his R. ft. Woman steps back on her L.

Bar 6.   1. Man hops on R. ft. swinging L. leg out sideways. Woman hops on L.
2. Man steps back on L. ft., woman on R.
3. Man hops on L. ft. swinging R. leg out sideways. Woman hops on R.

Bar 7.   1. Man steps back on R. ft., woman on L.
2. Man hops on R. ft. swinging L. leg out sideways. Woman hops on L.
3. Man closes L. ft. to R. Woman closes R. ft. to L.

Bar 8.   Pause.

Bars 9–12.   Both repeat bar 1 of D (2nd Copla) 4 times, man stamping on R. ft. making one complete turn to his right, woman on L. ft. making one complete turn to her left.

Bars 13–14.   Repeat bars 5, 6 with opposite feet.

Bars 15–16.   Pause and on last beat of bar 16, both step on L. ft., woman facing forwards and man facing backwards.

H. Bar 1.   1. Hop on L. ft. raising R. leg upwards and forwards.
2. Drop on R. ft.
3 Close L. ft. to R.

Bars 2–3.   Repeat bar 1 twice.

Bar 4.   1. Spring on to R. ft., L. leg pointed in front.
2. Spring on to L. ft., R. leg pointed in front.
3. Spring on to R. ft., L. leg pointed in front.

Partners now reverse direction, man moving forwards to front and woman to back.

Bars 5–12.   Repeat bars 1–4, twice starting on L. ft., then reverse direction and start on R. ft.

Bar 13.   Pause.

J. Bar 1.   1. Man steps on to L. ft.
2. Pause.
3. Brings L. heel to R. heel (cabriole). Woman steps on to R. ft. and also makes a cabriole. The couple both face forwards in this.

Bars 2–7.   Partners continue to cabriole from side to side moving to and from each other.

Bars 8–12.   Partners repeat bars 21–24 of 1st Copla, man kneeling first on R. knee, woman on L. After the turn man kneels on L. knee facing partner, and she places her L. ft. on his R. knee.

PORTUGAL

Although many Portuguese and Spanish dances look alike and there are strong racial connections between the two peoples, both having descended from the same tribal ancestors, there is a fine distinction to be made which is due primarily to the different climatic and geographical conditions, and thus to the different kinds of work performed. Spain has large, desert-like areas, where it is extremely difficult to scrape a living from the soil. Portugal on the other hand is largely green and fertile, and therefore where the Spaniards display dramatic arrogance and perhaps a spirit of defiance towards natural phenomena, the Portuguese show an easy grace and cheerfulness towards the natural gifts bestowed on them. There is a greater simplicity of movement, except in the south, where the Moorish elements prevail. Perhaps, too, some of this greater simplicity comes from the fact that Portugal is largely a country of fishermen and seafaring folk, and its fascinating fishermen's dances reflect the calm, unruffled manner of a work which requires endless patience. The coiling of the ropes, the casting of nets, the long waits for the catch, its sudden hauling in, or the slow hauling of boats and swinging of oars seen in the dances along the coasts and on the banks of the Tagus, are coupled to strangely elusive rhythmic tunes, which must have derived from the particular work process involved, or from the still undefined qualities of their ancient Basque ancestors. In some of the fishermen's dances in the northern Provinces remarkable use is made of the high leaps and turns usually associated with the Basques, which seems further to indicate their influence on Portuguese dance and music.

Another important difference between the dances of Spain and those of Portugal is in the attitude of the people towards the historical events that have affected them. Being a seafaring nation, the Portuguese show rather strong individual characteristics and a love of independence, and have not submitted so easily to outside influences, except those of the Catholic church which regulates much of their life.

Until the eleventh century, Portugal went through the same historical process as Spain, but when the Christian kings began to drive the Moors from the Iberian Peninsula, it seems that the Portuguese did everything possible to throw off Moorish influence, under the guidance of the English and Flemish Kings and the Catholic priests who accompanied the crusading armies. It is likely that from this early contact with these two more sober nations the Portuguese have developed so many dance forms similar to those performed in England. The steps, too, bear some resemblance in that they are simple and related to the music in much the same way. Running, *chassés* (Ex. 26, page 101), easy *pas-de-basques* with a good travelling movement (Ex. 63, page 188), waltzing, a smooth hopping *polka* or *schottische* step, and a passing of the right foot first in front of and then behind the left, usually match the regular beats or half-beats of their favourite 3/4 or 2/4 time signatures.

This contact between England and Portugal has always been closely maintained. The two are seafaring nations, have been allies in several wars, or have entered into friendly rivalry when both were developing their trade and exploring the world. There was a particularly close association during the Napoleonic Wars, when undoubtedly English and Scottish soldiers introduced later country-dance forms such as La Virra Extrapassado, or the Pretinho (versions of Strip the Willow), and similar dances of the Northern Provinces.

Portuguese dance also shows the influence of the courtly Provençal troubadours, who were particularly active during the early Crusades and undoubtedly reinforced the strong relationship of song and dance which was an important aspect of their performance and is still a vital part of many Portuguese dances. These often fall into two parts; during the verse, the couples walk round solemnly in a ring holding hands, and during the refrain, which is usually quick, they perform very lively but simple steps, clapping their hands or snapping their fingers at each other. Occasionally one also finds dances with very strong aspects of courtly mime, similar to those found in other areas influenced by the Provençal courts.

As in Spain, the dances and rituals are closely bound to the church calendar. Many of these have the same forms as the Sword and Morris dances of other European nations. There are no solo dances, although there are several couple dances, such as the Fandango, which have emanated from Spain. In these the two partners (sometimes two men) take it in turns to display their virtuosity. The first dancer sets the rhythm to be picked up by the second, who elaborates, if he can, the efforts of the other; and in the case of man and woman both finish their dance together.

Unfortunately the real folk dance in Portugal seems to be disappearing. The Andalusian style of dance in the south and the forms evolved by the gipsies are beginning to displace the older forms, and although groups of professional folk dancers are trying to save their heritage the people are perhaps too readily allowing themselves to be entertained by others instead of dancing the old dances for themselves; moreover they now indulge in the modern ballroom dances, which gain character by being performed on the great threshing-floors, the traditional ballrooms of the real folk dancers.

ROMANIA

Romania was the furthest north-eastern province of the Roman Empire, from which it derived its Latin tongue (see Map 2, facing page 52). It is without contact with any other nation speaking a similar tongue, and its folk dances, music, and arts are a mixture reflecting the activities of the many national groups which flowed in and out of this area during the first 1300 years of the Christian era. The majority of these dances and rituals are akin to those of the neighbouring Slavs, whose culture was impressed upon the Romanians between the tenth and fourteenth centuries, when the Slavs were being driven from place to place by Goths, Teutons, Magyars, and Bulgars. Within Romania there are also large minority groups with their own distinctive forms of dance.

Romania's history, like that of the rest of the Balkan countries, is complex. Its rich agricultural plains and well-wooded mountain slopes, its precious mineral and oil deposits, and its particularly easy routes through the mouth of the Danube or across lower mountain slopes, have made it a prey to advancing armies and exploiting landowners. After forming part of the Greek Empire, the original Eurasiatics were overrun by the Gauls, and later colonized by the Roman Emperor Trajan (A.D. 106), who made Latin the official language of this Province and gave it its name. This language gained so strong a hold that later conquering Gothic and Slav kings and their armies gradually adopted it for their own as they were converted to Christianity by the Greek Orthodox Church. This helped to mould the inhabitants of Romania into a united people, for its more tolerant attitude towards pagan ritual allowed the priests to encourage the peasants to practise their ancient dances in honour of their new God; thus dances with similar features belonging to the different tribes were amalgamated and became communal rites. This process was furthered when the whole area was conquered by the Ottoman Emperors, for the ruthless behaviour of the Turkish Janissaries caused many a group to flee into the mountains, where they continued to rehearse their rites in secret.

The break-up of the Ottoman Empire was a very long process, during which Romania was sadly split between the various warring kings. At one time some part of her territory would be annexed, and at another her boundaries would extend into other areas. In this way, many minorities found their way inside the political boundaries by which she is known to-day, and it is their dances as well as those of the Slavs that one must study to get an overall picture of Romanian dance.

In Transylvania, for example, there are many Hungarians, whose dances remain in their original form, each member of the group working opposite the partner with whom he is most in harmony, and indulging in wonderful feats of improvisation.

Among the German minority of southern Transylvania and the Banat are found several old, close-turning dances and more solemn, Teutonic processionals. Elsewhere there are Albanian, Armenian, Turkish, and Greek dances.

The most interesting dances are those of the Vlach shepherds, a strange nomadic group of people always travelling with their flocks through the wide Carpathian mountain ranges and paying little heed to political boundaries. Their methods of performance are similar to those of the Hungarians, Basques, and gipsies. Their wonderful leaps and turns are contrasted with statuesque stepping and complicated changes of épaulement, and punctuated by deep bending of the knees, or dainty batterie like the Highlanders. The rhythms are very complicated for they are dictated by the dancer to a drummer, the piper merely creating an atmospheric melody on his shrill shepherd's flute or soft bagpipe.

There are many gipsies in Romania, and they influence all dances, for they are often the only musicians available and therefore impose their will on the dancers. But when the Romanians accompany themselves by mouth music, or on the popular accordion, they have the same musical features that are found in Slav and Middle Eastern countries, and the most popular dance of all is the ancient circle and chain, or Hora. This usually starts with a slow stately stepping and develops into a dance of incredible speed, lightness, and gaiety. The circles often break into a couple dance, in which the partners whirl round taking two steps on the heels or the balls of the feet to each full turn, the partners holding each other round the waist and leaning backwards away from each other. There are the same three forms of Kolo or Hora as found in Yugoslavia and Bulgaria, which are performed according to the ground they are danced on. But they are far gayer than those of the true Slav countries, except such ritual dances as those of the Calusari, and the ones performed at weddings.

CHAPTER XVII

The Basques

WHO are the Basques, and where did they originate? If it were possible to answer these questions it might be possible to solve some of the interesting problems that arise from the study of this ancient people, and their relationship to the rest of Europe. They are said to be the most ancient of all European races and they speak a unique language, only a few words of which are found elsewhere among the Turki-Tartar tribes of the Caucasus. They still practise many ancient rituals and have customs peculiar to themselves. At the same time, in their dances are found similar elements to those in the southern half of Europe and parts of Asia. Four-fifths of them live below and the rest above a boundary line drawn by Spain and France, who have fought for the ownership of this territory, but the people themselves know no division, and were at one time united under their own democratically elected government.

Were they some nomadic tribe, originating in the Middle East, who gradually spread throughout the southern half of Europe, and then were pushed farther and farther westwards by other tribes until they finally came to rest where the western edges of the Pyrenees are bounded by the Atlantic Ocean? That they are a mountain people is very evident from the exciting upwards leaping of their male dance, whose steps are so like those of other mountain people. Did these dances originally belong to the Basques, who, as they passed on their way, left their strange capers and queer twists of the body among the Georgians, who also "wriggle" as they do their *entrechats*, or the Vlach shepherds, who have similar leaps? Or did they acquire them from the Celtic tribes who were later to spread through the British Isles into Scotland, since the Basque male solos, Arresku in particular, are extraordinarily like some Scottish solos, such as the Seann Triubhas? The strange thing, too, about the Arresku, is that in construction it is extremely like the Georgian Lezghinka-Lekouri, the male showing off his prowess before asking the girl to dance, and the couple then dancing together.

That the Basques were a tribe led by the male is immediately apparent, for he dominates the dance, which is tremendously exciting and, like that of the Georgian, full of significant gesture, fire, and spontaneity. But, unlike the Georgian, the Basque dances are usually "set." Where the Georgian practises his individualistic "whiffling" and guerrilla-like antics with great curving swords or short knives, the Basque marches round with sword held aloft before linking it with others in formal, complicated patterns. Did the Basques originate these linked point and hilt Sword Dances, or did the Celts, on meeting the Basques and with them watching the sun sink into the western ocean, give form and

In threes, either two men and one girl or two girls and one man—

France (Burgundian Branles)   N. Yugoslav Kolos, Poland (Troyak, etc.)
Russia (Trepak)   Scottish and Irish Three-handed Reels

Handkerchief Dances—

Czechoslovakia   Denmark   Scandinavia   S. Germany

Couple Dances—

Principally in Italy and Spain; all other couple dances are of later origin.

Fertility Dances (i.e. those containing the fertility leap or other erotic element)

Alpine area Schuhplattler, etc.   Brittany and Italy: use of broomstick
Dalmatian Eagle Kolo   French Provençal La Volta and dances in
Polish Kujaviak   La Vendée
Russian dances, Scandinavian, Danish and a few Dutch dances

Fishermen's Dances (also Sailors' Dances)

France: Mediterranean coast   Italy   Poland
Portugal   Russia: Barents Sea and Black and White Sea areas
Sailors' Dances: France, England, Norway, Holland and Russia

Gipsy Dances

Czechoslovakia   Hungary   Romania   Russia
Spain   Yugoslavia

Guerrilla Dances

Georgia   Greece (particularly Macedonia)   Yugoslavia

Hunters' Dances

Czechoslovakia   Hungary   Russia   Poland

(N.B. These sometimes become Courtship dances, i.e. the Georgian Lekouri.)

Moon-worshipping Dances

Russia   Yugoslavia

Morris Dances (Morisco or Maresca)

Basque countries   England   France   Italy
Portugal   Romania   Yugoslavia

Processionals

Nearly everywhere. (N.B. Helston Furry Dance, Abbot's Bromley Horned Dance and Breton Piler-Lan.)

Recreational Dances

> Everywhere

Recruiting Dances

> Czechoslovakia   Hungary   Russia   Yugoslavia

Ritual Dances (see also Circles, Serpentine, Processionals, etc.)

> Cramignon to Easter Hymn: Holland
> Dancing on fire: Yugoslavia
> Dancing round bonfires: very widespread
> Maypole Dancing: Basque countries, Czechoslovakia, England, Finland, France, Germany, Portugal, Sweden, Switzerland
> Funeral Dances: Balkans, Greece, Portugal, Spain
> Jack-in-the-green, etc.: Austria, England, France, Germany
> Tug-o'-war by girls in Czechoslovakia and by men nearly everywhere
> Witches' Ceremonials: Austria and Pyrenees
> Easter Dances: Seville Cathedral and outside Echternach Cathedral

Serpentine Dances

France, Portugal, Spain, Greece, and Italy all have forms of the Farandole. Yugoslavia and the Balkans have other forms.

Sun Dances (i.e. mill-wheel)

> Denmark and Switzerland

Sword Dances (various forms)

Austria	Sweden	Yugoslavia	Denmark
England	Bulgaria	Czechoslovakia	Italy
France	Germany	Holland	Spain
Poland	Portugal	Scotland	

Tree-Dwellers' Dances (with Whifflers)

> England   France   Romania   Yugoslavia

War Dances (in which actual sword play is practised)

> England   France   Georgia   Greece
> Yugoslavia

Wedding Dances (in which the bride's work is shown)

Armenia	Azerbaijan	Czechoslovakia	Finland
Georgia	Hungary	Poland	Romania
Russia	Sweden	Yugoslavia	

Work Dances (in which actual work is indicated)

Armenia: Carpet-weaving, Harvesting, Cowmen, Vintage, Cradle dance
Austria: Salt-miners
Bulgaria, Caucasus, and Crimea: Rose-harvesting, Vintage
Czechoslovakia: Poppy-harvest, Ploughmen
Denmark: Mill-wheel
England: Sailors, Bean-setting, Gathering Peascods
Finland: Woodcutters, Fishermen, Carters, Cowmen
France: Bellringers, Harvesters, Grooms' Dance, Woodcutters, Vintage
Hebrides: Weaving Lilt
Holland: Harvesting
Italy: Vintage
Portugal: Harvesting, Fishermen, Ploughing and Sowing
Russia: Fishermen, Sailors, Harvesting, Sowing, Cowmen, Woodcutters, Vintage
Spain: Vintage, Harvest
Switzerland: Cowmen, Mill-wheel

Appendix II

The following is a brief list of composers who have introduced, either consciously or unconsciously, their own national music into their original work.

Armenia. Balanchivaidze, Ippolitov-Ivanov, Khachaturian, Tigranian. (See also Russian Composers.)

Azerbaijan. See above, and also Russian Composers.

Basque Countries. Guridi, Usandezago.

Bulgaria. Vladigerov (Panchu).

Czechoslovakia. Bartók, Dvorak, Janăček, Smetana.

England. During the Tudor and Stuart periods, and for a short while after the Restoration, their names were legion, therefore a few contemporary composers only are mentioned. Bax, Moeran, Warlock, Vaughan Williams; also Percy Grainger for arrangements of folk tunes.

Finland. Sibelius.

France. Only one composer appears to have used any folk idiom at all—Vincent D'Indy in his "Symphonie Montagnarde."

Georgia. See Armenia and Russia.

Germany. Beethoven, Brahms, Mozart, Schubert, Schumann.

Hungary. Bartók, Kodaly. See also Brahms and Liszt.

Norway. Grieg.

Poland. Chopin, Scharwenka, Szymanowski.

Russia. Balakirev, Dargomirsky, Glinka, Ippolitov-Ivanov, Liadov, Mussorgsky, Rimsky-Korsakov, Stravinsky, Tchaikovsky, and many contemporary composers.

Spain. Albeniz, Manuel de Falla, Granados, Turina.

Yugoslavia. Hristic.

Appendix III

This short Bibliography gives suggestions for a further study of Folk Dance and its background.

Bartók, Bela: *Hungarian Folk Music*. (Trans. by M. D. Calvorcoressi. Oxford University Press, London, 1931.)

Chambers, E. K.: *The Mediaeval Stage*. (Oxford University Press, Oxford, 1903.)
The Elizabethan Stage. (Oxford University Press, Oxford, 1923.)

Childe, V. Gordon: *Man Makes Himself*. (Watts and Co., Ltd., London, 1941.)
What Happened in History. (Penguin Books, Ltd., 1942.)

Elyot, Sir Thomas: *The Governour*. (Published 1531—Everyman's Library.)

Farrington, B.: *Head and Hand in Ancient Greece*. (Watts and Co., Ltd., 1947.)

Featherstone, Christopher: *A Dialogue against light, lewde and lascivious dancing*. (Published 1582—can be seen at the Bodleian Library, Oxford.)

Fraser, Sir James, O.M.: *The Golden Bough*. Abridged Edition. (Macmillan and Co., Ltd., London, 1941.)

Graham-Dalyell, Sir John: *Musical Memoirs of Scotland*. (T. D. Stevenson, Edinburgh.)

Grecov, B. D.: *The Culture of Kiev Rŭs*. (Foreign Languages Publishing House, Moscow, 1947.)

Griffith, Wyn: *The Welsh*. (Penguin Books, Ltd., 1950.)

Harrison, Jane Ellen: *Ancient Art and Ritual*. (Williams and Norgate, Ltd., London, 1931.)

Howes, Frank: *Man, Mind and Music*. (Secker and Warburg, Ltd., London, 1948.)

Huxley, Julian, and others: *We Europeans*. (Penguin Books, Ltd.)

Kennedy, Douglas: *England's Dances*. (G. Bell and Sons, Ltd., London, 1949.)

MacLennan, D. G.: *Highland and Traditional Scottish Dances*. (Printed by W. T. McDougall and Co., Edinburgh, for the author, 1950.)

Martinengo-Cesaresco, Countess: *Essays in the Study of Folk Songs*. (Everyman's Library, No. 673, Dent and Sons, Ltd., London, 1914.)

Mellers, Wilfred: *Music and Society*. (Dennis Dobson, Ltd., London, 1946.)

Murray, Gilbert, O.M.: *Five Stages of Greek Religion*. (Watts and Co., Ltd., London, 1935.)

Nicoll, Allardyce: *British Drama*. (Harrap and Co., Ltd., London, Fourth edition, 1945.) *Mimes, Masques and Miracles*. (Harrap and Co., Ltd., London, 1931.)

O'Faolain, Sean: *The Irish*. (Penguin Books, Ltd., 1947.)

Playford, John: *The Dancing Master*. (Editions of 1651, 1652, 1665, 1670, 1675, 1679, 1686, and later editions published by others, 1690, 1695, 1698, 1701, 1703, 1713, 1716, 1718, 1721, 1728. Can be seen at the British Museum.)

Richardson, P. J. S. : Editor of *The Dancing Times*, a monthly publication, including numerous authoritative articles from 1910 to the present day.

Sachs, Curt: *The Rise of Music in the Ancient World*. (Dent and Sons, Ltd., London, 1944.) *World History of the Dance*. (George Allen and Unwin, Ltd., London, 1938.)

Spence, Lewis: *An Introduction to Mythology*. (Harrap and Co., Ltd., London, 1921.) *Myth and Ritual in Dance, Game and Rhyme*. (Watts and Co., Ltd., London, 1947.)

Steinberg, S. H.: *Historical Tables, 58 B.C.–A.D.1945*. (Macmillan and Co., Ltd., London, 1947.)

Thomson, George: *Studies in Ancient Greek Society*. Vol. I. "The Prehistoric Aegean." (Lawrence and Wishart, Ltd., London, 1949.)

Trevelyan, G. M.: *English Social History*. (Longmans, Green and Co., Ltd., London, 1942.)

Weaver, John: *An Essay towards a History of Dancing*. (London, 1712. Can be seen at the British Museum.)

Wells, H. G.: *The Outline of History*. (Cassel and Co., Ltd., London, 1925.)

Williams, R. Vaughan O.M.: *National Music*. (Oxford University Press, London, 1934.)

Viski, Karoly: *Hungarian Dances*. (Simpkin Marshall, Ltd., London, 1937.)

Index of Dances

Index